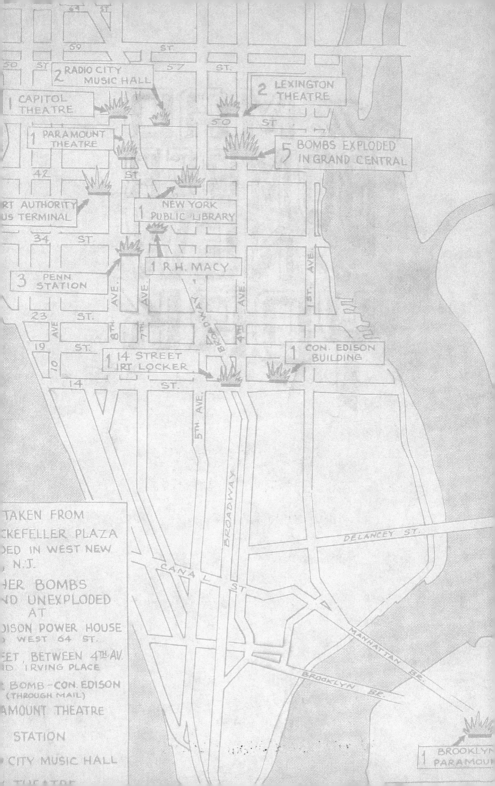

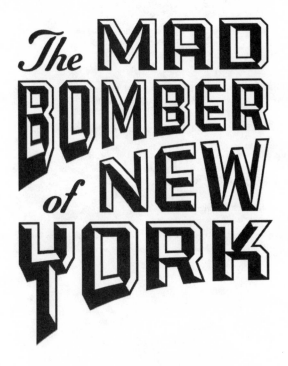

# The MAD BOMBER of NEW YORK

*The* **EXTRAORDINARY**
**TRUE STORY** *of the* **MANHUNT**
*that* **PARALYZED** *a* **CITY**

~

*Michael M. Greenburg*

UNION SQUARE PRESS
New York

UNION SQUARE PRESS
New York

An Imprint of Sterling Publishing
387 Park Avenue South
New York, NY 10016

**Library of Congress Cataloging-in-Publication Data**

Greenburg, Michael M.
  The Mad bomber of New York : the extraordinary true story of the manhunt that
paralyzed a city / Michael M. Greenburg.
    p. cm.
  Includes bibliographical references and index.
  ISBN 978-1-4027-7434-8
  1. Metesky, George P., 1903-1994. 2. Bombers (Terrorists)—New York (State)—
New York—Biography. 3. Mentally ill offenders—New York (State)—New York—
Biography. I. Title.
  HV6430.M48G74 2011
  363.325092—dc22
  [B]

2010038795

2  4  6  8  10  9  7  5  3  1

For information about custom editions, special sales, premium and
corporate purchases, please contact Sterling Special Sales
Department at 800-805-5489 or specialsales@sterlingpublishing.com.

Designed by Gavin Motnyk

*To my mother, Elaine Greenburg, who always provides love and encouragement.*

"Every normal person, in fact, is only normal on the average. His ego approximates to that of the psychotic in some part or other and to a greater or lesser extent."

—Sigmund Freud

# CONTENTS

# WAR AND PEACE

AT 7:55 ON THE EVENING OF DECEMBER 2, 1956, AS THE EPIC NARRATIVE of *War and Peace* began to unfold on the screen of Brooklyn's Paramount Theatre, there was no mistaking the sudden and violent explosion that ripped through the rear of the auditorium for anything remotely connected to that evening's movie presentation. In a blinding moment of fierce light, smoke, and fire, a locally powerful device had detonated at precisely the moment determined by the simple timing mechanism within.

A thirty-six-year-old postal clerk named Abraham Blumenthal, who had taken his wife, Ruth, out to the movies for the first time in what seemed like ages, was immediately thrown from his twelfth-row seat. Fierce pain began to radiate from his left leg, where shards of jagged metal had inflicted their damage. "Suddenly I heard a report like a grenade. Then a small column of smoke rose in front of me and drifted across the screen," Blumenthal would later tell reporters.

Panic began to envelop the room, and as *War and Peace* continued without pause, patrons began rushing for the exits. Seated about eighty feet from the explosion itself, a young mother, Doris Russo, and her sister Joyce were pummeled with scabrous debris, which settled deep in the face and scalp of each. Earlier that day the sisters had made their way through the retail menagerie of Fulton Street in downtown Brooklyn on a shopping spree with their mother, Mary Young, and Doris's two children in tow, and decided to cap off the evening with a movie. Mary Young would later say, "The shock and terror of what happened that evening will never leave my memory."

. . .

The unarmed outer casing of the "infernal machine" that he had hurriedly prepared for use earlier that day had already been assembled. He had many of them securely stored where only he could find them. To the maddening frustration of law enforcement authorities, the raw materials that composed these creations were commonplace and generic; they could be purchased in virtually any retail outlet throughout the country, and they provided little if any evidence as to their origin. In keeping with his meticulous manner, the Bomber purposely omitted any specialized or unique components that would betray their points of purchase.

A length of galvanized iron or "coupling" purchased from Sears and Roebuck had been carefully fitted on each end with metal plugs (prudently purchased elsewhere) that were machine tooled and neatly threaded into the cavity of the pipe. With the precision of a machinist, he had drilled a small hole into the cylinder to allow the later arming of the device with a detonative material, and a so-called "filling plug"—a 3/8-inch allen screw—was used to close the puncture. This, the Bomber would later state, ensured a "neater package."

Alone in his garage, his castle—"the one place on earth where nobody could bother me," he would later recall—he worked with painstaking resolve. The workspace was meticulously ordered; against one wall was a neat and sturdy workbench, and hanging above on evenly arranged hooks were rows of carefully polished tools. Situated around the structure in even intervals were seven windows of smoked glass that allowed neither sunlight nor view into this grim and very private world. An organized collection of blueprints lay on a wooden desk, and beside them, a worn Remington typewriter whose ribbon had been frequently replaced. Though the garage housed a rather out-of-place black English Daimler automobile, the focal point of the space was a metal machinist's lathe that ominously suggested craft beyond the typical household project. And beneath this well-oiled machine lay a small wooden box temporarily housing the various components of a deranged endeavor, stockpiled for later use and burrowed daily behind two soapstone tubs in the basement of his home. The ten-by-fourteen-foot detached garage, constructed of sheet metal and corrugated iron, was, in the later words of the New York City Police Department, "as clean and orderly as a hospital operating room."

On the morning of December 2, 1956, with the structure of the device complete, he began the process of converting this harmless assemblage of iron into an instrument of hate and potent danger. He fashioned a fusing mechanism by carefully grinding a flashlight bulb on an emery wheel to reveal a small hole that he perfected with a nail file and filled with black gunpowder. To the case and center conductor of the bulb he had soldered two silk-covered, multistranded copper wires that led to a chrome-protected no. 7 Burgess battery used to heat the filament. Interrupting this nefarious circuitry was nothing more than the distance between the hour hand of a shock-resistant Timex wristwatch and the contact point of a metal ignition terminal. With a steady hand, he slipped the fusing mechanism into place and screwed the iron plug back onto the body of the cylinder.

Then, as unaware New Yorkers made plans for an evening out on the town, he deftly funneled the fine, smokeless black powder from the cartridges of fifty .22-caliber long rifle bullets into the filling hole of the iron cap and reinserted the plug, completing the final step in the arming process.

The beads of sweat that had formed on his brow during this process in earlier years were missing on that December morning. To the contrary, he admired his workmanship, regretting only that no one would ever see it. By now the process had become rote to him. According to official police records, he had performed it no less than thirty-one times before; his own later estimates ranged closer to sixty. Yet his message, so clear, so right, so *just*, seemed lost on all but himself. Why were they not listening? When would justice prevail? This time, he pondered, would be different. This time they would be forced to reckon with him.

The Bomber wiped the "unit" (as he coldly referred to all of his bombs) clean of powder and fingerprints, placed it in what had become a signature red wool sock, and then he held it to one ear. Listening for the faint and soothing sound of the ticking Timex, he smiled with smug pride at the barely audible heartbeat emitting from his creation. He knew that later that evening the metal hands of the watch would make contact with the copper wires leading from the battery to the flashlight bulb, completing the lethal circuit and detonating the surrounding cache of powder.

The timing mechanism had been set for shortly before eight o'clock.

• • •

The sixty-mile drive from his home in Waterbury, Connecticut, to New York was well known to the Bomber. As he had done so many times in the past, he drove through the affluent suburbs of Westchester County and stopped in White Plains for a bite to eat at a local diner. On some occasions he had parked his Daimler outside of the city and traveled into Manhattan via the New York Central Railroad. Feeling uncomfortable as one of the only men on the midday train rides, however, he had elected on his more recent trips to park closer to the city and blend into the chaos of the New York subway system. On the afternoon of December 2, 1956, the Bomber drove straight into Brooklyn.

He had wrapped the wool sock that housed his device with a rubber band and attached a length of string. A few moments prior to the start of the movie, he entered the theater and found a seat toward the left rear of the orchestra section. As the opening credits of the film began to roll and the attention of each moviegoer was transfixed, he looked to his left and then to his right. With feigned nonchalance, he reached into the side pocket of his wool overcoat, and with eyes firmly affixed to the movie screen, grasped the string and gently lowered the device to the floor just behind seat 19 of row GG. With his foot, the Bomber carefully nudged the unit out of sight. Within twenty minutes, he had left the theater and was hurrying to his car.

• • •

The words of Tolstoy's voluminous classic leapt off the page and onto the silver screen with much the same fury as Napoleon's 1812 march into Russia. Though Henry Fonda himself had misgivings about his casting in the film, *War and Peace* was eagerly greeted by moviegoers and reviewers alike upon its release in August 1956. "There are sequences and moments of fire and beauty, and certainly the mighty spectacles of clashing armies and Napoleon's retreat from Moscow are pictorially impressive and exciting beyond words," wrote one New York critic. In a "Technicolored panorama," director King Vidor captured the fury of the Russian invasion— and the imagination of an engrossed American public with breathtaking scenes of battle that burst onto theater screens across the country. The film would later receive three Academy Award nominations, and by the end of 1956, nearly five months after its release, *War and Peace* was still drawing patrons into crowded movie houses.

Post–World War II America seemed to roar with a cultural vitality and social clamor. A young performer from Tupelo, Mississippi, stormed onto the national scene with his hit recording "Heartbreak Hotel," and before long Elvis Aaron Presley would redefine music and canonize "rock and roll" as America's signature form of entertainment in the twentieth century. The new medium of television, with broadcasts such as the *Ed Sullivan Show* and *Ted Mack's Original Amateur Hour*, would bring an endless variety of new musical acts, comedians, and drama directly into the living rooms of neatly aligned suburban tract homes. And development of an interstate highway system, the hallmark of the Eisenhower administration, would bring people and products together in a web of personal and cultural interconnectivity unseen prior to that time.

In the halcyon days of the American movie industry, however, a picture show often provided a singular respite from the rigors of life during the Depression. The Paramount Theatre arose in an era when competitive movie houses were owned by and often took the name of their founding production companies. The construction of the Paramount and several other rococo or Renaissance theaters, with their splendorous arrays of architecture, stole the show from the movies themselves and represented an early local foray into the entertainment business. They would become Brooklyn's theater district.

Located at the corner of Flatbush Avenue Extension and DeKalb Avenue in Brooklyn, New York, the Paramount was designed by the Chicago architectural firm of Rapp and Rapp, specialists in the creation of the so-called atmospheric theater. With an ornately decorated sixty-foot satin-embroidered stage curtain and 4,400 seats adorned in burgundy velvet, the Paramount at its 1928 opening was Brooklyn's largest and perhaps most opulent theater, and the second largest in New York City. According to the *New York Times,* the Paramount was fashioned along "the plans of an outdoor moonlit Italian garden." Nearly $3 million worth of elaborate sculpture, paintings, and tapestries together with domed and frescoed ceilings provided "scenic effects . . . not confined to the stage but made to envelop the audience by carrying a scenic architectural treatment completely around the auditorium." The rather drab exterior façade of the eleven-story office building to which the Paramount Theatre was appended was strikingly enlivened by the placement of a neon-powered sign that stretched nearly four stories in height above the roof. The massive glowing letters,

PARAMOUNT THEATRE

implored the bustling populace of Brooklyn, New York, to come and enjoy.

Though the Paramount was considered by some to be the area's "most famous movie place," the theater was by no means limited to film presentations. Behind the opulent décor lay a very practical and financial motivation for the owners, who demanded a diverse use of the property to help defray the ever expanding cost per seat. In its early days, frequent guests included musical performers such as Bing Crosby and Ethel Merman, and in the mid-1950s Alan Freed's renowned rock and roll shows introduced acts such as Chuck Berry and Fats Domino. Through the years, the Paramount would play host to other marquee names, including

Buddy Holly, Ray Charles, Bobby Rydell, Neil Sedaka, the Drifters, and many others, earning the theater the reputation as one of America's premier rock and roll venues.

With no warning of the distressing events that would follow, cheery moviegoers braved the cold northeastern winter winds and began lining up outside of the Brooklyn Paramount Theatre for the evening show. Nearly 1,500 New Yorkers, warmed with pre-holiday cheer, clamored with eagerness over that night's screening of *War and Peace*. As Horatio Tedesco, the theater's assistant manager, greeted patrons, he couldn't help but compare the refined makeup of the gathering to the raucous throngs attending the recent musical performances. He was grateful for the easy cleanup and closing that would follow.

It was sure to be another uneventful evening at the Paramount.

. . .

Horatio Tedesco heard the explosion and the muffled sounds of a commotion coming from the crowd. Rushing into the auditorium and scanning the escalating panic, he mustered his most authoritative voice and announced that a "firecracker" had exploded and that everyone should remain calm. He then summoned the police and rounded up several ushers to assist the injured through the lobby and into his private office. Ambulances from Cumberland Hospital joined officers from the 84th squad of the New York City Police Department in response to the call. As the injured were removed and order was restored, investigators from the mobile crime laboratory, under the direction of Captain Howard E. Finney, and detectives from the New York City Bomb Squad took over the scene. They conducted a row-by-row search of the theater and roped off a section of about twenty rows closest to where the explosion had taken place in an effort to gather evidence. Through the years the detectives had investigated many of the other bombings that had plagued the city, and it took them little time to pinpoint the usual markings of their elusive suspect. Soon after, Kings County district attorney Edward Silver huddled with police detectives and pronounced to the gathering of newspaper reporters that "old screwball" had struck again. The citizens of New York knew him better as the "Mad Bomber."

· · ·

As Doris Russo fought for her life following surgery to relieve the pressure that had developed from a depressed fracture of the skull, the Bomber watched and waited. Would the world finally stand up and take notice of his plight? Would the "dastardly deeds" of his enemies be redressed? Would he finally make them pay?

On no less than thirty-two separate occasions, he had slid into his automobile, his jacket pocket bulging with iron and gunpowder, and traveled from Waterbury to New York City with a deluded rage and nefarious intent. For sixteen years, he had imperiled unsuspecting New Yorkers, placing his insidious units in locations all over the city, without so much as a sniff of suspicion from family members or an inquisitive glance from frustrated police departments. For sixteen years, the man who could "easily pass as a person who could be your next-door neighbor" had evaded investigators, detectives, patrolmen, and citizens alike from Connecticut to New York, avoiding the killing of innocents only "through some quirk of fate." He had planted his bombs among women, children, workers, and patrons, and he had solemnly pledged to continue until he was either apprehended or dead. He bore no lofty social goals or political objectives. He harbored no broad civic message or popular agenda. He espoused neither government overthrow nor violent rebellion. He sought no extorted money and gained no pleasure from indiscriminate injury. The Mad Bomber simply held a grudge—a grudge that was relentlessly fueled by a simmering madness.

Across America people began to ask, who is this person, this Mad Bomber, and what does he want? And in New York City, Police Commissioner Stephen P. Kennedy announced "the greatest manhunt in the history of the Police Department."

# I

# "A REAL BOOM TOWN"

THE CALL CAME IN TO THE 20TH SQUAD OF THE NEW YORK CITY POLICE Department, located on the upper west side of Manhattan. Shortly after noon on November 18, 1940, an employee of the Consolidated Edison Company, in one of a maze of Con Ed buildings located within the West Sixty-fourth and Sixty-fifth Street city blocks bounded by Amsterdam and West End Avenue, had come across a curious sight while on break from his duties. A small wooden toolbox had been left on a second-story windowsill, containing a length of iron pipe about 4½ inches long and neatly capped on each end. Upon further examination, the employee observed what appeared to be a sheet of paper wrapped around the pipe. Not particularly alarmed by the article—a pipe in a toolbox was not an especially ominous sight at a power delivery company—the employee grasped the object and began unraveling the sheet.

There had been a chill in the air all morning long, and it promised to be a raw and sunless day throughout. As the employee opened the sheet of paper his pulse immediately quickened and, though comfortably shielded from the elements, the cold of the day shot through him like a charge. There, in neatly printed block lettering, appeared the words

CON EDISON CROOKS, THIS IS FOR YOU.

Then, printed in what appeared to be a coarse grey substance (which upon later analysis proved to be gunpowder) was ominously written

**THERE IS NO SHORTAGE OF POWDER BOYS.**

Carefully, the employee set the device back into the toolbox and scurried for his superiors, breathlessly exhorting them to call the police.

The New York City Bomb Squad was in no mood for pranks. Five months earlier, on July 4, 1940, a suitcase containing sixteen sticks of dynamite had been found at the British Pavilion of the World's Fair held in Flushing Meadows, New York. While being examined on the outskirts of the fairgrounds, the container exploded, killing two bomb squad detectives and critically injuring two other police officers on the scene. Though the explosion was felt throughout the 1,260-acre park, most of the holiday throng mistook the blast for a rather raucous feature of the patriotic celebration. For the New York City Bomb Squad, however, the tragedy would have broad implications. Following World War I, the squad took on the name Bomb and Radical Squad and focused its efforts on the militant leftists that threatened the city in the early 1920s. In 1935, as a result of duplication of effort in analyzing threatening and hostile writings, the bomb squad merged with the forgery unit to form the Bomb and Forgery Squad. Following the World's Fair tragedy, not only would the bomb squad be restructured into its modern incarnation as an independent entity, but it would forever adopt the operating procedure of allowing not more than one member of the squad to examine any device at any one time.

Despite the immediate roundup of "agitators and other suspects," the World's Fair bombing was never solved. Adopting a more rigorous training program and specialized protective gear, the bomb squad, mourning its own, would continue its mission with a greater sense of vigilance and purpose, and, for the next sixteen years, it would be tested at every turn. Among police, the work of the squad would be called "the world's most dangerous job."

The precinct officers who arrived at the Con Ed building at 170 West Sixty-fourth Street on November 18, 1940, immediately knew they were beyond their pay grade after observing the length of pipe in the toolbox. A call from headquarters went out to the bomb squad, and until the squad's arrival the officers on the scene secured the area and waited for what seemed like an eternity.

Upon arriving at the scene, the squad detectives assigned to the case immediately understood that they were indeed dealing with an "infernal machine"—a device, typically homemade and "'maliciously designed to explode and destroy life or property,' which can be deactivated by a man (other than its maker) only at the peril of death."

Knowing this, the detectives acted strictly in accordance with squad procedures. As one detective stated, the difficulty was that "[E]very problem is a new one. Every infernal machine is different. The ones that work on acid, the ones that work on a watch, the ones that work on position. We get the people away and then figure what we're going to do." Exactly what the New York City Bomb Squad, a team of eight to ten specially trained, dedicated volunteers, would do involved an often harrowing process of evaluation and removal, which would be performed in the coming years more times than any of them—or their wives and children—cared to dwell upon.

The preference of the bomb squad detective was almost always to detonate any small device bearing a volatile trigger mechanism on the scene if at all practicable, once the area had been fully cleared and evacuated. Though it was not the best outcome for the property owner, since the explosion would almost certainly result in damage, detectives preferred a controlled detonation on their own terms, rather than an explosion at an unexpected time on the bomber's terms. In some cases the device was simply nudged or "teased" with a long poker by a shielded officer, and at other times a length of twine was attached and, from a distance, yanked to agitate or incite a response. Creative methods to test devices and provoke detonation were routinely employed, and all carried their own distinct set of hazards and risks.

The Con Ed employee had already handled the pipe found at the West Sixty-fourth Street location and removed the handwritten note that previously surrounded it, and thus it was fairly evident that this was not a so-called position-control bomb—one that is set off by movement, drop switch, or liquid. Nonetheless, slowly and meticulously one detective approached the device and listened for the barely audible ticking of a timing mechanism. Having heard none, he used a device consisting of a gripping mechanism placed at the end of a five-foot pole operated by a handle at the reverse end—a bomb squad staple. Wearing protective body armor, steel-mesh gloves and shoes, and a steel-plated bucket-shaped helmet, and shielded behind a sheet of bullet-proof glass, the detective carefully turned the device over.

"Ninety-nine times out of a hundred, the innocent-looking object is just what it looks like—innocent," recounted one bomb squad detective. "It's that one in a hundred that sprays a quarter pound of rusty steel into you." To the detective's relief, his prods failed to detonate the device, though he knew the danger was far from over.

Once it was determined that the object was not reactive to movement, it was carefully placed into a woven steel-cable bag, which had come to be known affectionately as the "envelope," and carried out of the building at the center of a fifteen-foot pole manned on either end by two armored squad detectives. The package was then safely deposited into a specially equipped containment truck and transported with a blaring escort of police motorcycles and emergency vehicles to a secluded area for detonation or simple further analysis. The vehicle, officially named the Pyke-LaGuardia Carrier for the police lieutenant that conceived of the idea and the sitting mayor of New York, was a fifteen-ton semitrailer flatbed truck outfitted with a monstrous arched cage constructed of 5/8-inch-thick woven steel cable left over from the construction of the Brooklyn Bridge. Introduced shortly after the World's Fair bombing, the vehicle was "designed to take a bomb from a congested area to a remote or suburban district and to do so in a manner that will protect the public and the police."

Removed to the relative safety of an isolated location, the Con Ed object was dusted for fingerprints and then suspended in a vat of motor oil to clog the moving parts of any timing mechanism and to prevent an electrical or chemical reaction so that further examination could be conducted. Though the technique would in later years fall into disuse, it was for a time considered helpful in the detection and neutralization of bomb components. In a typical situation, an earphone, similar to a doctor's stethoscope (which would still operate in oil) would be applied to the device to determine if its timing mechanism, such as a ticking watch, had been disabled by the oil. Once satisfied that any dangerous internal apparatus had been neutralized, another technology adapted by police officials after the World's Fair tragedy, the fluoroscope, could be used to X-ray its contents. Only then could bomb squad detectives make a definitive pronouncement on the hazards of the device.

Having undertaken these procedures in the Con Ed incident, and confident that the imminent danger had passed, the officers transported the object to the police laboratory, located at the Centre Street headquarters in Manhattan, for further analysis. While the neatly capped pipe casing did contain some typical bomb components such as a flashlight bulb, a battery, a steel spring—and curiously an atypical Parke-Davis throat lozenge (the significance of which would remain a mystery to detectives for years to come)—technicians agreed that the device itself was imperfectly constructed and incapable of detonation. The question then became who had placed the bomb and why.

Con Ed, as it is today, was a large conglomerate company employing thousands and serving millions. While it was clear to all that the person who planted the device bore some grudge against the company, the task of identifying that person through the Con Ed system of record keeping would prove all but impossible. Many of the company's files, dating back decades, were housed in vaults and warehouses scattered throughout the city without method or organization. To make matters worse, each of the nearly two dozen separate entities that had merged to form the power conglomerate in the mid-1930s had maintained its own set of records, many of which were long since lost or destroyed. Within the company headquarters itself, the more recent claims of disgruntled and angry employees littered the personnel department record room, and hundreds of customer complaints poured into the company daily. The device could have been laid by almost anyone, and even the most painstaking search of the records, it was theorized, could never pinpoint a suspect. And so the police investigation ended, without result, as quickly as it began. "The episode was filed and forgotten."

· · ·

Serial bombings as a cultural phenomenon were not new to New York, or America as a whole, in the early to mid part of the twentieth century. As far back as 1906, a so-called Italian squad, the first incarnation of the bomb squad, had been formed as an arm of the New York City Police Department for the sole purpose of protecting the Italian immigrants of the city from the extortionist methods of a clandestine underworld cartel calling itself the Black Hand. The ex-convicts and outlaws that made up the group preyed on immigrant populations, blackmailing and extorting payments with threats of murder, certified with sticks of dynamite. "Recognizing the inability of the present small force of Italian detectives to drive out these criminals," wrote the *New York Times*, "Police Commissioner Bingham ordered . . . the organization of a secret service which is expected to be recruited and conducted as secretly as the operations of the men against whom it will work."

In 1908, just two years after the formation of the squad, police had apprehended five men, including the "master bomb-maker for the Black Handers." Among the evidence uncovered by the raid was a book containing carefully drawn diagrams and formulas for the manufacture and placement of explosive devices. "The book is not mine," said the captured bomber. "I know nothing about it. I am an honest grocer. I do not know the Black Hand and I do not make bombs." Less than a year later, Lieutenant Giuseppe Petrosino, the first commissioner of the Italian squad, was murdered in a town square in Palermo, Sicily, while investigating the notorious band.

With the approach of American involvement in World War I, concern over domestic bombings took on a more geopolitical and militaristic quality. By 1914, the New York City police commissioner had taken all bomb-related matters from the Italian squad and placed them under the jurisdiction of the newly created bomb squad. As German espionage efforts ensued in New York, the central focus of the squad became the protection of allied assets bound for Europe and the preservation of American neutrality. With America's entry into the war quickly becoming an inevitability, however, the bomb squad was placed under the direct control of the War Department.

Anxiety over the German espionage campaign in the United States culminated in 1916 with the sabotage and destruction by German agents of a munitions depot in New Jersey called Black Tom, located on a promontory extending into New York Harbor. The series of explosions was so powerful that the Brooklyn Bridge wavered and windows shattered in the buildings of lower Manhattan. The investigation and the ultimate assignment of blame for the Black Tom bombing was argued and litigated for years, but what is absolutely clear is that by the end of World War I the American public had become accustomed to the reality of random bombings that killed and maimed without discrimination.

By 1919 America's anxiety over domestic terrorism would shift from the work of militaristic spies to the radical statements of anarchists and foreign leftists. In April 1919 militant followers of the outspoken revolutionist Luigi Galleani, the so-called Galleanists, deposited into the mail dozens of bombs intended for prominent American politicians, officials, and capitalists. Though the devices were discovered and ultimately defused, a few months later a similar coordinated attack was successfully carried out across eight American cities, where explosives ripped through the homes of a series of government officials including various congressmen and the attorney general of the United States. Anarchist literature and leaflets were strewn about the sites of each bombing, proclaiming that the "revolution" had begun. Then, on September 16, 1920, a horse-drawn cart laden with one hundred pounds of dynamite exploded on Wall Street in front of the headquarters of J. P. Morgan Bank, instantly killing thirty people and injuring hundreds more. Shortly before the explosion, flyers were found in a nearby mailbox with hand-stamped red lettering reading:

REMEMBER
WE WILL NOT TOLERATE
ANY LONGER
FREE THE POLITICAL
PRISONERS OR IT WILL BE
SURE DEATH FOR ALL OF YOU.
AMERICAN ANARCHIST FIGHTERS

The backlash was both harsh and predictable. These bombings, juxtaposed against the patriotism and nationalist pride generated by World War I, would be the catalyst for the systematic xenophobic assault of immigrants, socialists, and left-wing groups across America. Though based on the palpable fear of radical insurrection, the "Red Scare" would envelop the country and evoke a period of civil rights violations that would endure from 1918 to 1920.

Through the ensuing years, most of the incidents involving planted explosives involved lone reprobates with unexplained motives or racketeers hurling "pineapples" at one another from moving vehicles. The rash of political bombings that would mark later decades would strike New York with harsh and bewildering force. Left-wing militant groups issuing declarations of war against the power structures of America would prompt one New York police commissioner to declare that the problem had reached "gigantic proportions." The *New York Times* would describe the city as "[a] real boom town."

• • •

In the days following the Con Ed incident, the Bomber anxiously scanned newspaper after newspaper searching for any mention of the unit that he had quietly placed on the windowsill of the West Sixty-fourth Street office building. Though some sources have concluded that the device was a live explosive filled with volatile black powder, the evidence appears to indicate otherwise. "It wasn't loaded. It was complete, but instead of powder, there was a note," he would later explain. "It was a[n] empty bomb."

Knowing that the writing would have been obliterated by the force of a detonation, police theorized that the culprit either inserted the note to satisfy some inner compulsion, aware that it would be destroyed, or that the bomb had been purposely constructed to deliver nothing more harmful than a sinister message to its recipient. The Bomber's own words would suggest a non-lethal intent. "That first unit was just a sample of what was to come."

War was raging in Europe and the American public and media were focused on other, more pressing, matters. To the Bomber's dismay, his handiwork would never find its way into the newspapers. He gained no satisfaction from the "message" that he had served upon the power company, feeling instead that it had been ignored and even ridiculed. The lack of public interest in his initial bomb-making endeavor served only to anger and embolden the already seething miscreant. He knew that further steps would have to be taken to focus the world's attention on the misdeeds of the corrupt Con Ed.

• • •

On September 24, 1941, traffic in and about the area of Nineteenth Street between Fourth Avenue and Irving Place was disrupted by the discovery of a strange object in the roadway. Crammed into a red wool sock was a contraption similar in construction and appearance to the pipe bomb found the previous November on the Con Ed windowsill. Though there was no note or identifying markings, bomb squad detectives quickly recognized the neatly capped four-inch length of galvanized pipe—and, once again, the inexplicable throat lozenge. This, coupled with the fact that the object had been placed within mere blocks of the main headquarters of Con Ed at 4 Irving Place, led them to the inescapable and disturbing conclusion that both devices had been conceived and assembled by the same individual.

Though single-minded and persistent in his deluded vocation, the Bomber had also become supremely cautious in his planning and execution. The ultimate target for his second bomb had, no doubt, been the twenty-seven-story Con Ed office building, but his attention had been diverted, perhaps by a lurking patrolman, and the bomb was abandoned short of its intended target. The unalterable resolution that dominated his mind, however, was to him logically conceived and, therefore, to be patiently revealed. A meticulous attention to order demanded no less.

In the weeks and months following the planting of his initial devices, the Bomber engaged in an incessant letter-writing campaign. Angry and insidious declarations postmarked from areas such as White Plains, Mount Vernon, and Morris Heights in New York, and Pittsfield, Massachusetts—locations that prudently gave no hint of the writer's true address—found their way into mail slots across Manhattan. "I was very careful," he later said. "I meticulously removed all my fingerprints . . . in mailing my letters. I carried with me a small piece of cloth and wiped the envelope clean. I would put this cloth over my knuckles and push the envelope into the mailbox."

With an air of narcissistic and intellectual superiority, the letters, addressed to newspaper editors, hotels, clothiers, department stores, and, of course, Con Ed, spoke of the "dastardly deeds" and "ghoulish acts" of the power conglomerate and demanded justice for wrongs perpetrated against the writer and others. As police detectives duly noted, some of the notes were typewritten; most, however, were hand-printed on postcards or simple white typewriting paper and displayed characteristically neat block letters, with clauses that were, intriguingly, separated with dashes rather than commas or periods. Many of the letters contained threats to bomb the recipients, and several were sent "with the compliments of the 'mobsters' at #4 Irving Place—for further information—see the Mayor."

And all of the letters were signed with the cryptic and baffling cipher "F.P."

. . .

Dispatches of the "Day of Infamy" spread to the mainland and America once again found herself at the doorstep of war. The attack on Pearl Harbor "was just the kind of unexpected thing the Japanese would do," lamented Franklin Roosevelt. "At the very time they were discussing peace in the Pacific, they were plotting to overthrow it." On the evening of December 7, 1941, as Roosevelt began dictation of his clarion "call to arms" to be delivered to Congress on the following day, men and boys from every corner of the nation set aside best laid plans and lined up outside of recruitment offices to enlist in the United States armed forces. The palpable anger that arose from Battleship Row on the island of Oahu roared through small towns and major cities alike and every American knew that the world, as they knew it, had changed forever.

The Bomber bore his own form of anger following the attack on Pearl Harbor. He was not lacking in patriotic feeling, as later events would clearly demonstrate, but his initial reaction to the news was peculiar and oddly self-centered. He knew that the attack would bring a single-minded national undertaking that would marshal all of the public's effort and attention. His ordained role to alert the world to the evildoings of Con Ed would now be sidetracked. The country would simply be too distracted by the war effort to take notice of the great service that he was performing for society. The jealously welled in him like a fever.

On the evening of December 7, 1941, as President Roosevelt completed the finishing touches on his address to the nation, the Bomber once again placed pen to paper. In a torrent of letters—nine in all—addressed to the managers of Bloomingdales, Bonds Clothes, the Capitol Theatre,

Radio City Music Hall, the Roxy Theatre, the Paramount Theatre in Times Square, the Strand Theatre, the Astor Hotel, and Hotel Commodore, he lambasted Con Ed with accusations and condemnations that, under the circumstances, went far beyond the pale of propriety.

With America reeling from the devastating losses at Pearl Harbor, the letters were received with a mix of curiosity and distaste—but mostly stoic disregard. Though he cajoled, implored, and, of course, threatened the recipients with harm, the Bomber, in reality, knew painfully well that his letters could not achieve the goals that he so compulsively clung to. Convinced that disparate forces of the world had conspired against him, he reasoned that punishment for Con Ed's misdeeds would have to be postponed.

After enumerating the usual litany of offenses perpetrated by Con Ed, the Bomber, in his last penned letter on the evening of America's Day of Infamy, concluded with the following statement neatly printed in block letters:

> I WILL MAKE NO MORE BOMB UNITS FOR THE DURATION
> OF THE WAR—MY PATRIOTIC FEELINGS HAVE MADE ME
> DECIDE THIS—LATER I WILL BRING THE CON-ED TO
> JUSTICE—THEY WILL PAY FOR THEIR DASTARDLY DEEDS
> . . . F.P.

In a self-indulgent fit of control over uncontrollable events, knowing that his portentous objectives had been delayed, the Mad Bomber vowed never to be forgotten.

# HELL GATE

THE MENACING STRUCTURE THAT WAS THE HELL GATE POWER PLANT spanned two city blocks along the East River and reached eight stories skyward in a gloomy morass of faded redbrick and terra-cotta. Four smokestacks spewing their black and sickly gases erupted from the base of the plant, taking aim at the skies above. By the time of the Great Depression, the power plant at Hell Gate was the primary supplier of electrical current to Manhattan, the Bronx, Queens, and Westchester County.

The plant's interior was dominated by two mammoth 160,000-kilowatt turbine generators with a combined capacity of more than 420,000 horsepower, and was served by a tangled mesh of piping, pumps, condensers, and boilers. At the dedication ceremony in 1929 marking the installation of these machines, the chairman of the New York Public Service Commission declared: "What we are doing here is forging a link with the industrial genius of other lands to form that indefinable, great force called civilization." Some would beg to differ.

Iron-grated floors and staircases crisscrossed the building, and asbestos-laden dust infused the air, flaking from aging mortar while unsuspecting workmen brushed against the gray and deteriorating walls. "Cement dust was everywhere in the air," complained one plant worker. "We came out filthy, dirty and coughing at the end of a day's work." In later years, the Hell Gate power plant would be identified as the source of pulmonary illness and disease in many of its workers, but in Depression-era America a job was the only thing that sheltered a man from certain destitution.

By the mid-1930s the Hell Gate plant and some two dozen other energy suppliers would be swallowed up in a complex series of mergers and acquisitions resulting in the new and mammoth Consolidated Edison Company of New York—or simply Con Ed, as it would come to be known by millions of New Yorkers. The smaller and independent United Electric Light and Power Company—the original owner and operator of the Hell Gate plant—was to be no more.

If the massive turbine generators were the cerebral center of the power plant, it was, in fact, the catacomb of coal-fired steam boilers that represented the cardiac muscle that pumped life into the plant. In the boiler room, a dense labyrinth of steel tubes, meters, gauges, and coal transport tracks served nine aisles of steam-generating boilers—twenty-one machines in total—arranged in narrow and orderly rows like iron-clad machines of war. Millions of gallons of purified condensing water from Long Island Sound were heated to temperatures approaching 1,000 degrees Fahrenheit by the intense flames of the coal and air confection created in the heart of each boiler. The high-pressure torrent of steam thus created was then fired through ten-inch valve connections to spin the turbines of the massive generators. According to the plant owners, the boiler room was constructed for "ultimate capacity."

Manning this 53,000-square-foot lattice of heat, water, and steel was a crew of hard and sturdy workmen who oversaw every aspect of the boiler room operation and of the plant as a whole. Engineers, dispatchers, operators, and menial workers alike labored long hours under difficult and dangerous conditions to operate and maintain the mammoth structures and equipment of the Hell Gate generating station in an effort to bring a reliable flow of current to the homes and businesses of New York. In a rather foreboding admonition that implied the dangers of the Hell Gate workplace, the standard application for employment with the United Electric Light and Power Co. contained the following "Notice to Employees Seeking Employment": "Unless you are willing to be careful to avoid injury to yourself and fellow workmen, do not ask for employment.

We do not want careless people in our employ." Most of the men signed the contract without a thought. They just wanted to feed their families.

Joining this hardnosed and obdurate collection of plant workers in December 1929 was one shy and somewhat peculiar twenty-eight-year-old who seemed out of place. George Metesky had temporarily moved from his Waterbury, Connecticut, home to a rooming house on West Eighty-eighth Street in Manhattan to find work following his discharge from the Marine Corps. Though meticulous and painstaking in his duties, Metesky appeared rather undaunted by the strains of the enveloping Depression or the rigors of daily life at the plant.

His sheepish eyes rarely met with those of his coworkers, and his courteous demeanor was infrequently mistaken for affability or friendliness. Unlike many of the plant's workforce, Metesky established few, if any, relationships on the job, and he rarely engaged his fellow workers in idle chat or conversation. In striking contrast to the nature of his job and its surroundings and in keeping with his fastidious nature, Metesky was incessantly neat and always clean-shaven, with his hair adroitly combed into a pompadour. With a starting salary of $30.12 per week, he had counted himself among the fortunate to secure a job at the Hell Gate plant in 1929.

His position did not utilize the electrical skills that he had earlier developed, but Metesky inoffensively went about his business as a maintenance worker at the plant. His specific job titles were "generator wiper" and later "gallery man," but Metesky dutifully performed whatever job was asked of him. Initially, his work entailed the simple cleaning from plant generators of the incessant buildup of grease, dust, and condensation, but later he received a promotion with the attendant duty of throwing switches and blocking feeders to safeguard the proper flow of electricity. As menial as many of his assigned tasks were, for nearly two years he always performed them more diligently than the job required, earning him a "top rating" at the power plant. He would later question his unfailing loyalty to Con Ed, but by 1931 George Metesky had become a model employee of the Hell Gate station.

. . .

"[He] looks like the usher who passes the collection plate in a small-town church. He would be a deacon, probably and certainly might lead the weekly sing at Rotary or Kiwanis and, in his spare time work hard for the Community Chest," wrote one observer. Opinions of George Metesky were as diverse as the confused machinations of his inner thought process. Some found him pleasant and friendly, even jovial, while others described him as aloof and solitary—a "lone wolf," said one co-worker. By most outward appearances, he was an introverted man with a gentle and inoffensive demeanor. He was regularly seen at Sunday mass in St. Patrick's Roman Catholic Church in Waterbury, Connecticut, and he was generally considered to be a simple, albeit odd, man. The record would ultimately reveal, however, that beneath whatever exterior he chose to exhibit on any particular day, George Metesky would soon develop a raging and deluded anger that would dominate his every breath.

He was of stocky build and medium height, and he often wore a gray fedora that covered his thin and well-oiled dark hair. Gold-rimmed spectacles accentuated studious light blue eyes, and his clothing, though modest in style, was always clean and meticulous in appearance. He would later be described as having a "spinsterish air about him," or bearing the outward look of a "schoolteacher."

Born George Peter Milauskas on November 2, 1903, in Waterbury, Connecticut, to Lithuanian immigrant parents, he was the youngest of four siblings. George's parents, George and Anna, settled the family in the ethnically diverse and divided community of Waterbury, where they built the family home at 17 Fourth Street. A stolid and hardworking man, George Senior worked first as a teamster then as a night watchman at the J. E. Smith Lumber Co. He would be remembered fondly by the owner of the company as "[e]fficient and well liked. He was a strong man, not big, but powerful . . . He used to leave notes for the day side after he went off duty. They were classics . . . he wrote beautifully, but spelled phonetically . . . [O]ne word he used all the time—'desdesem.' It [meant] 'just the same.' He wrote as he pronounced." George Senior brought a workingman's pride and a strong respect for rules and regulations to his job. "Gangs used to break into the lumber yard," continued the company owner. "[A]nd George would go right after then [*sic*], eight or ten at a time. He was all guts. He'd chase them too."

As a child, the younger George attended the St. Joseph's Parochial School at the Roman Catholic Church of "Brooklyn's Lithuanians." Later he would transfer to Duggan Elementary School, a weathered redbrick and mortar building, where he quickly gained a reputation as shy and withdrawn. A fellow student would later remark, "George would literally not step on an ant, he was that averse to hurting anything. He was a meticulous boy. Always dressed well. He wouldn't talk to you unless you made the first advances. He never went in for athletics. I should say he was quiet to the point of eccentricity."

A teacher at Duggan School who was afflicted with a mild stutter had difficulty pronouncing George's last name. She converted "Milauskas" to "Metesky," and ultimately the name stuck. The family surname would, in fact, prove to be a source of continuing confusion. At any given time the family would refer to themselves or be known to others variously as "Metesky," "Milauskas," "Miliauskas," "Mallauskas," "Mulesky," or "Molusky," and the mailbox at the front of the family home listed three of these variations.

Though he was of above average intelligence and showed proficient mechanical aptitude, Metesky managed only one year of high school. Feeling superior to his fellow students and even teachers, he dropped out of Crosby High School in 1918, later explaining, "I just had no interest in the subjects they were teaching." Upon leaving school, Metesky worked several menial jobs as a theater usher and soda dispenser as well as a short stint as an apprentice machinist at the Farrell Foundry in Waterbury. A coworker at the foundry observed, "Well, he was a strange one. He came to work all dressed up in a suit and collar and necktie. He tried to learn the machine business dressed like that. And he hated to get his hands dirty. After a while he left the job and I lost track of him."

In further pursuit of a technical vocation following school, he took on and ultimately completed an L. L. Coke correspondence course in electricity. Several months later, at the age of sixteen and a half, his "wanderlust" (as he called it) led him to enlist with the United States Marine Corps. In an initial two-year tour that began on April 13, 1920, at Parris Island, Metesky served eighteen months in Mexico and the Dominican Republic, where his service ultimately won him the Good Conduct Medal. In April 1922 he was honorably discharged from the Marines with an official service classification of "excellent."

During the next three years of civilian life, Metesky worked as an auto mechanic's helper and a stock clerk, but in August 1925, yearning for the order and regimentation of the military, he chose to re-enlist with the Marine Corps. His record indicated that he had grown an inch from the time of his first enlistment, now standing 5′ 9 ½″, with "eyes blue, complexion ruddy." During this period, PFC George Metesky spent a year in Guam and twenty-two months at the United States consulate in Shanghai, China (and later Peking), where he received formal training as a specialist electrician—and as a chief ordnance mechanic in charge of a munitions powerhouse. Again, Metesky received high praise for his "excellent" service and character in the Marine Corps.

Following his honorable discharge from the service in 1929, Metesky, then age twenty-six, moved back into the family home at 17 Fourth Street in Waterbury. The property was situated at the top of a short but steeply inclined street in an unattractive section of town, cut off from the rest of the city by the Naugatuck River—"a dreary, shabby area of old homes falling into disrepair, weedy, rubbish-strewn lots, grimy-windowed factories and warehouses. The local name for the area was Brooklyn. Its residents were first- and second-generation Middle Europeans, Irish and Italians." Though Waterbury had long since lost its character as a prosperous industrial center, it clung through the years to the appellation Brass City like a long-lost friend.

The Metesky home was a gray and dismal three-story frame building with faded wooden pillars that extended across the exterior of each floor. Porches, sagging at the middle, tenuously clung for the support of each pillar and gave the property the befitting appearance of an urban tenement. To the rear of the house, along a dusty and unpaved driveway, was a small garage of corrugated metal. Though the property was barren and in need of care, it was not untidy. "The house was not loved," wrote one observer, "It was only maintained."

Not long after he returned home, Metesky's mother, who had favored young George as the baby of the family, passed away, and in 1947 George Senior died, leaving the family home and a moderately sized cash estate to be divided among the four siblings. By this time, Metesky's brother, John, had married and moved to another part of town, leaving George alone in the house with his two gaunt and dour unmarried sisters, Anna and Mae.

The three siblings presented a strange and mysterious spectacle to the neighboring families. The top two floors of the home were rented to others, and Metesky resided on the first floor with his sisters. Following the death of their mother, Anna and Mae had taken on a maternal role and had set about to shelter, support, and pamper their younger brother, providing for his every material and financial need, often to their own sacrifice. It wasn't long, however, before dark and sinister rumors began to spread throughout the neighborhood and the moniker "crazy house" was soon ascribed to the property. Though both of the sisters held jobs in nearby factories, they were roundly thought of as stern and severe. The private and impenetrable nature of the family would serve only to heighten local suspicions.

Content with this reclusive lifestyle, Metesky remained friendless and largely alone. He showed little interest in women and, like his spinster sisters, remained unmarried. He accepted their unconditional love and admiration yet shared with them nothing of himself or his private world. Other than the short time Metesky spent in New York working at Hell Gate, this peculiar living arrangement would endure for nearly thirty years.

• • •

Summer in the Lower Bronx is often slow to depart, and the sweltering heat of September 5, 1931, provided little hint of the promised change in the season to come. The stairways and catacombs of Hell Gate seemed to magnify the outside heat, and as George Metesky made his way through the columns of deafening machines ominously arranged in the boiler room, he gently padded a folded handkerchief against his now profusely sweating brow.

Each of the twenty-one coal-fired boilers at Hell Gate represented a complex maze of cast iron and steel that was designed to operate under the most severe conditions, constantly confronting enormous pressure and temperature, and continually requiring a complex array of repair and maintenance. The obvious and foreboding danger of malfunction was a constant presence, and despite the implementation of safety measures, a palpable sense of concern was prevalent throughout the plant.

Metesky scanned the meters of the high-tension board, and the usual tumult of the boiler room suggested good order. He made his way blithely along the gray aisle with his eyes focused ahead of him, thinking only of his assigned tasks—and heedless of the danger that lurked before him.

Obscured by the racket of raging boilers and unbeknownst to Metesky, one sick and heaving machine lay along his path. The technical maintenance of this particular cistern had failed, and sinister residues of coal and soot now clogged the gaps between its iron segments—the so-called "baffles"—and the boiler thrashed in a suffocating dance to free its pressurized air channels of the foul obstruction. Drowned by the noisy clamor of the other boilers, the groans that would have announced the malignant condition of this particular machine went unnoticed by Metesky. He strolled forward, unaware of the dangers that lay ahead. As he approached, disparate forces within the boiler reached a breaking point and, with a deafening burst, a toxic potion of soot and sickly gases expulsed through the intakes and directly into the path of George Metesky.

# THE SEEDS OF MADNESS

THE BOILER ROOM FILLED WITH AN ACIDIC ODOR THAT SUGGESTED a metallic decay or perhaps even the merging of discordant chemicals. George Metesky staggered backward, one hand clutching his constricted throat, the other reaching out for balance that instantaneously waned. As the searing combustion gases filled his lungs, he gasped and began to cough violently and uncontrollably. One knee settled to the concrete floor and then the other, and soon the harsh and burning sensations in his chest were accompanied by a gurgling bark, suggesting the presence of blood. Metesky instantly recoiled as the carmine film sprayed the floor and his trousers like a macabre work of art.

Two plant workmen named Cavanaugh and Casey heard the commotion and came upon Metesky lying on the floor and struggling for air. Upon viewing the splatters of blood the men nervously eyed one another as Metesky, through staggered breaths, attempted to explain what had happened. After regaining somewhat his strength and composure, he reported the episode to the foreman, a Mr. Purdy, who, according to Metesky's later statements, all but ignored the incident and even ordered the stricken worker to assist in the non-plant-related task of loading of wood into a car owned by one Lawson, the floor boss. "Apparently," recalled Metesky, "the coughing and blood were normal occurrences at Con Edison because when I told these . . . three guys [Cavanaugh, Casey, and Purdy] they weren't a bit surprised . . ."

After the twenty minutes of laborious effort required to assist the foreman, Metesky, per his own statement, fell to the concrete floor in exhaustion. It was two o'clock in the afternoon, and he was forced to remain on that spot for nearly two hours without comfort or assistance. "There were over 12,000 'Danger Signs' in the plant," Metesky would later recall, "yet not even 'First Aid' was available or rendered to me. I had to lay on cold concrete." Finally, according to Metesky, around four o'clock, he gathered his strength and was able to get up off the floor and make his way home.

In the coming days he remained alone and in bed in the rooming house on West Eighty-eighth Street, his condition growing progressively worse. He continued to experience episodes of uncontrolled coughing during which he would expectorate blood, and he grew more fatigued by the day. Increasingly concerned, he sent for a doctor, who, without the benefit of X-rays or medical tests, was unable to arrive at a specific diagnosis. He did, however, suggest that Metesky return home to Waterbury, where he could receive proper care and be looked after by family.

Following the doctor's advice, he called on his brother, John, to bring him home to Waterbury. He was promptly seen by a Dr. Max Ruby, and within two hours Metesky was admitted to Waterbury Hospital. There, doctors immediately diagnosed an aggressive form of pneumonia and confirmed that the pain, exhaustion, and bleeding that he was experiencing had been caused by a series of pulmonary hemorrhages. During his hospitalization he received antibiotic treatment for his conditions and came under the constant observation of physicians and hospital staff. After two grueling weeks, Metesky was finally stabilized enough to be sent home to continue with his recovery.

Despite continued aggressive medical therapies during the next eleven months, Metesky's condition did not significantly improve, and, in fact, his symptoms grew so pronounced that his doctors soon began to suspect tuberculosis. He endured such a constant state of pulmonary distress that he remained, for the most part, confined to home and bed and unable to return to his job at the Hell Gate plant. Somewhat alarmed, and aware that the facilities of Waterbury Hospital were inadequate to care for such an illness, Dr. Ruby referred his patient to a sanitarium in Tucson, Arizona. Metesky made the difficult journey west and, upon his initial examination by staff physicians, was definitively diagnosed with "active pulmonary tuberculosis."

Metesky was clearly a sick man, but he settled well in Tucson. He was provided with a small bungalow "like a tourist cabin," and though alone except for the visits of a nurse who occasionally stayed with him during his more acute periods of distress, he began his long road toward recuperation. Not two months into his stay, however, he endured another series of lung hemorrhages that required treatment with a painful array of pneumothorax therapies, which consisted of the introduction of nitrogen gas into the pleural cavity via long hollow needles. Progressively, over a period of nearly three years, these therapies started to take hold and the tubercular lesions in Metesky's lungs began to subside.

Though improved physically, his mental state had already begun to show signs of the irretrievable free fall that was to come.

• • •

In the mind of George Metesky the events of September 5, 1931, at the Hell Gate power plant boiler room were absolute and real, though later a lack of corroborating evidence would cast a mantle of uncertainty and conjecture over them. Con Ed never reported the incident to the Workmen's Compensation Board, and the three employees who came to Metesky's aid would later offer confused and differing accounts of what occurred. Though his physical illness was unquestionably genuine— George Metesky was clearly ailing—its derivation would be the subject of conjecture for years to come. What remains undisputed, however, is that the backdraft of gases that afflicted him, whether real or imagined, and the series of events that followed planted the seeds that would ultimately transform the seemingly inoffensive George Metesky into a psychotic and vindictive personality.

During his extended illness, Metesky had noted on many occasions that he had been discharged healthy from the United States Marine Corps in 1929. Indeed, in his yearly physical examination mandated by his employer, he was deemed "physically sound" as late as March 10, 1930. In the months and years that followed his employment at the power plant, however, he had been undeniably crippled by the effects of constant and debilitating lung disease. Though there remained no medical proof that a blast of hot gases could be the underlying source of tuberculosis, it was not difficult for him to make the causal link. There was no doubt in George Metesky's mind that the root of his enduring physical problems lay at the feet of the Consolidated Edison Company.

Understandably, from the first onset of his illness, Metesky had deep concerns not only for his physical well-being but also for his financial well-being. Immediately upon his accident, he applied for and was granted sick benefits from Con Ed. For six months the company paid him roughly eighty percent of his $38.16 weekly salary. He drew an additional $58.00 per month for roughly three years as a settlement on a company group life insurance policy.

Though Metesky incurred ever rising medical and living expenses, especially upon his admission to the Arizona sanitarium, he was able to nominally survive with some assistance from his father. By mid-1933, as the prospect of dissipating insurance benefits began to loom, however, it became clear that his expenses were going to be well beyond the means of his family to absorb alone. Metesky knew he was going to need further means of financial sustenance.

On the good days—the days when he felt physically well enough—Metesky would spend his time pistol shooting at targets in the yard surrounding his cabin in Tucson. The new hobby provided a welcome respite and served to pass many unfilled hours of boredom as his body healed in the dry Arizona climate. During these times his thoughts would drift, and as he fired the weapon his mind would invariably flash to the Hell Gate boiler room and the pure injustice of his present situation. His illness, his dwindling finances—they were all the fault of Con Ed. "They owe me," he would mutter. "Con-Ed owes me."

By the close of 1933, Metesky had already begun a campaign of what would become his signature form of communication—letter writing. With nothing but time and a growing disposition of anger on his hands, Metesky began incessantly hammering out typewritten missives to Con Ed that brashly demanded an increase in his benefits. By his own estimate, Metesky, while living in Arizona, would write two to three hundred letters to his former employer.

Initially his letters succeeded; perhaps out of sheer exasperation, Con Ed agreed to increase his insurance settlement to $180 per month. When that ran out, Metesky badgered the company to pay his medical bills and total living expenses. "I asked them to take care of me," he would later confess. As the barrage continued, the financial managers of the company finally concluded that they had fully discharged their obligations to Metesky and terminated all further benefits to him effective December 31, 1933. At wit's end, they suggested that if he wished to pursue the matter further he should contact the Workmen's Compensation Board. Of course, the disgruntled former employee construed this as "the run around."

• • •

New York's workmen's compensation system, one of the first in the country, was born in 1914 largely out of a tragic fire at the Triangle Shirtwaist Factory that killed 146 workers, almost all of them women. The Lower Manhattan sweatshop occupied the eighth, ninth, and tenth floors of the Asch Building off Washington Square and manufactured 10,000–12,000 women's blouses each week. Somehow, a bin of loose cotton beneath a worker's bench ignited and the fire quickly rose to the floors above. Panic-stricken employees encountered a partially blocked and unstable fire escape that collapsed and a stairwell door leading to the roof that had been locked to prevent employee theft. Many of the victims were faced with the unthinkable choice of burning to death or leaping from upper-story windows. In a matter of moments the fire had consumed the factory and ravaged many of its unfortunate workers. Through the time of George Metesky and for years beyond, the Triangle Shirtwaist tragedy would be considered "the worst work-place fire in the history of New York City."

The owners of the Triangle Shirtwaist Company were criminally tried on manslaughter charges but acquitted, and civil suits brought by surviving family members ultimately netted each family a pittance in damages. What would begin as a simple outpouring of grief by stunned New Yorkers soon turned to outrage and a clarion call for reform. The political strength of labor unions and progressive movements gradually increased following the tragic fire, and soon activist members of the New York legislature—and indeed legislatures across the country—would enact sweeping changes in workplace regulation and state labor laws. Within this progressive era would emerge state workmen's compensation legislation that created a statutory scheme of automatic no-fault payments to injured employees. The "compensation bargain" created by this system required the acceptance of an employee's damage award as an exclusive remedy for workplace injuries. In exchange for this prescribed benefit without proof of fault, all rights to sue the employer for negligence in the workplace were relinquished. This policy compromise ensured guaranteed protection for workers while providing employers with limited liability (usually covered by insurance) and the avoidance of costly and protracted litigation. The misery and destitution that followed the Triangle Shirt-waist tragedy would, it was theorized, never be repeated.

• • •

By the start of 1934, George Metesky had been repeatedly frustrated by what he viewed as the insolence and arrogance of the Con Ed conglom-erate. As part of the company's attempt to stop the unrelenting volley of communications, they sent Metesky an Industrial Commission form to be completed as the first step in the process of requesting workmen's compensation benefits.

Recognizing that Con Ed was not going to resume his sick pay, Metesky filed his initial claim with the compensation board on January 4, 1934. In it, he provided a detailed description of his September 1931 accident at the Hell Gate station, making out, in his view, a clear and compelling case for compensation payments. A hearing was scheduled for May 24, 1934, but was delayed as a result of Metesky's residence in Arizona and consequent inability to appear. The matter again came up for hearing on September 27, 1934, and this time the board summarily dismissed the claim in Metesky's absence. As justification, section 28 of New York's Workmen's Compensation Act was cited.

Of the many legalities that would confront George Metesky in the coming years, none would frustrate and confound him more than the provisions of section 28. In the 1930s, the section imposed a one-year statute of limitations on claims for compensation benefits; any claim, to be considered viable, had to be filed within one year from the date of injury or be subject to dismissal. Since Metesky had delayed his filing well beyond the imposed one-year period, his claim was doomed from the start.

Upon being notified of the board's rejection of his claim, Metesky inquired as to the reasons and was informed that Con Ed and its insurance carrier had, in fact, invoked the time limitations of section 28. The merits of his case—the injustice of his circumstances—had, to his indignation, never even been broached at the hearing. He had been lulled to sleep by Con Ed in the days following his accident. He was convinced that his obstreperous former employer had purposefully pacified him until it was too late to assert a claim for compensation.

By the spring of 1935, Metesky had been forced to abandon his treatment in Arizona and had returned home to Waterbury. Though his health had fairly stabilized, he was instructed to continue bed rest with minimal physical activity. In his mind, a job was still out of the question. Dwindling finances had forced the move and, according to Metesky, the unscrupulous Con Ed and an uncaring state compensation system were the cause.

Once home in Connecticut, the letter-writing campaign, which had now expanded to include members of the New York State Industrial Commission and its chief, Elmer Andrews, and even the governor of New York, Herbert Lehman, accelerated and became unbendingly fixed on securing a new hearing in which his grievances could be heard. Surely, mused Metesky, when the true facts emerged, his claim would be embraced and allowed by any fair-minded judge or jury.

As rambling and passionate as his letters were to that point, they contained no intimidation or hints of violence. His communiqués to public officials included prods and bold demands for intervention against Con Ed and the compensation board, but were not in any way viewed as dangerous or threatening. Though the sheer volume was somewhat disconcerting, the letters were reviewed, and in early 1936 Metesky was granted a reconsideration hearing.

This time he was present at the hearing and was represented by a Brooklyn attorney named Michael Jackowitz, but to Metesky's dismay, the result was the same. Con Ed again asserted section 28, and again the claim was abruptly dismissed for lack of timely filing.

With a seething frustration, Metesky once more took to the typewriter, and, remarkably, a third hearing—one promising to include testimony on the merits of his case—was granted. "It took a lot of letter writing," said Metesky, "but I got another hearing." He would finally get his day in court.

On April 2, 1936, an inquiry was held before a compensation board referee, and Metesky, again represented by his attorney, was allowed to submit his grievances. At first, the testimony went as planned and Metesky, pleased with its progress, would comment that the referee, a Mr. S. E. Senior, appeared "fair and honest." "He was a very nice man." It was with a certain uneasiness, however, that Metesky watched the Con Ed workman, Cavanaugh, and the supervisors, Purdy and Lawson—all present on the day of his injury—enter the hearing room prepared to offer their accounts.

With verbal skills somewhat lacking, each of the men appeared to contradict the other as to the events of September 5, 1931. Purdy testified that Metesky was working at the plant on the day in question but recalled only that he did not feel well. Cavanaugh merely stated that Metesky had suffered a nosebleed, and Lawson swore that Metesky was not even working on the day in question. To the claimant's delight, Referee Senior became completely exasperated with the differing accounts rendered by the men, and threatened to discount the entirety of their testimony. "The referee was going to make an award in my favor . . . ," Metesky later recalled. It appeared that his claim would finally be allowed.

At that moment, however, counsel for Con Ed and their insurance carrier, Hamlin and Company, rose with an air of smug confidence and once again asserted their rights under section 28 of the Compensation Act. Metesky visibly faltered as the referee listened intently to the arguments and reluctantly acceded. The undeniable fact remained that the written claim for benefits had been made beyond one year from the date of his accident. Senior had no choice but to once again deny Metesky's request.

An administrative appeal of the decision failed to yield better results. On September 28, 1936, the New York Workmen's Compensation Board conclusively denied George Metesky's final claim for benefits. Barring judicial appeals, which Metesky was in no position to finance, the ruling would stay undisturbed. Officially, it would remain so for twenty-one years. Later circumstances, however, would demand another look.

• • •

With the final appeal of the compensation case decided, George Metesky spent most of his time confined to home and bed, lamenting his misfortunes. Ever persistent, he again began writing a series of letters to Commissioner Andrews informing him of the great injustice performed at the Workmen's Compensation Board and imploring him to intercede in the matter. Andrews's failure to provide the desired results served only to frustrate the ailing Metesky and further provoked him to again escalate the use of his only available weapon—the written word.

A barrage of mail began arriving at the State Industrial Commission, the governor's office, and, of course, Con Ed. In droves, Metesky's letters, which by then had taken on an angry and ominous tone, poured into New York media outlets and public institutions, calling the world's attention to the "injustices" and "dastardly deeds" of the corrupt power company and the system that failed him—all without invoking so much as a flicker of interest or a furrowed brow of suspicion. "I had written thousands of letters to every newspaper, every radio station, every commentator of importance and just about every church. I even tried to purchase space in the press, even the papers rejected my offers," Metesky would later state. He estimated that he had written nearly 800,000 words during this period—enough to fill a 3,000-page book. (Tolstoy's *War and Peace* contains about 560,000 words). "I never received so much as one single penny postal card in reply."

His letters were long—some as many as nine hundred words—and filled with vitriolic ire. In one such letter to Con Ed, Metesky wrote:

> You know, I just refuse to be robbed by the law, or a Power Trust, of my health, my ability to earn a living, the best years of my life, my advancement in the world . . . You are paying me what is due me, or you are telling me why not. Said reason better be AIR TIGHT. If there is any TREACHERY, or DOUBLE-CROSSING, I may assume the role of JUDGE JURY AND EXECUTIONER, and straighten matters out. I am done fooling around with SCUM.

With the failure of his communications to induce any response whatsoever, Metesky's hostility and bitterness only escalated, and gradually his thinking became more illogical and his behavior increasingly irrational. Convinced that the failure of the newspapers to take notice of his sad chronicle was due to their incestuous relations with the influential Con Ed, he soon developed a broad mistrust that extended to people and institutions in general—all of whom, according to Metesky, seemed to be conspiratorially connected in some way to the sinister power company. With his prodigious letter-writing campaign in full tilt, his life seemed to be driven by the singular purpose of enlightening the world to the horrible injustices perpetrated by Con Ed against himself and thousands of its other employees.

And yet at the very time that George Metesky's mind had begun its decent into the vortex of fury that would dominate his every thought, a creative and intellectual side also began to take shape. He invented an electric snow shovel that he demonstrated for one of his Waterbury tenants, who delightedly observed, "It worked great too. It'd pick up the snow and threw it to the left." Later, Metesky rigged a hand-pushed lawnmower with a small electric motor and an extended durable cord that was featured in an article published in *Popular Science*. And in July 1938, he applied for and was ultimately granted a United States patent on a piston-driven circuit breaker for connecting and interrupting the electrical circuit of a solenoid pump. Ironically, this circuit completion technology would later prove to have broad application to a more devious and destructive venture engaged in by its inventor.

• • •

Though Metesky's technical nature occasionally distracted him from the anger and bitterness that permeated his thoughts, he would later confess, "I had a mission to perform," and his focus would invariably return to the injustices committed by Con Ed and its personnel. It was, however, this very ability to portray himself with an air of normalcy—even excellence—that permitted his increasingly impaired judgment and perception to remain undetected for much of his adult life.

Notwithstanding outward appearances, Metesky's mind was slowly descending into flights of twisted imagination and distorted perceptions. He reserved his most vituperative bouts of fantasy for the three Con Ed employees—Cavanaugh, Purdy, and Lawson—who, in Metesky's mind, had purposely provided false and slanderous testimony against him at the compensation hearing (this, despite the fact that the referee had clearly discounted their statements as unreliably inconsistent).

During the periods when his health permitted, Metesky would travel in and around Manhattan via the subway system. On one such occasion, as he sat holding the steel balance rail and peering silently out the window, Cavanaugh, Purdy, and Lawson boarded the car at one of its stops. Nothing could have persuaded him that he was mistaken as to their identities—though perhaps, and in all likelihood, he was. The three took seats directly across from him, and though he glared at them with confrontational eyes, they pretended, Metesky insisted, not to notice. As they sat in quiet conversation he was absolutely convinced that he was the topic of their exchange. Their smiles were derisive and their laughter, mocking—and it was all directed at him. He was sure of it. From that moment and for years to come, George Metesky's disordered thinking became accompanied by a new and dangerous component: violence. In his mind's eye, he saw, as clear as the perjurers' deceitful lips, an explosion that ripped off the right arms of all three of these men—the arms that rose in a solemn vow to tell nothing but the truth. He saw a bullet enter the chest of the president of Con Ed, the shameful and blameworthy source of the world's evils, and explode in his heart. And as for the elite power centers of New York City itself, he saw a plan of sabotage that would bring the metropolis to its knees—and at long last call attention to the condemnable acts of Con Ed.

As the scourge of fascism spread across Europe, the violent impulse that now inculcated George Metesky's ailing mind searched for expression. The decade that gave birth to radio and radar, Art Deco and swing, *The Grapes of Wrath* and *The Wizard of Oz;* that saw Olympic triumph in Berlin and Hindenburg disaster in New Jersey; that began with the hardship of depression and the repeal of Prohibition, would end with America edging ever closer to world conflict. And for an unpretentious man from Waterbury, Connecticut, ravaged with mental illness, the decade of the 1930s would end with a simple decision to use bombs to settle a personal score.

## IV

# "SELECTED BY DESTINY"

WITH THE GREAT MISSION OF HIS LIFE HELD IN ABEYANCE IN FAVOR OF HIS patriotic feelings following the attack on Pearl Harbor, Metesky withdrew deeper into his quirky and enigmatic world. His initial assaults against Con Ed had proven feeble at best, but the postponement of his objectives would allow him time and opportunity to prepare for the ultimate conflagration envisaged by his steadfast mind-set. Though his two spinster sisters, Anna and Mae, happily labored and sacrificed for the benefit of their younger brother, whom they still viewed as sickly and vulnerable, Metesky rarely conversed with them or shared any of his inner thoughts. His aging father, though still residing on the property, exerted minimal influence on George's life and contributed meagerly to the household. His sisters provided him with clothing, money, and all the necessities of life. "We would deprive ourselves for him," Anna would later recall. "We were sorry for him." It was a "classic study in over-protection," wrote one observer.

His daily routine began at eight o'clock each morning, after his sisters left for work, at which time he arose, tidied his bedroom, and prepared a light breakfast. Other than an afternoon nap of several hours and a short walk along Fourth Street, he would busy himself with his automobile, which he always serviced on his own, and would study electrical engineering from a series of books that he had accumulated through the years. By four-thirty in the afternoon, Metesky's day was typically over. He would prepare an evening meal, dine alone, and immediately go to bed. His reclusive lifestyle would later be described as "timid and dull."

Not a soul—his sisters included—had the slightest inkling of the rage and insanity that brewed within.

Metesky was true to his promise to forego bomb-planting activities during the war, but he used the hiatus to study the craft and hone his skills, confident that in time they would be put to good and productive use. Alone in his garage, he extended his knowledge of electrical properties and experimented with different kinds of galvanized metal and fusing mechanisms. He began to stockpile the essential elements of his later units, which would have greater power and more efficient mechanics than his early ones. While the war raged through Western Europe and the Pacific, Metesky essentially lay in wait. The distorted reality that preyed upon his paranoid mind, however, continued in earnest. The passage of time did not dissuade his seething hatred of Con Ed or the list of its co-conspirators, which, to his unhinged way of thinking, expanded by the day.

Shortly after the start of the war, Metesky, then thirty-nine years of age, received his draft notice. To add to his feelings of alienation, he was rejected for military service on the basis of his medical history. Several months later he attempted to enlist but, upon examination by the Waterbury draft board, was again rejected based on the results of a chest X-ray that evidenced prior lung disease. Sensing a scheme—a pervasive and surreptitious fraud—Metesky immediately lashed out against one of the draft board members, Miles Kelly, whom he suspected of being complicit. Kelly was a former tenant in Metesky's home, and the relationship was strained from the outset. Following his enlistment rejection, Metesky sent letters to the company where the man worked denouncing his actions and berating his character. At the same time, he wrote to the local draft board and even President Roosevelt, complaining of the man's improprieties and cynically suggesting that Kelly himself be drafted for service. The carefully constructed logic of Metesky's arguments was twisted to everyone but himself. "He was a person who always was ready to fight authority . . . ," said one Waterbury citizen.

In December 1942 Metesky cajoled the owners of the Waterbury Tool Company to give him a job. At first, the owner was hesitant to offer the position because of his prior health problems, but "after much discussion and medical examinations" Metesky was able to persuade him that his mechanical expertise would be a valuable asset to the company and he was hired.

During the next year, he maintained the appearance of a productive and functioning employee. Ironically, however, Metesky found himself working side by side with Miles Kelly, who was also employed at the tool company, and the personal rancor between the two stemming from the draft board incident continued. Metesky repeatedly complained about Kelly's work and often petitioned his employer to fire him. Despite this discord, Metesky eagerly worked with both the public and other company personnel, sorting, shelving, and selling tools and other mechanical equipment and earning a very respectable wage of between $60 and $70 per week. As time went on, however, his chronic lung disease had begun to resurface and his absences from work started to increase. Finally, in December 1943, Metesky suffered another pulmonary hemorrhage and was diagnosed with an advanced case of bilateral tuberculosis.

With the assistance of his doctor, Max Ruby, he was able to gain admittance to the Undercliff Sanitarium in Meriden, Connecticut, a state-run facility exclusively dedicated to the diagnosis and treatment of pulmonary tuberculosis, where he would remain for the next fourteen months. Though examined and treated on many occasions by facility personnel, Metesky's condition did not materially improve. By his own account, he was "miserable and lonely," and on February 25, 1945, he left the sanitarium against the advice of his doctors and returned home. A few months later he was re-examined and found to have "further progression" of the disease, but because of "the patient's lack of cooperation" further treatment became impossible. Spending most of each day at home and in bed, Metesky gave up all thought of employment, electing rather to independently follow the routines of the sanitarium and live off the hard work and good intentions of his father and doting sisters.

Predictably, Metesky lay blame for his troubles squarely at the feet of Con Ed. The persistent grudge that he bore against the company continued to advance, and on various occasions between 1941 and 1946 he again launched volleys of letters to concerns around New York, all containing the familiar vitriol, and all closing with the characteristic "*F.P.*" sign-off. For all practical purposes, however, through World War II and for several years beyond, George Metesky dropped from sight.

The record is practically void of specific detail regarding Metesky's life for much of the 1940s. His health remained in various states of advance and decline during those years, and perhaps his total focus was centered on the pursuit of physical well-being. By his own words, the period was marked by feelings of disillusionment, and even his letter-writing campaign had begun to subside. None of his actions had succeeded in drawing attention to Con Ed's evil conduct, and the ideal of the "unknown man battling for justice," as he preferred to view himself, had seemed a distant and faltering aspiration.

Disillusionment notwithstanding, there is also evidence that, during this reclusive period after the war, Metesky resumed his bomb-making endeavors. He would later admit to planting up to twenty-four units that would remain unexploded and undiscovered—several at locations in and around the offices of Con Ed in the late 1940s. Neither the police nor the public had taken any notice of these devices, but Metesky's later declarations against his own interest would suggest that the statements were reliable and consistent with the underlying resentment that continued to brew within him.

· · ·

With the war behind her, America had entered a new era of optimism and prosperity. Families would be reunited and the national ethos would turn from the horrors of war to the solace of social and economic renewal. For

George Metesky, however, the war against tyranny had just begun. To him, the advent of the 1950s would herald a rebirth of fury and a resurgence of fixated obsession.

As the 1940s drew to a close, the inherent and unmistakable traits of paranoia, though not fundamentally changed, had begun to broaden and steadily intensify, leaving him unrelentingly persecutory and pathologically self-absorbed. The focus of his anger, though still emanating from the deeds of his former employer, had generalized through the years, leaving him with the paranoiac view that "the world had done him wrong." The failure of newspapers, retail stores, theaters, dance clubs, hotels, and other New York institutions to respond to his letters and render aid to his cause was viewed not merely as indifference or confusion to his myriad claims, but as active and malevolent collusion with Con Ed to deny him justice. Alone against a vast conspiratorial network that penetrated into every crevice of society and threatened not only his own interests but those of countless others, he regarded himself as "the instrument selected by destiny to overcome this conspiracy." "[H]is fury of hatred so enveloped his mental faculties and impaired his judgment to such a degree that it excluded all conscious, rational behavior and thinking." With the advent of a new era and the apparent resurgence of his health, he had become convinced that the "great mission" of his life, his "messianic role," his "crusade" to provide society with a "great service" was now at hand.

Deep within the throes of a progressive and severely incapacitating schizophrenia, George Metesky once again declared war on the Consolidated Edison Company.

# "A MAN WITH A HAMMER"

ROWS OF CASKETS BEARING THE BODIES OF FALLEN AMERICAN SOLDIERS had become an all too familiar sight beneath the high vaulted ceilings of the Forty-third Street entrance to New York's Grand Central Terminal during World War II. The terminal had been used by the military as a stop-over point from which grieving families could retrieve their loved ones and then continue the final journey home. At the arched entrance of the terminal, the statuary metaphor of Progress rising from the American Eagle, with Physical Force and Mental Force at its feet, seemed burdened once again by the strains of war.

The celebrated story of Grand Central, steeped in triumph and tragedy, began with its 1913 opening. It quickly transformed the culture and economy of surrounding Manhattan. Covering seventy-nine acres and bragging a capacity of 30,000 people without crowding, the station, at various times, was home to movie theaters, art galleries, museums, schools, and a wide variety of exhibitions. Considered by some at its opening the "greatest railway terminal in the world," Grand Central would host, through the years, such famous long-distance trains as the *Fast Mail,* the *Water-Level Limited,* the *Wolverine,* and the *Twentieth Century Limited.*

With the advent of postwar suburban life and effortless automobile travel, however, interstate rail service had begun a steady decline, and by the early 1950s the condition of the once majestic terminal had suffered greatly, prompting murmurs of its possible demolition. Among the many legends and architectural oddities of Grand Central that had survived, however, was the so-called Whispering Gallery that lay beneath the tiled

Guastavino arches, extending across the ceilings of the lower concourse in front of the famous Oyster Bar, a seafood restaurant that opened in 1913 with the inauguration of the station itself. Created by the low ceramic structures of the domed ceiling, the unique architectural design allowed even faint whispers in one corner of the gallery to be heard clearly and distinctly across the expanse to the other.

As George Metesky stole into the lower level of Grand Central Terminal in the early afternoon of March 29, 1951, and placed his latest edition of revenge in a cigarette sand urn outside of the Oyster Bar, the acoustical quirk of the Whispering Gallery carried his footfalls throughout the passageway. The later explosive blast would fill the area with the same force and avid resolve as Metesky now brought to his reborn cause.

• • •

At 5:25 in the afternoon, at the peak of New York's rush hour, Metesky's unit detonated, spraying shards of sand and debris in all directions. By happenstance nobody was passing by the area at the particular moment of discharge, but the blast was heard throughout the station and into the confines of the Oyster Bar. There were no injuries and there was little, if any, panic by commuters and patrons, though the bomb squad investigation that ensued well into the evening was a curious and disrupting sight in a location that thrived on a certain frenzied order.

Investigators were immediately stumped. This did not appear to be a typical pipe bomb, and, since there was a detonation, a conclusion as to its design and construction would be a difficult task. The attempted bombings of the Con Ed buildings in the early 1940s were a fleeting memory, and no immediate connection was made by police.

In the following days, Metesky was gratified by several newspaper articles that covered the incident. Though some of the particulars conflicted, the story was picked up by the wire services and the news had spread across the country, albeit in small accounts beneath the fold or buried in the back pages. For the most part, these stories emphasized the homemade nature of the device and confirmed that no one had been injured. The *New York Times* contained a page 24 article titled "Bomb Blast in Terminal," which stated that the police attributed the incident to "boys or pranksters."

The Grand Central bombing was, in reality, intended by Metesky as more of a prototype of a new fusing mechanism rather than a full-fledged explosive device. It did not contain a pipe casing or a measure of volatile powder, only a .25-caliber cartridge and an ingenious apparatus designed to automatically discharge the round at a predetermined time. Though destroyed in the ignition, the focus of this mechanism was, once again, the throat lozenge that had so confounded bomb squad detectives in the past—and would continue to do so in the future.

Metesky knew that the "throat disc," as he called it, had a constant rate of dissolution when exposed to moisture. Through years of experimentation he observed that by applying varying amounts of water to a disc that had been meticulously filed down to a prescribed thickness, he could predict, with some accuracy, the time it would take for the disc to melt. A spoonful of water, for example, would disintegrate the disc in half an hour, while two to three drops would take several days. In his earlier units (which had failed to detonate either by design or defect), he applied these properties to complete the circuit between a battery and a flash bulb. As the lozenge dissolved it would bring the fusing wires into contact and thus, in theory, detonate the bomb.

His new method, though still crude, carried a greater level of ingenuity—and risk. In the Grand Central incident Metesky used the throat disc to compress a spring within a slot in the bomb housing. Once the disc sufficiently dissolved (the time this took depending on the amount of water added), the spring would release, driving a ball-bearing into a second spring, which, in turn, slammed a firing pin into the .25-caliber cartridge, causing its detonation. In his future bombings, the cartridge and the throat disc fusing mechanism would be used to trigger a larger cache of smokeless gunpowder contained within a pipe casing. On March 29, 1951, however, it was nothing more than the sound of a .25-caliber bullet that echoed through the lower concourse of Grand Central Terminal near track 27.

Metesky was now ready to begin what he called "the rough stuff." He had perfected several workable versions of his bomb units, and to give his crusade maximum exposure he would seek further high-profile targets in heavily traveled areas. He always insisted that it was never his intention to kill or injure any person, and thus he would purposefully design his bombs to be smaller in scale and less likely to inflict harm. "I've read," Metesky would later say, "that a man with a hammer can wreck a sixteen-inch naval gun, just by hitting it until it shatters. It takes a while. It's the same way with bombs. Individually, they couldn't knock a telephone off the wall. Collectively, they had an effect."

The New York City police would beg to differ. In each case, investigators would conclude that Metesky's bombs were purposefully placed in public locations and that each was capable of causing injury or death to anyone within proximity. Every so-called unit was, in fact, "lethal."

• • •

About three weeks after the Grand Central incident, Metesky struck again. He stole into a telephone booth on the basement level of the New York Public Library on Forty-second Street and Fifth Avenue, and placed a three-and-a-half-inch length of pipe fueled with smokeless gunpowder and a .25-caliber cartridge mechanism—throat disc fused—inside the metal fan casing at the top of the enclosure. At 6:10 in the evening of April 24, 1951, the bomb detonated, tearing through the booth's ventilation apparatus and horrifying (but remarkably not injuring) a library security guard who happened to be leaning against the booth at the time of the blast. Bomb squad detectives immediately saw the connection with the Grand Central bombing, both in the form of the mechanism and in the manner of its placement, and the newspapers were quick to recall the earlier police conclusion that they were dealing with "pranksters."

Over the months that followed, Metesky seemed to regroup and assess what, if anything, he had accomplished. He had successfully planted several of his units, each of which had detonated as designed, and each had garnered some minor publicity. Yet, whatever satisfaction he gained from these events was trifling and short-lived. With every painful and labored breath that he drew, he was reminded of his nemesis, Con Ed, and his mission to make them pay for what they did to him. He was compelled to finish what he had started.

On August 27, 1951, Metesky once again struck Grand Central Terminal. At 9:00 p.m., well beyond the evening rush hour, a length of galvanized pipe detonated in a telephone booth on the west concourse of the terminal, causing damage but no injuries. And several weeks later, in a direct assault against Con Ed, a five-inch pipe bomb, his largest to that point, exploded in a telephone booth in the lobby of the company's main offices on Irving Place. Again, in an apparent effort to minimize the possibility of injury, the unit was timed to explode at 6:15 in the morning, well before most employees arrived for work.

The New York City police downplayed the Con Ed incident, again insisting that they were dealing with a prankster and that damage had been "trifling." Privately, however, bomb squad detectives had begun to grow uneasy. Detective William Schmitt, an affable, brawny veteran of the force charged with the task of examining and cataloguing each fragmented component of the exploded machines, immediately realized that the city was dealing with a serial bomber. Though the contraptions thus far had been constructed on a small scale, he recognized the progressively improved workmanship of each and, along with the bomb squad as a whole, privately worried that the culprit would take the obvious next step of increasing the potency of his work. Contained in the official police record of the second Grand Central bombing was this ominous notation: "This is a well constructed mechanism. It shows considerable advance in technique as compared with earlier bombs."

In what would become the standing policy of the New York City Police Department for the next five years of the investigation, department personnel refused to provide any specific details of their investigation. "It would 'just build up the ego of the nut who did it,'" said one detective. The department was also concerned that heavy publicity about the bombings might panic the city and bring out the inevitable copycats. This position would prove to be a dreadful blunder. As Metesky himself would explain, "They got some stupid advice from some psychiatrist, 'If you don't bother with him, he'll stop.' And that just made me work all the harder."

Thirteen days after the Con Ed bombing, a clerk in the third floor Con Ed mail room accepted postal delivery of a large manila envelope that seemed to bulge at its seams. The package, postmarked "White Plains, NY," was hand-addressed to the personnel director of the company and contained, at the upper left corner, a printed return designation of "Lehman and Lehman." Though the Con Ed security force had advised all company personnel to remain alert for strange or unexplained devices in the building, the clerk was not cued to any obvious danger that might have been suggested by the package. Upon tearing it open, however, he identified the ashen hue of galvanized metal and dashed for security.

Following the usual protocol, a bomb squad detective, in full protective gear, examined the device via the portable fluoroscope, then jostled it from a distance in an attempt to test the trigger mechanism. When nothing occurred, the device was removed from the building in the mesh envelope and whisked, via the armored containment vehicle, to a safer locale. Upon closer scrutiny, the device seemed to contain all the familiar earmarks of the Bomber's handiwork, though the powder within the casing didn't look right. When it was deemed safe to do so, the detectives dismantled the contraption and out poured the phantom powder, which, upon further analysis, proved to be nothing more than sugar. Metesky's howls of laughter could almost be heard all the way to police headquarters. In describing the incident years later, one New York newspaper wrote, "The weirdie patently pulled this caper for laughs."

. . .

On October 22, 1951, a longshoremen's strike that had pressed its way up the New York waterfront had paralyzed thirty miles of docks and now expanded into shipments of rail freight, and at the White House an announcement had been made that the Soviet Union had once again conducted a test of an atomic weapon. News of the day had been coming in at a brisk pace, and the night crew of the *New York Herald Tribune* was hard at work bringing the next day's early edition to life. Decisions as to lead stories and copy position were being made at the usual breakneck speed, and interruption was the last thing the staff of the paper needed—but interruption was exactly what it got.

At approximately 10:15 on the evening of October 22, a special delivery letter found its way into the hands of the *Tribune's* city editor. With one angry eye focused on a staff writer who was protesting the deletion of certain passages from a feature article that he had proudly authored, the editor fumbled with the envelope whose late-night delivery carried the air of some import. As he began reading the missive, his full attention was abruptly garnered and the clamor of the writer's remonstrations slipped into the hum of background noise generated by the clattering office. In handwritten block letters stroked in pencil, the note informed the reader that a bomb had been planted in the ventilation system of the men's restroom located in the basement of the Paramount Theatre, at Broadway and Forty-third Street. The letter went on:

BOMBS WILL CONTINUE UNTIL THE CONSOLIDATED
EDISON COMPANY IS BROUGHT TO JUSTICE FOR THEIR
DASTARDLY ACTS AGAINST ME. I HAVE EXHAUSTED
ALL OTHER MEANS. I INTEND WITH BOMBS TO CAUSE
OTHERS TO CRY OUT FOR JUSTICE FOR ME . . . IF
I DON'T GET JUSTICE I WILL CONTINUE, BUT WITH
BIGGER BOMBS.

Within minutes word had reached the bomb squad and a quiet search of the Paramount had begun. As 3,600 unwitting patrons enjoyed that evening's movie presentation, an unexploded four-inch "cylindrical object" charged with black powder and a .25-caliber bullet was carried from the building and hurried from the area in the squad's containment vehicle.

In what would become a further signature of his operations, Metesky had provided an advance warning of his doings in an effort not only to curtail injuries but also to maximize the potential publicity garnered from the event. Beginning with the Manhattan Paramount, he would, on occasion, place a terse and angry telephone call to his targets or write advance letters warning of his bombs—and scolding the recipients of the consequences of their failure to blame Con Ed for the incidents. With the letter to the *Herald Tribune*, Metesky accomplished each of these goals. Though, for now, the *Tribune* itself had resisted publishing the contents of the letter, other local newspapers (as well as a prominent wire service) had obtained a copy and included full-length quotations, over the formal objections of the New York City Police Department.

The police and the public at large now knew that the person responsible for planting explosive devices in locations throughout the city bore a venomous hostility against the Consolidated Edison Company. Hungry for attention and retribution, Metesky had openly revealed his motives.

Even with the revelation to the *Tribune*, police detectives remained in the dark as to who was plaguing the city with these infernal machines. The obvious conclusion that the Bomber was in some way affiliated with Con Ed was muddled by the fact that bombs had turned up in other locations throughout New York, and, in any event, the universe of individuals bearing some kind of grievance against the power company could number in the tens of thousands. As frustration mounted, wild theories began to circulate through the department and the police groped for clues. Following the lead of a former New York City fire marshal in the investigation of a serial arsonist in the 1920s, it was observed that the Bomber seemed to follow a pattern of one bomb per month and that each of these was planted within three days of a full moon. Some in the department theorized that the culprit was a so called "mooner"—"one in whom flashes of lunacy are induced by lunar fullness." It was even successfully argued that extra manpower be devoted to possible targets during these full-moon periods. The lengths to which the department would go to apprehend the Bomber seemed to expand by the day.

Wild theories notwithstanding, police detectives pursued every practical lead and parcel of evidence available to them. They analyzed each word of the Bomber's letter to the *Tribune* as to both appearance and substance, and they pored through as many relevant Con Ed personnel files as time and manpower would permit. Finally, through the identification of a file from a particularly disgruntled former Con Ed employee and a positive comparison of handwriting samples, detectives began to focus on a possible suspect. In the first week of November 1951, it appeared that an arrest was imminent.

• • •

"This defendant is a particular source of annoyance to the New York City Police. We are firmly convinced that he is not of sound mind." Chief Magistrate John Murtagh regarded the words of the assistant district attorney with interest as the felony court arraignment began. The suspect, who silently looked on, had been arrested the previous day in his Connecticut home on a charge of sending a threatening letter and a package containing a sugar-laden "bomb" to the offices of Consolidated Edison Company. "He has been sending simulated bombs around the city the past few months," continued the attorney. "Hundreds of police have been called out at all hours of the day and night to investigate because of his actions."

The arrest had been prompted by the similarity of the suspect's handwriting to the block printing contained in the letter to the *Tribune* (a similarity that the accused himself was forced to admit), as well as a documented and ongoing dispute between the suspect and Con Ed that police had adroitly unearthed. Though at the time of the arrest there existed no direct evidence to link him to any of the other bombings around Manhattan, it was assumed that such evidence would soon pour into the department. Faced with these charges and potential charges, the prisoner waived extradition and willingly accompanied the officers to New York for arraignment. He was considered by police to be the prime—and only—suspect.

As a white-haired, fifty-six-year-old former employee of Con Ed, Frederick Eberhardt, was lead out of the courtroom bound in handcuffs and committed to Bellevue Hospital for thirty-seven days of psychiatric observation, his sobbing wife was heard to protest, "This arrest is an outrage. He never sent those things. He couldn't hurt a fly."

As to his confinement at Bellevue, Eberhardt would later recall, "They were the most harrowing days of my life."

• • •

In the days following the arrest, police officials held their collective breath, hopeful that the rash of bombings had finally come to an end. On November 11, however, as Frederick Eberhardt underwent a battery of mental testing at Bellevue, bomb squad detectives were once again called into action. Anonymous calls had been made to the East Twenty-second Street police station and to an operator at the Plaza exchange of the telephone company, reporting that bombs had been planted and were ready to explode at the Capitol Theatre on Broadway and a Roman Catholic church on East Twenty-eighth Street.

• • •

At 10:33 on the morning of November 28, 1951, air-raid sirens pierced through the chaotic drone of Times Square, bringing the usual tangle of traffic to a complete stop and sending drivers, passengers, and pedestrians alike for the cover of designated bomb shelters. "With horns silenced and other noises stilled, an eerie quiet settled on the streets, deserted except for policemen and a few defense workers," said the *New York Times*. "It lasted until the first wailing note of the all-clear was heard at 10:43 A.M. and then within seconds the city bustled back to life and New Yorkers went about their affairs as if nothing unusual had happened." In a three-minute exercise that the presiding civil defense director, Arthur W. Wallander, called a "pattern for survival," New Yorkers had ushered in the atomic age with a "remarkably successful," first of its kind air-raid drill. "I feel it would go just as well if an actual raid had occurred," gloated Wallander. "It was money well spent—If only for insurance."

Later that evening, in what would be considered troubling news to all but Frederick Eberhardt, a small explosion ripped through several coin-operated parcel lockers on the southbound mezzanine of the IRT subway station located at Union Square on Fourth Avenue and Fourteenth Street. Among the people passing near the lockers at the time of the blast was a lieutenant of the New York Fire Department, who told newspaper reporters that the explosion "sounded like a stick of dynamite." Remarkably, no one was injured, but George Metesky had placed his exclamation point upon the earlier events of the day.

• • •

At the start of the 1951 Christmas season, the *New York Herald Tribune* received another letter:

> TO HERALD TRIBUNE EDITOR—HAVE YOU NOTICE THE
> BOMBS IN YOUR CITY—IF YOU ARE WORRIED, I AM
> SORRY—AND ALSO IF ANYONE IS INJURED. BUT IT
> CANNOT BE HELPED—FOR JUSTICE WILL BE SERVED.
> I AM NOT WELL, AND FOR THIS I WILL MAKE THE
> CON EDISON SORRY—YES, THEY WILL REGRET THEIR
> DASTARDLY DEEDS—I WILL BRING THEM BEFORE THE
> BAR OF JUSTICE—PUBLIC OPINION WILL CONDEMN
> THEM—FOR BEWARE, I WILL PLACE MORE UNITS UNDER
> THEATER SEATS IN THE NEAR FUTURE. F.P.

• • •

On May 15, 1952, the case against Frederick Eberhardt was dismissed by a felony court magistrate for lack of evidence. A disheartened New York City Police Department was forced to hesitatingly admit what they had known for months: their serial bomber was still on the streets of Manhattan.

• • •

In 1952, Metesky struck three more times: once at a telephone booth in the Forty-first Street Port Authority Bus Terminal, and twice at the Lexington Theatre on Fiftieth Street and Lexington Avenue. Bomb squad detectives, now working from their new home on the top floor of the 84th precinct station on Poplar Street in Brooklyn, immediately recognized the familiar components and construction of each device and the pocketknife left within the torn recesses of the theater seats, and ominously noted that the Bomber's handiwork seemed to be improving.

The Lexington was one of the first of many movie theaters to be struck by Metesky, and in its bombing the Bomber established a method that he would repeatedly follow—a method that the New York Police would soon identify as uniquely his:

> He buys an admission ticket shortly after the theater opens in the morning, about 10:00 a.m., possibly the fiftieth patron. He has nothing in his hands, for his bomb is in one pocket of his coat and an ordinary cheap jackknife in another.

> This shadowy figure sits in an empty section of the orchestra, away from other persons. In the darkness of the show, he reaches to the seat next to him, slits the bottom with his knife, and slides in both the bomb and the knife (presumably so if anything goes wrong and he is searched before he leaves the theater, the knife will not be found on him).

Then he moves to another section of the theater and watches the show. As the theater fills up, and the early customers begin to leave—and the time for the explosion draws near—the machinist gets up, tags along behind someone who is leaving, and vanishes.

On December 8, 1952, Metesky's second bomb at the Lexington Theatre exploded and, for the first time, a patron was injured. A woman, innocently watching MGM's song and dance film production of *Everything I Have Is Yours*, was struck with shards of metal and debris that caused several deep lacerations on her feet and legs.

As a result of the official policy of secrecy and a police request that the particulars of the bombings be kept from the public, few, if any, details of the injuries at the Lexington Theatre, or any of the other 1952 incidents, found their way into the newspapers. Metesky wouldn't even learn if his devices had exploded—let alone injure anyone—for months to come.

There were no duds in 1952, and the bombs seemed to be growing in power and causing more and more damage. By the start of 1953, Metesky began to experiment again with flashlight bulbs and batteries (as opposed to .25-caliber bullets), as he had done in the 1940s, to mechanize his bombs. His decision to continue use of the infamous throat lozenge disc as a timer device, however, would be one that he would soon come to regret.

. . .

The "sweeping arches" and "choral staircases" that punctuated the largest indoor theater in the world adorned an architectural and entertainment icon. "Everything about Radio City Music Hall is outsized—from its sixty-foot-high foyer to its two-ton chandeliers . . . to its Wurlitzer organ (the mightiest on earth, with fifty-six separate sets of pipes)," wrote one observer. Dubbed the "American People's Palace," Radio City combined stunning Art Deco design with an affordable price of admission. The hall initially opened in 1932 with the intention of featuring splendid stage shows, but when the gala debut met with failure, Radio City immediately shifted to movie presentations. Since then, hundreds of film classics, such as *Mr. Smith Goes to Washington, An American in Paris,* and *Singin' in the Rain*, would premier at the hall, "virtually [guaranteeing] a successful run in theatres around the country." As George Metesky stole into the nearly 6,000-seat auditorium on the afternoon of March 10, 1953, however, his mind was far from the elegant surroundings of the house or the movie themes that filled it.

With his latest creation safely wrapped in a signature red wool sock and stowed in the pocket of his overcoat, Metesky casually took a seat in row L of the orchestra section of the hall. He had previously armed his four-and-a-half-inch galvanized pipe bomb with a quantity of black powder and a throat lozenge timing mechanism carefully calibrated by a measure of water to create a defined rate of dissolution. At a voluble moment of the movie presentation, *The Story of Three Loves*, when he was certain that all eyes would be fixed on the screen, Metesky removed a pocketknife from his overcoat and ripped a hole into the undercushion of the seat next to him. At an awkward slant, he reached underneath and, with a dexterous backhanded scoop, thrust the bomb and the knife into the gap, where he left both. A few moments later he was headed out of the auditorium and toward the lobby.

Though an ingenious fusing apparatus, Metesky's use of the throat lozenge wafer was fraught with danger—and he knew it. For the most part he could predict fairly well when the disc would dissolve, thereby triggering the detonation, but the variables, such as degrees of thickness and measures of water, could also prove imprecise. The result was often a somewhat unstable and unpredictable timing mechanism. In short, though he had performed experiment after experiment and perfected the system as best he could, there was really no sure way to predict the exact moment of detonation.

As Metesky reached the exit doors of the Radio City auditorium, his bomb exploded much earlier than planned. The blast—a "funny" sound—echoed off the eighty-four-foot ceilings and through the hall. "[It] sounded like a rocket. It went zzzzzz—BANG!" recalled Metesky. Realizing what had happened and beginning to hear the harried sounds of confusion, if not panic, behind him, he rushed from the theater. As he passed through the lobby, Metesky was detained by the sudden grasp of an usher who had caught hold of his arm. He froze in near panic.

"We're sorry about this sir. We regret the inconvenience."

Eyes squinting with quizzical amazement, Metesky freed himself from the usher's grip and nervously informed him that he was fine but that he still wished to leave. Foisting a free movie pass into his hand, the man urged him to please come back at a later date and promised that it would never happen again. As Metesky exited Radio City Music Hall, the wailing sound of police cars converging on the building had already begun. He smiled and whispered to himself, *If I come back, it'll happen again all right.*

The morning newspapers played down the Radio City incident, calling it a "mild 'pop'" and noting that the device caused little damage and no injuries. The *Herald Tribune* attributed the bomb to the work of a "psychopath," and weeks later, when Metesky struck at Penn Station and yet again at Grand Central Terminal, blowing apart a locker on the lower commuter level of the latter, the *New York Times*, quoting the police, described him as a "publicity-seeking jerk" and a "mental case."

Metesky was outraged by the statements of the press and by their lack of detailed reporting on his bombings. Unceasingly self-consumed and utterly narcissistic, he vowed to show the world that he meant business. He would now sharpen and advance his campaign of terror—and, once again, focus the world's attention on the malevolence of the evil Con Ed.

• • •

EDITOR + STAFF OF N.Y. HERALD TRIBUNE: UNLESS
SLOPPY OR NO REPORTING IS CORRECTED ABOUT
BOMBINGS—PUBLIC WILL GET INFORMATION BY WAY OF
MOSCOW.

GET THIS INTO YOUR HEADS—THE CONSOLIDATED
EDISON CO. WILL BE BROUGHT TO JUSTICE. ALL OF
MY PHYSICAL, MENTAL AND FINANCIAL SUFFERINGS
WILL BE PAID FOR IN FULL.

YOU KNOW THAT BOMBS ARE GETTING BIGGER. SO FAR—
THE HAND OF GOD—HAS SPARED EVERYONE FROM DEATH
OR SERIOUS INJURY. BELIEVE ME—I KNOW.

IN THE PRESS, NOW AND THEN I AM CALLED A "BAD
NAME." JUST WHAT NAME FITS YOU PEOPLE WHO
DENIED ME THE PURCHASE OF "SPACE" TO TELL MY
STORY—YOU WHO ARE TO [SIC] "YELLOW" TO PRINT
THE FACTS WHICH CONCERN THE SAFETY OF SO MANY?

I AM BEWILDERED BY YOUR ATTITUDE. I CAN ONLY
RESPOND WITH MORE AND LARGER BOMBS. EVERY DAY
THAT PASSES—MEANS A DAY CLOSER TO ANOTHER BOMB

• • •

The return address on the envelope of Metesky's letter of May 24,
1953, read simply:

CONSOLIDATED EDISON CO.
4 IRVING PLACE
NEW YORK CITY

• • •

With the narrow escape of the Radio City bombing and the antagonism of the New York press harping at his mind, Metesky resolved to draw attention to his crusade through increasingly more powerful and effective bombs, albeit with safeguards in place to avoid risk of detection. His next bombing, that of the Capitol Theatre, his last of 1953, would represent the final installment of his earlier small-scale and unpredictable design.

At home in his garage Metesky developed a safer, more reliable timing mechanism based on inexpensive and untraceable wristwatches, to replace the erratic throat lozenge method that had failed him at Radio City. Removing the second hand, he was able to accurately set his devices for up to twelve hours by simply dialing the hour hand to the desired interval from the contact point. Once the designated time had passed and the terminal connection was made, the charge from the battery would surge through a circuit and into the powder contained in the flashlight bulb, thereby exploding the larger cache within the bomb itself. It was a design the New York City Police Crime Laboratory and bomb squad detectives would become all too familiar with in the coming years.

Though undeterred in his overall mission, the incident at Radio City had raised Metesky's threat awareness, prompting him to take other extraordinary measures to avoid detection, some divorced from logical reality. He was compulsively "careful and wary as a cat," later observed one newspaper, and, therefore, arrogantly sure of himself.

On one occasion, he spotted an advertisement in a New York newspaper offering wristwatches from a discount store at bargain prices. The hyper-suspicious Metesky haughtily laughed at the ad and tore it to shreds, certain that it was a police trap set specifically for him. The component parts of his bombs were commonplace items that could be purchased almost anywhere, and he took pains to avoid buying from the same store more than once or twice. He would not be unnecessarily drawn to any particular outlet to make his purchases, let alone one that he was sure had conspired with Con Ed and the police to snare him.

On another occasion, he was traveling on a New York subway when he spied a woman sitting opposite him holding a handbag connected to a shoulder strap. Convinced that this was the trademark of a New York policewoman, Metesky got off at the next stop—and when the woman did as well, he *knew* that she was following him. Before he could panic and begin running, however, she turned a corner and was gone.

Paranoiac idiosyncrasies aside, Metesky's endeavors obviously entailed the balancing of actual and grave dangers. The Radio City incident had proven this. He never risked apprehension by driving erratically or above the speed limit when he carried a bomb in his car, and he frequently parked far from his targets, opting to take the subway to the targeted areas to avoid the linking of his car in any way to the crime scenes. In each of his missions through 1952 and a portion of 1953, he had carried a container of explosive powder with him and armed the fully constructed bombs in his car prior to boarding the subway. This method ensured that he wasn't transporting an armed explosive device any longer than was absolutely necessary—but it also presented a risk that would, on one afternoon, materialize into near disaster.

Sitting in his car on Ninety-sixth Street, Metesky readied an iron coupling for use against his chosen Manhattan target of that day. He quickly eyed the rearview mirror and reached for the vial of black powder that was safely stowed beneath his bench seat. As he began pouring the powder into the pipe casing to arm the bomb, a New York police officer pulled alongside the car and eyed its occupant. Nervously, Metesky had settled the bomb between his feet and readied himself to turn the ignition and hit the gas when the officer informed him that he was parked in a restricted zone. With a gasp of euphoric relief, Metesky apologized for the infraction and, exercising due care, left the parking spot and headed for home. "I thought my number was up," Metesky would later say. "I was so frightened I could hardly speak."

In the moment of his near-apprehension, Metesky was not content to declare victory and cease operations, happy to escape with his freedom. Empowered by the feeling that he had once again outsmarted the authorities, he simply decided to arm his future units within the safe confines of his private garage and out of broad daylight, prior to his trips to New York. Satisfied that he had taken effective measures to decrease his risk of capture, Metesky's brush with danger had an evolutionary side effect. He was now free to increase the size and intensity of his devices.

. . .

Though Metesky would strike only three times in 1954, each of his bombs would prove dangerously effective, and the injuries began to mount.

A blast in the lower-level men's washroom of Grand Central Terminal on March 16, timed precisely for the start of the heavily traveled rush hour, slammed fragments of iron and debris into several porcelain fixtures, causing extensive damage and sending three commuters to the hospital for treatment of shock and bruises. The explosion echoed through the depot, causing hundreds to rush toward the sound in a "fervor of excitement" and prompting the washroom attendant to complain, "My ears are still deaf."

And true to his vow, Metesky did return to Radio City Music Hall—this time with injurious results. During a 1954 pre-holiday viewing of Bing Crosby's *White Christmas,* a "crude, home-made time bomb" ripped through a seat cushion in row 14 of the orchestra level, sending a concussive sound through the auditorium, "as if a big electric bulb had been broken." The capacity audience of 6,200 that had crammed into the orchestra level as well as three balconies of the theater were confused and panicked by the commotion, and four patrons received an array of puncture wounds and contusions that required a trip to the hospital for treatment.

As was the usual case with Metesky's bombings, the actual damage to the facility was fairly limited but the disruption was immense. He was aware of the popularity of the musical and had purposefully chosen the busy Sunday evening showing as his target to maximize the effect. "All seats were taken and there were a number of standees in the auditorium, while a line numbering about a thousand stretched through the lobby and into the street," wrote the *Herald Tribune.*

Within moments of the blast, police cars from the 16th squad on West Fifty-fourth Street, ambulances from Roosevelt Hospital, bomb squad vehicles, the mobile laboratory unit, and four fire engines together with two hook-and-ladder companies from Engine 3 converged on Rockefeller Center. As the injured were removed from the theater and the immediate area surrounding the blast was roped off pending a detailed search and examination, firefighters and police detectives, including Deputy Chief Inspector Edward Byrnes, a veteran New York cop in charge of the Manhattan West detectives known for his calm and efficient demeanor, quieted fears and quelled what could have grown into full-blown chaos. Among the jagged bomb fragments recovered from the scene under the direction of Inspector Byrnes was a small generic wristwatch and the remains of a cylindrical battery casing that surely formed the familiar firing mechanism of this latest device.

Mere weeks after the second Radio City bombing, thirty New York police officers and bomb squad detectives again rushed to the Eighth Avenue Port Authority Bus Terminal, where a bomb had detonated in a telephone booth, driving metal fragments and debris through a pedestrian corridor and startling throngs of weekend bus travelers. A Port Authority attendant and Navy veteran, in the process of checking the lights in the "suburban concourse" telephone booths, threw himself facedown on the ground upon hearing the blast, then, regaining his composure, rose and contacted the authorities.

Investigators easily identified the shattered bus terminal bomb components as similar in style and design to those used at Radio City and in prior bombing incidents throughout Manhattan. With each new episode, detectives were learning more and more about the infernal machinist that plagued their city.

As Metesky's bombings grew more brash and potent, local as well as national newspapers would find it very difficult to ignore what was occurring around New York City. By the start of 1955, the requested and hitherto honored police policy of secrecy would ultimately be sacrificed in the name of circulation. Front page stories with inflammatory headlines began appearing in tabloid papers and broadsheets alike, chronicling the bombings—and, in the process, unnerving everyday New Yorkers. Soon, feeding on this air of anxiety, the New York scandal sheets would designate a moniker for the disgruntled miscreant who imposed his resentment and rage upon the citizens of Manhattan. They began calling him the "Mad Bomber."

# CHASING SHADOWS

Now, Metesky's pace began to quicken and confusion seemed to reign within the press as well as throughout the floundering police force. On January 11, 1955, he struck Penn Station during the evening rush hour, blowing a two-inch gouge into a concrete wall and sending clouds of smoke billowing through the lower level of the terminal. As detectives cordoned off the surrounding area and conducted a detailed search for fragments and additional devices, Metesky placed a telephone call to the switchboard operator of Grand Central Station, warning that a bomb had been placed in a coin-operated locker on the south side of the building and that it would detonate in fifteen minutes. A frenzied team of thirty additional officers rushed to the scene and conducted a painstaking search that turned up nothing.

Though there were no injuries from the Penn Station blast, the New York newspapers were almost comically inconsistent with their descriptions of the effect the bombing had on the public. Clearly torn between their responsibility to report the news and their desire to honor the continued police requests to play down the details, the *New York Times* buried the story on page 11 with the restrained headline "Penn Station Bomb Blast Is Ignored by Commuters." The effusive *New York Daily News*, however, brought the story to page 3 with the lead "Bomb Goes Off, Panics LI Rush-Hour Throng." And, in a clear attempt to compromise, the *New York Herald Tribune*, though placing the story at the bottom of page 1, went with the less controversial "Penn Station Bomb Startles Commuters." Two months later, the New York newspapers similarly reported on another of Metesky's Penn Station bombings, but it was, ironically, an unexploded device planted by him, again at Radio City Music Hall, that would capture the attention—and fears—of the city.

At 5:34 on the evening of May 2, 1955, an editor of the *New York Herald Tribune* received an anonymous phone call from a man who informed him that a bomb had been placed at Radio City. The voice, bristling with anger, insisted that the act was carried out "to get even with the Consolidated Edison Co." Within minutes, an army of sixty firemen, police officers, and bomb squad detectives converged upon the theater, roped off the area, and, for the next hour and a half, conducted an extensive search of the premises. The investigation yielded nothing, and detectives nervously reopened the theater to movie patrons, concluding that the scare had been nothing but another maddening false alarm.

Later that evening, after the theater had closed and the cleaning crew had begun its nightly task of removing candy wrappers and soda cups from the seats and floors of the auditorium, one of the workers, while scouring the floor beneath seat 125 of the orchestra section, banged into a strange object with his mop handle. With curiosity aroused, the worker knelt down to investigate and there spotted what an extensive ninety-minute police search had failed to reveal: the Mad Bomber's latest creation wrapped in a red wool men's sock.

For the second time that evening, police and emergency personnel descended upon Radio City Music Hall. With the usual array of armored bomb squad detectives and equipment on hand, the neatly capped three-and-a-half-inch length of galvanized iron pipe was removed from the premises and transported to a deserted area near the waterfront at West Fifty-third Street, where it was examined and guarded by technicians. As morning approached, the device was brought to the stark concrete military bunkers of Fort Tilden, Queens, a United States Army installation commonly shared with local police for the storing and dismantling of the Bomber's creations.

After three days at Fort Tilden it was determined by squad detectives that the bomb could be safely defused. An option that earlier had been considered and rejected was the use of a so-called "shaped charge" to direct a quick and controlled explosion specifically focused on the end cap of the device, thereby opening the bomb and exposing its undamaged inner workings. While the technique worked in theory, oftentimes the intense charge would have the unintended result of exploding the bomb itself, and it was therefore considered too risky to attempt under the circumstances. In short, the detectives simply did not want to risk a rare opportunity to inspect the Bomber's latest handiwork.

Using specially fashioned tools, squad detective William Schmitt slowly unscrewed one of the iron plugs, careful to avoid the possibility of a detonative spark. With the device open and its mechanics exposed, he cautiously removed the wires running to the battery, thereby neutralizing the bomb.

Once deactivated, the technicians examined the familiar design and components of the device and confirmed what they already knew: the bomb was the creation of the same individual that had eluded them for years. Fortunately for the 4,500 moviegoers who were in attendance that evening at Radio City Music Hall, the timing mechanism of the device, set for 6:30 p.m., had malfunctioned. A defect in the cheap watch chosen by the Bomber had caused it to stop dead before the hour hand could reach its baleful point of contact. The intact bomb now held by police, however, would serve as a roadmap for the future of the investigation—and an unintended turning point in public awareness of the case.

• • •

Further police analysis would reveal that the Radio City bomb, as was the case with most of Metesky's other devices, was capable of causing death or serious injury to anyone in proximity had it detonated, and the police department officially branded it a "lethal weapon." The New York media—television, radio, and print—were quick to react with detailed and inflammatory coverage. Unlike the newspapers' treatment of the prior incidents, there was nothing equivocal or restrained in the reporting of the attempted Radio City bombing. The *New York Journal-American* chillingly proclaimed, "Radio City Bomb Found to Be Deadly," while the front page banner headline of the *Mirror* shrieked, "City Hunts Mad Bomb Planter." And across America, the wire services informed anxious readers of a "Mad Bomber Being Hunted in New York."

As the doings of the Mad Bomber became more public and the citizens of New York more uneasy, the pressure on the New York City Police Department to make an arrest began to increase. Some of the top brass of the department, including deputy chief inspector Edward Byrnes, chief of detectives James Leggett, inspector in charge of technical services Edward Fagan, captain in charge of the police laboratory Howard Finney, and even police commissioner Stephen Kennedy himself, assumed greater organizational roles and became more involved in the day-to-day activities and decisions of the investigation as opposed to mere policy making. From a detailed study of the bombings, these officials knew that the "diabolical genius," as he was called by one New York newspaper, was capable on a whim of dramatically increasing the size and potency of his bombs and even attacking a bridge or a crowded train. A palpable fear began to stir in the city of New York, and a growing frustration brewed within the police department. The Mad Bomber needed to be stopped.

In the coming months of 1955, as New Yorkers nervously went about their business, infernal machines continued to turn up throughout the city. In August, a cheap pocketknife and an ominous-looking length of pipe wrapped in a wool sock slipped from a tear in a movie seat as it was being repaired by an upholsterer at the Roxy Theatre. Though unexploded, the bomb caused the usual ruckus and traffic snarls, as detectives, using their steel-mesh envelope, whisked the device out of the building with five hundred curious bystanders looking on from behind police lines. The signature dud had been left by Metesky some two years earlier and had remained undetected since then. In October, a man was slightly injured as a bomb exploded in the twelfth row of the Paramount Theatre in Times Square during an evening showing of *Blood Alley*, and in December, emergency crews dispersed a large crowd of rush-hour commuters in Grand Central Terminal who had gathered for a look after an explosion ripped through the upper level in the main men's lavatory.

With city newspapers maintaining a foreboding (though often inaccurate) count of the Bomber's sorties, the police department was forced to divert extraordinary resources to the case. Time, money, and manpower typically expended in other crime-fighting or community endeavors was redirected to the investigation, and officers with little formal training in explosives became adjunct deputies of the city bomb squad. Following the second Radio City incident, extra details of detectives—fifty additional men in all—were assigned to covertly watch rail stations, bus terminals, and movie theaters, with special instructions to search for suspicious characters carrying packages of any kind. Crime lab technicians conducted detailed technical analyses of past unexploded devices as well as fragments from the ones that had exploded, and opinions and conclusions were taking shape as to the Bomber's motives, capabilities, and vocations. An exhaustive study of numerous samples of handwriting as well as reliable firsthand descriptions of the Bomber's voice (derived from the various advance warning calls that had been placed) provided a baseline source of comparison as well as clues into his background and even ethnicity. His routines and assumed habits had been examined and re-examined. Police detectives had, in short, become intimately familiar with the behaviors and persona of the Mad Bomber. As one commentator wrote of the police investigation, "You are dealing with a man who can be described in such detail that at times you feel he is sitting in the room with you, just across from you . . . The picture of him that has slowly been blocked in over the years almost comes alive before your eyes . . ."

Yet for all the police did know about him, the Bomber remained as elusive and faceless as he was on the first day of the investigation. Even the mundane tasks of simple police work frustrated detectives at every turn. The Bomber's assiduous selection of commonplace materials for use in his devices made tracking them virtually impossible, and, to the utter consternation of the bomb squad, rendered analysis utterly fruitless.

"I personally have taken the watch-timing mechanism from one of the bombs this clown has made to 75 stores around Times Square," lamented Detective William Schmitt. "Every one stocked that watch."

Investigating the possible origins of the bomb casings, squad Detective Joseph Rothengast remarked that he "once spent a solid day going to plumbing-supply stores. Every one stocked the kind of pipe I had. And every one looked at me as if I had holes in my head when I asked if there was any way to trace this particular piece."

By the start of 1956, frustrated by the lack of any concrete leads in the case, police again found themselves chasing shadows. On February 21, a seventy-four-year-old porter named Lloyd Hill, who was working on the lower level of Penn Station, was informed by a young man that there was a clog in a toilet in the men's washroom. Shortly before four o'clock in the afternoon, as Hill applied a plunger to the obstruction, the fixture exploded, firing shards of metal and porcelain in every direction—and into Hill's head and legs. "The whole inside of the booth was wrecked. People were running in every direction, scared. So was I," reported one witness. "The porter must have been seriously hurt. He was bleeding all over. I could see blood on his face, hands, arms and legs as police arrived." Hill would recover from his injuries, but the thirty detectives investigating the explosion, led by Chief James Leggett, were dismayed to find threads of a familiar red wool sock, charred remains of a watch frame, and fragments of an iron pipe casing that had been carefully waterproofed with a paraffin coating among the rubble of the Penn Station washroom. The next day, newspapers reported that the FBI had joined city and railroad police in the search for the Mad Bomber.

In the coming years, Metesky would insist that he felt "sick" over the prospect of causing injuries, but in the same breath he blamed the police for failing to properly evacuate targeted areas after receiving prior warnings. In any event, he would continue, "I took an oath to keep on placing them until I was dead or caught."

By the end of summer 1956, Metesky would strike an IRT subway train (by chance containing only three passengers), a telephone booth at Macy's in Herald Square, and the RCA Building in Rockefeller Center. He would later admit to planting several other bombs in 1956 that apparently failed to detonate and were ultimately unaccounted for—including one in the Empire State Building—which, as far as anyone knows, could still be unceremoniously lodged into a little-noticed cranny of the 37 million cubic foot structure a half-century later. The RCA bomb, however, would immediately illustrate the untoward consequences and unpredictable results of Metesky's endeavors.

On the afternoon of August 4, a security guard at the RCA building had stumbled upon what he thought to be a harmless length of pipe that he thought could be put to good use. He gave the pipe to another guard, one William Kirwan, who, near the end of his shift, showed his prize to a third guard named Thomas Dorney, who was preparing for the 5:00 p.m. to 1:00 a.m. shift. As the two men talked, Kirwan playfully batted his palm with the end of the pipe and told Dorney that he could have it if he wanted. "You never know when a piece of pipe is going to come in handy," said Dorney, accepting the gift. Dorney carried the pipe with him all that evening throughout his guard duties and during the bus ride home after work. Upon arriving at his house on Fifty-ninth Street, West New York, New Jersey, he removed from his pocket the length of pipe and a small card bearing a picture of Jesus that he got earlier in the day at a friend's funeral, placed both on the kitchen table, and went to bed.

At precisely 6:00 a.m. the Dorney family was awakened by what they described as a sound "like two cars coming together." Rushing into the kitchen, Dorney, fighting the pungent smoke, witnessed what his wife would later describe as "a mess . . . like an atomic bomb hit it." "I haven't been as religious as I ought to be before," explained Dorney. "[B]ut I'm very religious now; that's a cinch."

With each new incident, the police learned more and more about the Bomber—except for his identity. Their files brimmed with fascinating and for the most part disjointed and worthless pieces of information. As the winter of 1956 approached, the top brass of the department were forced to admit that their investigation was going nowhere. "His face remains a blank no matter how you try to visualize it," wrote one reporter, summing up the mood of the police. "And this juxtaposition of feelings, knowing so much yet nothing at all, can suddenly give you the sensation, after hours and days of talking with detectives and thumbing through records, that you are walking down the streets crowded with gray and faceless men, looking for a man you wouldn't recognize."

. . .

The New York police were not the only ones frustrated with the flow of information. With all the destructive energy George Metesky had brought to bear upon the greatest city in the world, his seething hatred of Con Ed had yet to be sated. The newspapers were printing the details of his bombings but had failed, in any meaningful way, to capture the purpose and significance of the campaign—to expose to the world the brutal actions of his mortal enemy and to exact, once and for all, his full measure of vengeance upon them. The frustration churned within like an ulcer.

    . . . WHILE VICTIMS GET BLASTED—THE YELLOW
    PRESS MAKES NO MENTION OF THESE GHOULISH
    ACTS. THESE SAME GHOULS CALL ME A PSYCHOPATH—
    ANY FURTHER REFERENCE TO ME AS SUCH—OR THE

LIKE—WILL BE DEALT WITH—WHERE EVER A WIRE
RUNS—GAS OR STEAM FLOWS—FROM OR TO THE CON
EDISON CO.—IS NOW A BOMB TARGET—SO FAR 54 BOMBS
PLACED—4 TELEPHONE CALLS MADE. THESE BOMBINGS
WILL CONTINUE UNTIL CON EDISON IS BROUGHT TO
JUSTICE—MY LIFE IS DEDICATED TO THIS TASK—
EXPECT NO CALLS ABOUT BOMBS IN THEATERS AS
YOUR ACTIONS—NO LONGER WARRANT THE EFFORT
OR DIME—ALL MY SUFFERINGS—ALL MY FINANCIAL
LOSS—WILL HAVE TO BE PAID IN FULL—IT MUST
ALARM—ANGER AND ANNOY THE N.Y. YELLOW PRESS &
AUTHORITIES TO FIND THAT ANY INDIVIDUAL CAN BE
JUST AS MEAN—DIRTY AND ROTTEN AS THEY ARE. I
MERELY SEEK JUSTICE.

F.P.

The editors of the *Herald Tribune* again delivered the letter to police brass and wondered, along with the rest of the city, what the Bomber's next move would be. Meanwhile, the evening showing of *War and Peace* was only hours away as George Metesky rolled down his driveway and headed for the Paramount Theatre in Brooklyn, New York.

VII

# THE "TWELFTH STREET PROPHET"

THE MODESTLY APPOINTED TENTH-FLOOR APARTMENT IN GREENWICH Village had become one part family home, one part psychiatric office, and one part bird sanctuary. Parakeets flying freely throughout the Twelfth Street high-rise could be seen fluttering before the thin face of the eccentric homeowner, stealing bite-size parcels of food strategically placed between his upper and lower front teeth—a position typically reserved for his smoldering pipe. A pencil-line mustache accented otherwise gaunt and wiry features that provided only a hint of the brusque and authoritative nature of the man within. "It is a comfortable enough face . . . ," he would write in his memoir. "It is an ordinary human face, marked by the tracks of many years." A New York columnist would describe Dr. James A. Brussel as simply, "Bow-tied, Mustachioed and Natty."

From his office at one end of the apartment, family members on the other could hear him, on any given day, impatiently shouting at patients undergoing heartrending psychoanalysis. His more subdued moments were spent composing crossword puzzles for the *New York Times* and other syndicated newspapers across the country. His submissions were so frequent that he was often forced to present his puzzles under assumed or pen names. A prolific and incessant writer (in 1959 he boasted 250,000 words in a period of ten months), Brussel authored a variety of books on psychiatry and a full-length published novel titled *Just Murder, Darling*, in which the antagonist commits murder—and gets away with it. "[A] man has to be paranoid to turn out something like that," he once said with a broad smile. "So I guess

I am. I have a dirty, rotten, no-good mind and my wife and I laugh about it all the time."

He was a product of the Roaring Twenties—collegiate culture, raccoon coats, the Charleston, fraternity pranks, and jazz. His brash and uninhibited talent for self-expression gave him an air of supreme confidence—and some would say downright arrogance. On one of many working vacations abroad with his family, a tour guide aboard a sight-seeing bus pointed out a cement plant along a highway outside of Rome, and from the back of the bus came the sarcastic quip in a distinctive Damon Runyon–styled New York accent: "Is that where they make the bread?" His uninhibited mind could coin a phrase, in rapid-fire fashion, tailor made for any moment. "There is a kind of poetic justice in the fact that James A. Brussel, M.D. . . . really exists," observed a friend. "He should be found only in fiction."

A native-born New Yorker, James Brussel graduated from the University of Pennsylvania Medical School and performed his psychiatric residency in the early 1930s at Pilgrim State Hospital in Brentwood, New York. Following the attack on Pearl Harbor, he volunteered for the army and, for a time, provided psychiatric services aboard the *Queen Mary*, which had been used during the war to transport troops and prisoners from the front. Later, he served as head of the army's neuropsychiatric service at Fort Dix, New Jersey, and as a psychiatrist at the military prison in Greenhaven, New York. During the Korean conflict, Brussel was once again called into military service as chief of the Neuropsychiatric Center in El Paso, Texas. As a civilian in the mid to late 1940s, he worked as assistant director of Willard State Hospital in New York's Seneca Lake region and as a criminological consultant, focusing his curiosities on the mind of the criminal offender as he had done in the military. Returning home to New York following Korea, Brussel was appointed director of the Division of New York City Services, and in June 1952 was named assistant commissioner of mental hygiene for the state of New York—a position he would hold, in addition to maintaining a flourishing private psychiatric practice, for the next twenty years.

Throughout his career, Brussel's extensive range of professional writing would distinguish the broad intellect and creative composition of the man. Though he focused some of his early authorship on military psychiatry, he developed an intriguing interest in the personality traits of the masters and published psychiatric studies of Dickens, Van Gogh, and Tchaikovsky (who he argued suffered from an unresolved Oedipus complex). In 1948, while working at Willard State Hospital, Brussel was awarded first and second prizes in a national contest of the American Physicians Literary Guild for his satirical operatic rendition of *Dr. Faust of Flatbush* and a short story titled "Café Au Lait." Through his career, he would weigh in on subjects ranging from the practical aspects of geriatrics to the dangers and concerns of hypnosis, and would even later posit that cognac should be recognized as an acceptable treatment for a number of heart ailments. He would be called upon as a psychiatric adviser to the National Broadcasting Company and as an expert witness in a variety of criminal trials where competency or sanity was at issue.

Though his high-energy constitution demanded a blossoming creative outlet that would find written expression throughout his life, Brussel's professional interests would focus, through the 1950s and beyond, on the plight of the mentally ill and the work of the Department of Mental Hygiene.

Established in 1926, the stated function of the Department of Mental Hygiene was to afford protection for the mental health of the people of New York. The changing face of psychiatric treatment and institutionalization in the mid-twentieth century, and the social and political challenges that constantly faced the department from its inception, resulted in an ever shifting organizational history. The department's own view of its professional mission remained steeped in realism yet optimistic promise. "The history of mental disease," began the department's 1948 annual report, "is a story of ignorance and cruelty, of suffering and bitter despair, but the white light of science and the gentle hand of kindness and understanding have shown the way to the promise of a happy ending." As extensive as Brussel's intellectual interests were, he would spend little time pondering the existential philosophies of his profession. Rather, his mind would focus on the practical applications of psychiatry and the known and yet to be discovered scientific methods that accompanied them.

Early on, his professional interests leaned toward the study of criminal behavior, and much of his work at the Department of Mental Hygiene focused on the analysis of deviant conduct and criminology. Throughout his military and civilian career, Brussel struggled to weave together that often incongruent marriage of crime and psychiatry, studying the mentally ill and drawing conclusions as to rational cause and effect. Though he was often prone to draw snap—and often erroneous—conclusions, he would think about "the great mystery of human behavior" and, "with an attitude of cool scientific inquiry—neither judging nor condemning; simply ask . . . why the criminal has behaved this way and how he can be helped to behave in a less self-destructive way in the future." Through years of studying hundreds of psychiatric criminal cases, however, Brussel developed a hunch—a gut feeling—that if he could apply these "common psychiatric principles in reverse," using a "private blend of science, intuition, and hope," perhaps he could predict by a study of prior acts, not what a known man might do in the future, but what kind of person an unknown offender might be. Might not the body of evidence surrounding a crime allow one to deduce something of the character and personality of the perpetrator?

In his position with the Department of Mental Hygiene, Brussel had established many contacts and friendships at the New York City Police Department. He would, on occasion, share speaking engagements with department chiefs and often seek information from officers and detectives about offenders to whom he was rendering treatment. As a criminologist-psychiatrist, his work necessarily brought him into constant contact with police personnel, and they knew of his interest in and reputation for the study of criminal behavior. Though Brussel had never formally provided professional assistance on any ongoing police investigation, it seemed to be only a matter of time before police brass would recognize that nebulous link between crime and psychiatry, and enlist his opinions.

. . .

"That the human mind works at all—that anything so fantastically complex could even begin to operate as a unit—is itself rather remarkable," wrote Dr. Brussel in his 1968 memoir, *Casebook of a Crime Psychiatrist*. "That most of us manage to keep this intricate and enormously variable mechanism under some sort of control most of the time, living with one another in tolerable harmony, is more remarkable still." In December 1956, as the nervous citizens of New York waited in dread for the Mad Bomber to strike again and while a reeling police department grappled with the pressure of a growing public anger, Brussel—a man who would soon earn such mythical titles as "Sherlock Holmes of the Couch," "Psychiatric Seer," and the "Twelfth Street Prophet"—a man who understood the fragility of the human mind and its tenuous grip on sanity—was about to receive a call that would change his life, and the face of law enforcement forever.

# "THE GREATEST MANHUNT IN THE HISTORY OF THE POLICE DEPARTMENT"

IN SIR ARTHUR CONAN DOYLE'S CLASSIC *THE SIGN OF FOUR,* SHERLOCK Holmes, with characteristic mastery of logic, if not frustration, scolds Dr. Watson: "How often have I said to you that when you have eliminated the impossible, whatever remains, *however improbable,* must be the truth?" As 1956 drew to a close, it seemed that the New York City Police Department had fully processed the impossible and the improbable in the search for the Mad Bomber. Truth, it seemed, had proven an elusive abstraction.

In the aftermath of the Brooklyn Paramount bombing, police commissioner Stephen Patrick Kennedy had clearly had enough. In the days before, he had mobilized every asset his department could muster in the search for the Bomber, and his inspectors had scrutinized lead after sparse lead in the case. The crime laboratory, under the educated guidance of Captain Howard Finney, had studied bomb fragments, handwriting samples, and fingerprints, and detectives had assessed hundreds of possible suspects, and yet the Bomber was still on the loose. In his announcement of the "greatest manhunt in the history of the [New York City] Police Department," Kennedy promised a refocused department-wide effort and condemned the actions of the Mad Bomber as the ravings of a deluded and dangerous mind.

Labeled by J. Edgar Hoover as "New York's 'finest career officer,'" Stephen Kennedy had risen, in a period of twenty-six years, through the ranks of the department from probationary patrolman to police commissioner, a position often referred to as the city's "number one headache."

"Deceptively gentle in appearance, with thin graying hair combed straight back and rimless bifocal glasses, he looks—and usually talks—more like a college professor than the stern commanding officer of the largest police force in the country," wrote the *New York Times* in an exposé about the city's "No. 1 Cop."

He grew up in the tough Greenpoint section of Brooklyn and initially was not able to complete his high school education because of financial concerns. Before joining the New York police as a patrolman in 1929, he worked as a seaman aboard a British freighter, a longshoreman along the East and North rivers, and a clerk-stenographer for a steel corporation, and even became a respected amateur boxer. Hardnosed roots notwithstanding, Kennedy would soon develop a bookish and polished manner that would follow him throughout his professional career. In 1943, already a lieutenant on the police force at the age of thirty-six, Kennedy went back to school during off-hours and earned his high school diploma. Soon after, he attended St. John's University, where he earned an undergraduate degree, and then New York University, where he graduated in 1950 with a law degree. In 1951 he was promoted to inspector of the department, and a year later he was admitted to the New York bar, though he would never practice as an attorney.

Kennedy's appointment as police commissioner by Mayor Robert F. Wagner Jr. in August 1955 was not met with universal acceptance, and he would soon be viewed by the rank and file of the department as somewhat odd and arrogant. His leisure time was spent reading books and talking about theater and the arts, and though he had a reputation as "all cop," he was never considered "one of the boys."

"Mr. Kennedy is a man of suavity and polished speech," wrote the *Times.* "There is in his tone none of the over-meticulousness of the self-consciously cultured man, though there is a hint of the 'Harvard A.'"

One of the attributes that Kennedy brought to the New York City Police Department was a philosophy of strict discipline and fierce adherence to the rule of law. Though this authoritative deportment would ultimately cost him the admiration of his men, his reformist and forward thinking would also pay dividends.

Prior to his appointment as commissioner, Kennedy had undergone specialized training at the Federal Bureau of Investigation National Academy in Washington, D.C., where he received detailed and advanced federal instruction on scientific crime-fighting methods and crime lab techniques. He acquired a deep admiration for what he saw as the incorruptible image of J. Edgar Hoover and the FBI, and was determined to bring that professionalism and innovative technology to the New York City Police Department. By 1958, the department would boast the largest most encompassing crime laboratory in the world, second only to that of the FBI.

Kennedy was confident that it would be through the painstaking scientific analysis of evidence that a break in the Mad Bomber case would come. He could never have imagined where that bumpy road of science would lead.

• • •

On the day following the Brooklyn Paramount Theatre bombing, Commissioner Kennedy called a meeting of 350 borough and division chiefs in the lineup room at police headquarters. He briefed the gathering on the most up-to-date information regarding the Mad Bomber investigation and he directed the commanders to instruct each of the 23,000-plus uniformed officers and detectives of the force, regardless of their current assignments, "to make every effort to ascertain the identity of the perpetrator." In a sea-change of department priorities, and noting the increasing potency of the Bomber's devices, he exhorted his department to take swift action to avoid an inevitable fatality. "The man is not in his right mind," roared Kennedy. His activities constitute "an outrage that cannot be tolerated." He concluded the conference by offering an "immediate good promotion" to any member of the force who was able to make an arrest of the Bomber.

Following the closed-door meeting, the commissioner called together the throng of reporters that had gathered in and around police headquarters. In a rare departure from the stated police policy of secrecy, Kennedy had determined that circumstances now required a measured but definite public involvement in the Mad Bomber investigation. Wary of instigating a rash of copycat bomb scares or perhaps even feeding the ego of the Mad Bomber himself, but finding himself with little alternative, Kennedy delivered a statement to the gathering. "I appeal to members of the public to come forward and give to the police whatever information they may have concerning this man. The identity of informants will be kept a closely-guarded secret." Informing the reporters that he, indeed, considered the effort to be the "greatest in department history," he acknowledged that the Mad Bomber is "our No. 1 most wanted criminal . . ."

In the coming days, the department released small excerpts of the Bomber's handwritten letters with photostatic samples of his distinctive block printing. In newspapers around the city, words such as "GHOULS," "JUSTICE," "YELLOW PRESS," and "CON. EDISON CO," appeared in obtrusive stories beneath headlines such as "DO YOU RECOGNIZE THIS WRITING?" and bewildered New York citizens were encouraged to take notice and report any information to the police.

Eager reporters began independently consulting with psychologists, graphologists, munitions experts, scientists, and watchmakers, and wild and inconsistent theories as to the Bomber's age, appearance, ethnic origin, and motives began appearing in the media. "A 'faceless man' driven by a desire to have the power of life and death over others . . . ," wrote one newspaper. "He is searching desperately for sympathy . . . [W]hat this man really needs is love," wrote another. The *New York Journal-American* provided a detailed schematic of a typical pipe bomb, including everything but an instruction manual, and the *World-Telegram and Sun* included an artist's rendition of the Bomber's face based on information solely provided by a handwriting analyst.

After years of crime lab analysis, and the application of common sense, the police themselves had developed several working assumptions about the Bomber. Based upon the phrasing of his writings and the use of certain distinctive and characteristic lettering, they theorized that he was of German extraction and most likely middle-aged. They knew, by examination of bomb fragments and the unexploded devices, that he possessed some mechanical expertise, and the flood of threatening letters against Con Ed led them to the obvious conclusion that the Bomber had, in some way, been connected to the power conglomerate. Abstract generalities, however, did not equate with solid evidence. The task of generating reliable information that would lead to the identity of the Bomber still lay before the department.

The revitalized police investigation mandated by Commissioner Kennedy was spearheaded by a newly formed Bomb Investigation Unit that worked exclusively on the Mad Bomber case and reported directly to the chief of detectives. The so-called BIU acted in a liaison capacity alongside both the bomb squad and the crime laboratory, coordinating and developing the entire body of evidence. Initially organized with a staff of nine investigators, the ranks of the BIU would swell to nineteen, then to thirty-four, and ultimately to seventy-six members in the days following the commissioner's announcement.

BIU detectives canvassed the streets of New York in a coordinated web, checking and verifying any possible clues in the case. They visited jewelry stores and watch shops on a regular basis to determine whether any "regular" customer had been purchasing an inordinate number of cheap watches. They went to Army surplus stores and plumbing supply houses in an effort to trace the pipes and iron plugs regularly used by the Bomber. They checked sporting goods stores and hunting supply shops, hoping to jog the memory of an owner or a clerk as to any large purchase of bullets or other powder-based munitions. They checked and double-checked the personnel files of disgruntled or terminated Con Ed employees and sought court records for any lawsuits filed against the company. They painstakingly scoured the patient files of surrounding mental institutions where the Bomber might have sought treatment or suffered commitment, such as Bellevue, Brooklyn State, and Grasslands, and they reviewed thousands of records of discharged World War II servicemen.

Yet, for whatever information detectives had been able to generate in the department's most extensive manhunt, they had little in the way of solid, actionable evidence. In the days following the Paramount Theatre bombing, the department was forced to admit that its search for the Mad Bomber had drawn to an impasse. As one New York newspaper reported, the police had "reached the end of their investigative rope."

# A CITY IN TURMOIL

As it became apparent that the New York police had no real insight into the identity of the Mad Bomber, the public began to withdraw into a cocoon of fear. "I didn't see any reason why he shouldn't put a [bomb] under my bed!" recalled one New Yorker decades later, summing up the fears of children throughout the city.

In the winter of 1956, neighbors began casting a suspicious eye upon neighbors, and the bustling streets of New York City and beyond seemed to drone with an uncharacteristic air of apprehension. Train stations, bus terminals, and movie theaters, all favorite targets of the Bomber, reported dramatic reductions in patronage, and a palpable drop in local retail activity marked an overall sense that people had begun to avoid the city. "A whole generation of New Yorkers never felt entirely comfortable in public places," wrote Jamie James for *Rolling Stone* in his 1979 retrospective on the Mad Bomber. "You thought twice before you used a phone booth or went to the movies. You heard lots of Mad Bomber jokes—you'd laugh, but they weren't really funny," a local resident recalled. "He had the whole city in panic," stated another.

It was an era when Americans lived under the threat of nuclear conflict. Evening news reports warning of Soviet aggression and targeted warheads fueled a Cold War cynicism that became part of the undercurrent of daily life. The ominous markings of carefully situated fallout shelters and the presentation of coordinated training programs on survival techniques in the event of nuclear attack presented a constant reminder to adults and children alike that annihilation was only a mushroom cloud away. Americans had received training and preparation for a nuclear conflagration that seemed palpable but, at least, perhaps, politically avoidable. The citizens of New York, however, were demonstrably unprepared for the anxiety of an ongoing and daily war of munitions that existed in reality within the confines of their own retail markets, theaters, and transportation systems. "It is one thing to live under a cloud of fear . . . but it is another thing altogether when lightening strikes again and again," wrote the *New York Times,* reflecting on "Terror in the Age of Eisenhower." The siege of an unknown assailant bore upon the beleaguered city like a pungent curse.

It wasn't long before the wave of panic would develop into a seething anger. Newspapers began to question the competence of the police department, and the public at large soon followed. With all the available evidence, such as intact bombs, writing samples, and known methods of operation, why, asked New Yorkers, was the department at such a loss for clues in the Bomber investigation? The political pressures on Commissioner Kennedy grew by the day, and he, in turn, began commuting those pressures to his department chiefs. The New York police seemed to shudder beneath the weight of a fermenting urgency.

Amid this agitated turmoil, police brass bonded together and attempted to fuse the expertise of the varying districts and bureaus within the department. In a concentrated effort to share information and develop innovative and imaginative methods to corner the Bomber, active communication became the cornerstone of the investigation. Implementing this posture of interaction, the chief of the department's missing-persons bureau, a career officer named John J. Cronin, in an offhand conversation with Captain Howard Finney of the crime laboratory, relayed a bold and innovative idea.

The two had an ongoing course of dealing involving the technical analysis of evidence in missing-person cases, typically teenage runaways, and had developed a fairly open and friendly relationship through the years. Aware, of course, that the commissioner had been pressing Finney for quicker and more constructive results on the technical end of the Bomber investigation, Cronin happened to mention a psychiatrist friend with whom he had appeared at several police chief conventions, and whom he knew to have a broad and working interest in the behavior of criminal offenders. Cronin posited that perhaps this psychiatrist could be of use to the investigation. The highly educated and broadminded Finney listened intently to Cronin's description of the man, and his imagination began to swirl. Could the field of psychiatry actually assist in a criminal case? If a physical description of the Bomber was unavailable, could a trained individual develop a psychological description—a profile of sorts? The pressures of the investigation had clearly worn upon the fatigued director, and he was eager to explore any possible methods, regardless of novelty, in the case. Perhaps, he surmised, this was just the innovative thinking that the investigation needed.

Finney was an accomplished technical presence on the New York City Police Department. His tough and understated demeanor betrayed no hint of the three college degrees that he held—including a master's in forensic psychiatry. "He has been described as poker-faced," wrote one newspaper. "[B]ut when he gets angry . . . he looks like he's going to explode right out of his well-tailored business suit." As commanding officer of the police laboratory, Finney gained a reputation as a "Book of Rules," or one whose expertise kept him buried in the numinous confines of the crime lab offices. A short and stocky man with thinning gray hair, Finney was a well-respected scientist through every rank of the department and into the upper echelons of New York law enforcement. His 1956 contribution to the *Manual for Prosecuting Attorneys*, titled "Forensic Evidence and Scientific Police Methods," would provide technical guidance on crime lab techniques to New York district attorneys for years to come. In later years, his hardnosed deportment and celebrated credentials would land him in the commissioner's seat of the Buffalo Police Department, but in December 1956 Finney would find himself consumed by the beleaguered search for the Mad Bomber.

. . .

Dr. James Brussel eyed the ever growing stack of files and reports that cluttered his high-rise Manhattan office at the State Department of Mental Hygiene. Through 1956, the department had overseen an institutional population of approximately 120,000 patients, and it was witnessing an annual increase of nearly 3,000 per year. Though the arcane methodology of custodial care had given way to the more enlightened approach of prevention, it seemed that Brussel's patient caseload and administrative functions had risen steadily through the years, taking its toll on his private practice and family life. He was really looking forward to a holiday vacation.

When his friend Captain Cronin called to initiate a meeting with the director of the New York City Crime Laboratory to discuss the Mad Bomber case, Brussel wavered. Not only had his already jam-packed schedule of lectures, appointments, and paperwork left him with little time for extraneous endeavors, he had failed to see what assistance he could provide to the case. "I had real people to deal with, not ghosts," Brussel would later write.

Up to that point in time, psychiatry and crime fighting had joined only in theoretical studies and fictionalized detective novels. For years, Sherlock Holmes had successfully postulated logical and dispassionate deductions in apprehending his man, but in practice the two disciplines were, for the most part, separate endeavors having little to do with one another. Through the early 1950s, the pervasive attitude among law enforcement toward the untested realm of psychiatry was one of disdain and mistrust. Tracking criminals, they held, was the job of the police—and psychiatrists generally agreed.

"I don't know what you expect me to do," Brussel said to his friend. "If experts haven't cracked this case in more than ten years of trying, what could I hope to contribute?"

"Maybe you'll come up with something. Inspector Finney needs a break. The Commissioner is pressing him for results . . . Come on. Give it a whirl, doctor. Sometimes the difference between failure and success is a new thought."

Brussel paused for a moment and then hesitatingly agreed to meet with Finney. Though he didn't know it at the time, his decision would be remembered as a pioneering step on the road to a new discipline of law enforcement.

# PROFILE OF A BOMBER

DR. JAMES BRUSSEL WOULD LATER ADMIT THAT HIS PROFESSIONAL CURI-osity had been aroused by the Mad Bomber. He had followed the intense media coverage of the case and, like all New Yorkers, wondered what kind of person would engage in such a fiendish and perilous pattern of conduct for so many years. Privately, Brussel had constructed several speculative notions about the nature of the perpetrator and the makeup of his char-acter, but such thoughts were general and fleeting, without purpose or substance. His professional opinion had never been formally or officially requested in connection with an ongoing police investigation—indeed, no psychiatrist's opinion had ever been so requested. When Brussel greeted Captain Finney and two associate detectives in the Manhattan office of the Department of Hygiene on that brisk December day in 1956, they were navigating uncharted ground.

. . .

Though the process of attributing probable physical, personality, and character traits to a criminal offender based upon an analysis of crime scene evidence and behaviors—what would later become known as crimi-nal profiling—had never been specifically used in the United States by a police force to assist in the identification of a criminal suspect, the technique is deeply rooted in history, lore, and literature. Homer's eighth century BC classic *The Iliad* spoke of the ugly and deformed features of a character as being indicative of criminal tendencies, and Plato, in *Hippias Major,* suggested a relationship between physical ugliness and psychological comportment. During the Inquisition, an early form of pro-filing was embodied in the Latin publication *The Malleus Maleficarum*, or *The Witches' Hammer*, which was, in essence, a handbook for the identi-fication and prosecution of witches. Published in 1486 and sanctioned by the Catholic Church, the document asserted divine authority to dispose of heretics and heathens, and set forth a series of general characteristics such as birthmarks, solitary lifestyle, and pet ownership as evidentiary badges of witchcraft and devil worship.

A more scientific, though still flawed, application of profiling began to emerge in the nineteenth century with the work of the Italian physi-cian Cesare Lombroso. In a methodical attempt to classify and predict criminality, Lombroso announced in his 1876 book *The Criminal Man* that physical and anthropological characteristics found in certain groups of offenders suggested the existence of what he called "born criminals," as opposed to those driven to crime by illness, insanity, or circumstances. Based upon a study of 383 Italian prisoners and postmortem analysis of various offenders' bodies, Lombroso concluded that certain physical fea-tures of some criminals denoted a primitive or lower evolutionary order. "I seemed to see," said Lombroso, "all of a sudden, lighted up as a vast plain under a flaming sky, the problem of the nature of the criminal—an atavis-tic being who reproduces in his person the ferocious instincts of primitive humanity and the inferior animals."

Pursuant to his anthropological theory, Lombroso developed a series of eighteen physical and congenital characteristics, including asymmetry of the face, excessive dimensions of the jaw and cheekbones, deformities of the nose, swollen and protruding lips, excessive arm length, and so on, the presence of five or more of which, in his view, suggested the born crimi-nal. Lombroso believed that the identification of these physical attributes could be used, like a "mark of Cain" to predict future criminality.

Since Lombroso's day other criminologists have made similar attempts to classify and predict criminal behavior based upon such factors as race, intelligence, and anatomical attributes. Though most of these theories have been scorned and discredited through the years, the concept of behavior as a reflection of personality has endured as an axiom of modern psychology.

The practical application of the behavioral sciences to criminology found perhaps its greatest influence in the pages of fictional literature. In November 1887, an English doctor and writer, Sir Arthur Conan Doyle, published the first of his Sherlock Holmes mysteries, *A Study in Scarlet*. In a series of four novels and fifty-six short stories and articles that made up the classic adventures, "Conan Doyle continually referenced observation, logic, and dispassion as invaluable to the detection of scientific facts, the reconstruction of crime, the profiling of criminals, and the establishment of legal truth," wrote renowned forensic scientist Brent Turvey. Sherlock Holmes and the renowned Dr. John Watson would engross aspiring detectives for years to come, and inspire future forensic scientists and profilers with their legendary nonbiased inferential study of crime.

Perhaps influenced by the fiction of Conan Doyle, the first actual interpretation of crime scene evidence to infer details of an offender's personality took place in Great Britain in 1888 in response to the Whitechapel murders—the fabled case of Jack the Ripper. Baffled by a series of gruesome and sadistic murders of women, London authorities enlisted the help of a police surgeon named Thomas Bond to examine the evidence and, based upon his medical expertise, draw conclusions as to the personality of the killer. By a careful examination of the stab wounds and an analysis of the extensive mutilation of the bodies, Bond extrapolated that all five murders had been committed by one individual who was physically strong, dispassionate, and brazen. His comprehensive profile continued:

> . . . A man subject to periodical attacks of Homicidal and Erotic mania. The murderer in external appearance is quite likely to be a quiet inoffensive looking man, probably middle-aged and neatly and respectably dressed. He would be solitary and eccentric in his habits, also he is

most likely to be a man without regular occupation, but with a small income or pension.

The Whitechapel murders were never solved, and thus the accuracy of Bond's inferences remain unverified, but his detailed findings stand, to this day, as a historical example of a pragmatic criminal profile.

The technique and theories associated with the study of modern profiling underwent comprehensive development in the early to mid twentieth century through the work and teachings of dedicated teachers and criminologists such as Dr. Hans Gross, August Vollmer, Dr. Paul Kirk, and Dr. Walter Langer. In a famous American account of a psychological study conducted during World War II, the US Office of Strategic Services enlisted the assistance of Dr. Langer to develop an evaluation of Adolph Hitler for planning and tactical purposes. In a 135-page assessment later published under the name *The Mind of Adolph Hitler,* Langer noted a series of psychological characteristics such as an unresolved Oedipus complex, evidence of sadism, and an irrational fear of germs and disease. Of strategic significance was Langer's prediction that Hitler would likely fight to the end and commit suicide rather than endure capture—a calculation that would prove entirely accurate. Though Langer's assessment was confined to the study of a known subject rather than providing aid in the search for an unidentified offender, his work nonetheless represented a practical attempt to predict patterns of future behavior and would lay the foundation for further study in the field.

Yet, despite the steady historical development of the behavioral sciences in the context of criminology by academics and practitioners alike, there existed prior to 1956 no reported case of a professionally generated criminal profile being sought by an American law enforcement agency as a tool to identify and apprehend a criminal suspect.

• • •

Captain Finney sat expressionless across from the desk, waiting for Dr. Brussel to say something. It was a cold and variably cloudy winter afternoon in Manhattan, and the occasional yellow hues of sunlight filled the seventeenth floor office and then faded like a fleeting whisper. Finney and the two detectives had brought with them a large satchel stuffed with every accumulated document that made up the official police record on the case of the Mad Bomber. The bundled contents of the file had been spread across the desk, and the men waited patiently as Brussel painstakingly sifted through the hundreds of letters, reports, photographs, and memos that they hoped somehow might contain an unseen clue or the missing element, drawing authorities closer to an arrest.

Though he had never met Finney, Brussel immediately recognized him as a direct and intelligent man who demanded honest appraisals or none at all. "I knew I wasn't going to fool him with psychoanalytic doubletalk," wrote Brussel. The two plainclothes detectives, however, did not share the captain's intellectual curiosity and carried in their skeptical eyes the contempt that had marked law enforcement's traditional attitude toward the field of psychiatry. Brussel captured the moment in his memoir, *Casebook of a Crime Psychiatrist*: "I'd seen that look before," he recalled,

> most often in the Army, on the faces of hard, old-line, field-grade officers who were sure this newfangled psychiatry business was all nonsense . . . The two detectives were obviously quite sure [Captain] Finney was wasting his time and theirs. They fidgeted, they sighed, they exchanged glances of alternating amusement and impatience. Catching criminals was police work. What could a psychiatrist know about it?

Despite the intimidating circumstances, Brussel seemed to immediately recognize the significance of the moment and the far-reaching implications of what he'd been asked to do. He felt a certain stress at the meeting, and would later articulate in his memoir a sense of insecurity about the overwhelming nature of the task:

I felt that my profession was being judged as well as
myself. And curiously, I was one of my own accusers in
this bizarre trial of wits. Did I really know enough about
criminals to say anything sensible to [Captain] Finney?
I'd seen hundreds of offenders in my career, but had I
learned enough from them and about them? . . . Did I
actually have any business at all sitting here and talking
to these three highly trained, experienced policemen?

I stood up from my desk, went to my window, and looked
down at City Hall, seventeen floors below . . . The streets
were crowded with cars and trucks, the sidewalks with
pedestrians. Millions of people live in New York and more
millions travel in and out every day. Any one of those people
I saw below could have been the Mad Bomber . . . So little
was known about . . . [him] that virtually anyone in the city
could be picked at random as a suspect. Anyone—and no one.

He seemed like a ghost, but he had to be made of flesh and
blood. He had been born, he had a mother and father, he
ate and slept and walked and talked. He lived somewhere.
Somewhere people knew him, saw his face, heard his voice
. . . He had a name. Probably thousands of people in and
around New York had some fleeting contact with him at
one time or another. He sat next to people on subways
and busses. He strolled past them on sidewalks. He rubbed
elbows with them in stores. Though he sometimes seemed
to be made of night stuff, unsolid, bodiless, he patently did
exist. This was one of the few things about him that were
known for sure. It narrowed the search to perhaps ten million people in and around the New York metropolitan area.

On that cold afternoon in the glimmer of the 1956 Christmas season, as Brussel studied the letters and photographs that had so perplexed the leading analysts of the New York City Police Department, he quickly reached one clear and quite obvious conclusion: "At large somewhere in or near New York City was a man who was quite definitely mad."

. . .

"A psychiatrist's dominant characteristic is his curiosity," wrote Dr. Brussel. "Sometimes he gets satisfying answers, and at other times he doesn't, and all the time he is aware of vast unknown territories that he and his colleagues have only begun to explore." Drawing upon his exhaustive knowledge of psychological disorders and the behavioral characteristics of each, but aware of the daunting challenge ahead, he scanned the material before him for particular items of psychologically relevant data. Each such item, he surmised, could be individually analyzed for specific meaning and impact, and then combined to form an overall picture of the Bomber's mental status and underlying psychopathology. He knew that certain behaviors were indicative of certain disorders, and that each disorder carried a set of known and predictable characteristics and symptoms. Thus, if he could make a diagnosis of sorts based upon the Bomber's behaviors and add a modicum of intuitive insight, general knowledge, and pure luck, he could then extrapolate a series of personality traits and, perhaps, even predictions as to future tendencies. It would, in effect, become an innovative brew of science and art.

Brussel gazed, almost hypnotically, at the collection of crime scene photographs strewn across his desk, and one in particular suddenly caught his eye. The fully intact unexploded device that was left at Radio City Music Hall on May 2, 1955, had become an archetype of sorts for study, evaluation, and publication, and it piqued Brussel's curiosity. He raised his eyes to Finney's, and in a loud, staccato-paced voice suggestive of quick wit and confidence he asked, "These mechanical affairs . . .

What's your opinion of them . . . Do your bomb experts consider them well or clumsily made?"

"Highly skilled work," said Finney. The man has obviously had some training."

It was an evident point, previously considered by the police department, that the Bomber had some level of mechanical skill, enabling him to construct fairly sophisticated explosive devices. Every homeowner, Brussel mused, had some knowledge of household repairs and was thus capable of using tools even on a perfunctory basis. But these infernal machines indicated a greater range of mechanical aptitude and a clear ability to use complicated metal shaping machines not typically used by the layman. The evidence, Brussel concluded, weighed in favor of the Bomber having some vocational training as a metalworker.

The assumption had always been that the Mad Bomber was a man, though some newspapers and even several police investigators had entertained the possibility that perhaps they were dealing with an angry or disgruntled woman. Brussel's personal notions toward women were aligned with the traditional and chauvinistic attitudes prevalent in the mid-1950s. Based on this mind-set, it was a simple and natural matter for him to point out that the precise mechanical skills required for bomb construction and the very act of bombing are "alien to the feminine personality." Though he noted several historical anomalies to this axiom, most notably the role of female bombers in the 1918 Russian Revolution, he quickly advised the officers that the manufacture and placing of explosive devices had been, through history, the work of men. Consequently, Brussel indicated that, as a preliminary matter, he was satisfied that the Bomber was male.

The myriad typed and handwritten letters sent by the Bomber to concerns throughout the city had contained the common thread of a deep-seated anger directed at Con Edison for a series of injustices that had, according to the Bomber, resulted in his injury or disease. Through the years, his anger had broadened to include the press, libraries, theaters, bus and transit systems, and department stores, leaving Brussel with the obvious impression that the Bomber's feelings of persecution had extended to the world in general. "WHERE EVER A WIRE RUNS—GAS OR STEAM FLOWS—FROM OR TO THE CON. EDISON CO—IS NOW A BOMB TARGET . . . ," the Bomber had written in his March 2, 1956, letter to the *Herald Tribune*, now scrupulously examined by Brussel. The threats had continued for more than fifteen years, and the Bomber had ominously promised that "MY LIFE IS DEDICATED TO THIS TASK." The diagnosis was unmistakable: According to Brussel, the Mad Bomber suffered from a textbook case of paranoia.

The two detectives stifled cynical grins, but Finney leaned forward with interest as Brussel provided his definition of the condition: "a chronic disorder of insidious development, characterized by persistent, unalterable, systematized, logically constructed delusions." Over time, he explained, the disorder typically broadens and grows worse and can often last a lifetime. "These are the people who eventually go on to become God," he continued. "They feel they are omnipotent." "The paranoiac is the world's champion grudge-holder," wrote Brussel in his memoir,

Once he gets the idea that somebody has wronged him or is out to hurt him, the idea stays in his mind . . . Nothing you can say will make the paranoiac change his mind . . . He can marshal all kinds of compelling evidence to support his central premise. His delusion is rooted in reality in such a way that it baffles efforts to dispel it. He'll walk down a street with you and say, 'See I *told* you I'm being followed—why there's a man right behind us now, *following me!*' And you look back, and sure enough there's a man behind you . . . You figure the man just happens to be going your way. The paranoiac is convinced the man has some sinister purpose. The paranoiac is pathologically self-centered—in psychiatry we say 'narcissistic.' His delusion is essentially a defense of his love object—himself. It's the cornerstone of his being; without it he'd collapse . . . Instead of admitting failings or weakness in himself, he attributes all his troubles to the machinations of some powerful agency that is out to destroy him . . . [A] paranoiac doesn't believe he has a mental disorder. He *knows* he is intellectually superior.

The definition seemed to fit everything that Brussel knew about the Mad Bomber. The widening pattern of bombings, the arrogant and threatening tone of the letters, the obvious ability of the Bomber to blend inconspicuously into a crowd without detection—they all added up to the workings of a paranoid mind. Armed with this diagnosis, the personality traits and even physical characteristics of the Bomber now began to crystallize in Brussel's mind.

"He's symmetrically built. Perpendicular and girth development in good ratio. Neither fat nor skinny." The abrupt delivery caught the officers off guard and they regarded him quizzically, as if uncertain of what they had heard.

"How did you arrive at that?" asked a perplexed Finney.

Brussel spoke in assured tones seemingly confident of his opinions, though he knew he was proffering nothing more than a statistical guess. Citing the work of the German psychiatrist Ernest Kretschmer, Brussel explained that a correlation had been observed between body type and psychological disposition. In a study of 10,000 institutionalized individuals, Kretschmer found that a large percentage of schizophrenics, including paranoiacs, possessed what he called the "athletic" body type, that is, medium height to tall with a well-developed and proportioned frame, as opposed to the "asthenic" type, marked by a thin and narrow body, or the "pyknic" type, possessing a more fat or rounded appearance. Brussel told the officers that according to Kretschmer's study, the odds were seventeen in twenty that the Bomber would fall into the "athletic" category. Assuming a diagnosis of paranoia, the statistical odds were with him.

Then, like a shifting gust, Brussel's mind seemed to snap to a higher focus and his brow furrowed with nascent curiosity. He flipped furiously though the documents and searched for the earliest police record of the Bomber's activities. Noting that the first crude bombing attempt occurred in 1940, Brussel's eyes widened and he almost shouted, "He's middle-aged."

Captain Finney leaned forward and soberly inquired as to the basis of the conclusion. Again, drawing on his extensive knowledge of the likely characteristics of paranoiacs, Brussel explained that the disorder typically grows slowly and insidiously over time, and in most cases does not become fully symptomatic until well past the age of thirty. It was a logical assumption that if the Bomber had first reached the point of acting on his rage nearly sixteen years earlier, he was at least approaching his mid-forties, and perhaps was even older.

As the men pondered the precise age of their suspect, Brussel was already assessing his next deduction. He knew that another primary characteristic of paranoia is a feeling of superiority that would necessarily manifest itself in physical orderliness, precision, and neatness. Since the Bomber's overriding contempt for others would make it difficult to hold a job and thus he wouldn't have much money, his clothing would likely be of an older style but his appearance would otherwise be scrupulously smart and clean. The careful workmanship and precision of the unexploded bombs bore out the meticulous nature of the Bomber, and his ranting letters, though long and irate, appeared carefully written, with few erasures or smudges. "He wants to be flawless," said Brussel. "He wouldn't stand out as overtly different from anybody else . . . [H]e's probably very neat, tidy, cleanshaven . . . He goes out of his way to seem perfectly proper, a regular man. He may attend church regularly. He wears no ornament, no jewelry, no flashy ties or clothes. He is quiet, polite, methodical, prompt." Captain Finney nodded with understanding. Slowly, the wraithlike shape of a man was beginning to emerge before his eyes. He could almost reach out and touch him.

For years, the Bomber's letters had been scrupulously analyzed by police investigators and graphologists for any evidence of origin. Repeated use of odd phrasings such as "DASTARDLY DEEDS" and "GHOULISH ACTS," together with a distinctively Teutonic letter formation—the G's in particular, which contained a horizontal double bar within the opening of a capital C—led police to the initial conclusion that the Bomber had been born and educated in Germany. Another theory, inexplicably gleaned from the letters, which police adamantly refused to elaborate upon, held that the Bomber had a facial defect of some kind. As Brussel reviewed the same letters, his practiced imagination began to churn. His conclusions regarding handwriting would test the officers' patience like none other.

It was not the G's that leapt out at Dr. Brussel but the W's. It was his immediate perception that the Bomber's bold and neatly printed block lettering was almost perfect in form. Any flaw in this otherwise obsessively rigid and tidy composition would, to a trained psychiatrist, carry considerable significance. Studying the character formation, he was struck by the shape of the writer's W's which, in Brussel's view, often formed a literal double-U with distinctively curved lines, as opposed to the typical double-V with sharp and pointed features. "It was like a slouching soldier among twenty-five others standing at attention, a drunk at a temperance society meeting. To me, it stood out that starkly," Brussel would later write. He theorized that something deep within the Bomber had permitted this graphic anomaly to occur—"something inside him so strong that it dodged or bulldozed past his conscience." Brussel's Freudian mind-set began to take hold. Almost predictably, he concluded that the Bomber's W's resembled female breasts or, perhaps even, a scrotum. "Something about sex seemed to be troubling the Bomber," he thought. "But what?"

He was hesitant to broach the question to the skeptical officers, whose vacant stares betrayed little comprehension of the strange deliberations whirling through the eccentric doctor's mind:

Once again, I realized that the things I was thinking about might seem farfetched to my visitors, for, in trying to get at the reasons why people do otherwise unexplained things, a psychiatrist must allow himself to consider possibilities that would seem rather wild to the layman. It was obvious to me that I'd never crack the puzzle of the Mad Bomber by considering only the man's superficial characteristics or his conscious and obvious motivations.

Brussel returned his attention to the police files and specifically the crime scene photographs, which he urgently scanned anew. His eyes were drawn to a photograph of a slashed theater seat, and he immediately recognized it as the Bomber's odd method of planting his devices in movie houses. The photograph seemed to indicate a savage stabbing and tearing at the bottom of the seat as if by violent impulse, and Brussel silently understood the risky and troublesome nature of the deed as being inconsistent with the otherwise cautious and wary disposition of the man. Again his Freudian mind turned to the sexual character of the act and wondered, "Could the seat symbolize the pelvic region of the human body? In plunging the knife upward into it, had the Bomber been symbolically penetrating a woman? Or castrating a man? Or both?" The implications went to the very heart of his psychiatric philosophies.

Brussel believed strongly in the power of the unresolved Oedipus complex to cause psychological havoc in the male mind. The repressed sexual attraction that a young boy may feel toward his mother and the consequent rivalry he may adopt toward his father are typically reconciled in the childhood years, and a normal, sexually well-adjusted individual emerges. According to Brussel and others sharing his beliefs, however, in some cases, as is found in the paranoiac, the process becomes muddled, and psychosexual problems can result. Brussel was convinced that at the root of the Bomber's behavioral trouble was an Oedipus complex gone awry.

Noting the obvious contempt that the Bomber felt toward Con Ed and the police department as a whole, Brussel drew the broader psychological inference that these male authority figures represented in the Bomber's mind a general disdain for his father. "And now," thought Brussel in the ultimate nod to Freudian principles:

> I had a plausible explanation for his unexplainable act of slashing theater seats. In this act he gave expression to a submerged wish to penetrate his mother or castrate his father, thereby rendering the father powerless—or to do both . . . It [fit] the picture of a man with an overwhelming, unreasonable hatred of men in authority—a man who, for at least sixteen years, had clung to the belief that they were trying to deprive him of something that was rightfully his. Of What? In his letters he called it justice, but this was only symbolic. His unconscious knew what it really was: the love of his mother.

The "inferential mosaic," as Brussel called it, of the Bomber's personality now began to crystallize, and a quick-paced torrent of impressions flowed from his lips. "A loner," he said. "He [wants] nothing to do with men—and, since his mother [is] his love, he [is] probably little interested in women either." Despite this lack of interest in the opposite sex, Brussel explained, the Bomber was not overtly homosexual. He is a classic "lone wolf." He has no friends and is untroubled by his inability to form lasting relationships, though his fastidious nature requires him to be courteous and well-mannered to all.

"He [is] unmarried [and] quite possibly . . . even a virgin . . . I'll bet he's never even kissed a girl," he said. The plainclothesmen smiled wryly, but Finney nodded in agreement. The police had earlier theorized that the Bomber, in all probability, lived in a house where he could likely maintain an elaborate workshop, as opposed to an apartment, where noises of his craft would bother neighbors. Since men typically don't reside alone in houses, Brussel theorized that the Bomber would most likely be living with "some older female relative who reminded him of his mother."

Turning again to the writing samples that were now scattered across his desk, Brussel perceived a certain expressive aptitude (though certainly not eloquence) in the wording and diction. The conveyance of ideas, angry and convoluted as it was, indicated that the writer had some level of academic competence. To Brussel, the letters did not reflect a college education, but they did suggest "at least two years of high school." The actual language of the Bomber's missives, however, seemed to reveal even more about the writer. The strange phraseology repeatedly found in the letters such as "DASTARDLY DEEDS," "THE HAND OF GOD," and "FRUSTRATED GHOULS," once again caught Brussel's attention. He flipped through the pages, finding example after example of what he called a "stilted tone" and "a total lack of slang or American colloquialisms." Even the constant reference to "*the* Con Edison" as opposed to the simple and commonly used "Con Ed" suggested to Brussel an odd, uncustomary use of language. These strange word choices, Brussel told the officers, indicated a man who was either foreign born or living within a non-English-speaking community. The letters almost read as if they had been conceived in a foreign tongue and translated into English during their writing. He paused for a moment, then, as if emboldened by the mounting interest of the three officers, Brussel exclaimed, "He is a Slav."

With head bowed, Finney folded his hands in front of his mouth in a deliberative, almost prayerful, pose. He was aware of the department's speculation that the Bomber might be of German descent, but he had heard no plausible theory to support any other cultural point of origin. He looked up and in a bemused tone asked the doctor for the basis of his audacious conclusion.

"Historically," responded Brussel, "bombs have been favored in

Middle Europe. So have knives. They're used in violent acts all over the world, of course—but when one man uses *both*, that suggests he could be a Slav." The skeptical expressions on the officer's faces did not abate, but Brussel plowed forward without hesitation. "Now, if he's a Slav," he continued, "the odds are he's a Roman Catholic—and this would mean he's a regular attendant at a Catholic church, as he is regular in all his habits."

But Brussel wasn't finished. With the question of ethnic origin addressed, he now attempted to credibly determine the Bomber's current geographic area of residence. He once again scanned the stack of letters, but now focused on the postmarks. Noting that each of the letters had been mailed from either New York City or Westchester County, and knowing that the Bomber's hyper-meticulous personality would never permit him to use a post office near his home, Brussel theorized that the letters would likely have been mailed somewhere between New York and the Bomber's place of residence. "To play the odds again," explained Brussel, "let's ask where some of the biggest concentrations of Slavs are in this part of the country. One of the biggest I know of is in Connecticut. Bridgeport has an enormous Polish population. And to get from Connecticut to Manhattan, you've got to go through Westchester."

Satisfied with the plausibility of Brussel's analysis, Finney inquired about a possible illness or disease suffered by the Bomber and wondered about its nature. The letters had alluded to the Bomber's health and his angry conclusion that his former employer had been the cause. "I AM NOT WELL," he had written. "AND FOR THIS I WILL MAKE THE CON EDISON SORRY." Brussel deduced that, because of the passage of time, they were, in all probability, talking about a chronic illness of some kind. Recognizing that thousands of such conditions existed, he again placed his wager on the most statistically common chronic afflictions of the day: heart disease, cancer, and tuberculosis.

He quickly ruled out cancer, since grim survival rates would make the long period of bombings unlikely. "Heart disease is my guess," he said. In what he would later call a failure "to make every possible allowance for the known facts," Brussel had ruled out tuberculosis, noting that the disease had been fairly treatable with several modern drugs. What he had failed to take into consideration, however, was the probable unwillingness of the paranoiac to heed the suggestions of doctors or to follow a prescribed regimen of treatments. "The Bomber was God, punishing an unjust world that had made him suffer and had failed to recognize his superiority," Brussel would write in his memoirs. "What could any doctor do for God?"

. . .

The long shadows of the day now began to submerge Manhattan in their cold December gloom. The early dusk of winter had cast its tenebrous veil upon the office, though the men had seemingly failed to notice. Nearly four hours had passed, and a rising sentiment of hope seemed to infuse the air like vivid sunlight. The faceless ghost that the New York police had so painstakingly sought through the years had, at last, taken shape—and a technique, developed through history as a curious blend of science and intuition, had suddenly come of age in the office of a New York crime psychiatrist.

"Tell me something," Dr. Brussel asked. "What are you going to do with what I've given you?"

"Well, it'll help somehow," said Captain Finney. "We know where to start looking at least."

Brussel frowned and sarcastically noted that the department could not possibly position an officer at every city intersection searching for a "neat, single, middle-aged Slav from Connecticut."

He thought for a moment and said, "I think you ought to publicize the description I've given you. Publicize the whole Bomber investigation, in fact." He leaned forward and his voice seemed to erupt. "Spread it in the newspapers, on radio and television."

Finney peered dubiously at the animated Brussel and reminded him of the department's general policy of nondisclosure regarding the Mad Bomber case. "I don't think the commissioner would favor that," he said.

Brussel pressed the issue. "I think he *wants* to be found out now." He insisted that the Bomber craved attention and was becoming progressively more frustrated by his inability to secure the public's notice. The arrogant superiority of the paranoid mind, Brussel theorized, could not resist the direct challenge of the police actually describing the unseen man. Given the right circumstances, he thought that the Bomber might actually reveal himself.

Brussel rose from his desk and fixed his eyes on the pensive gaze of Finney. "By putting these theories of mine in the papers," he pleaded,

you might prod the Bomber out of hiding. He'll read what I've said about him. Maybe a lot of my theories will be wrong, maybe all of them. It'll challenge him. He'll say to himself, 'Here's some psychiatrist who thinks he's clever, thinks he can outfox me—me the Bomber! Well he's all wet, and I'll tell him so.'

Finney listened intently to Brussel's lecture and reluctantly conceded the point. Though he was certain that every crackpot in the city would plague the department with hoaxes and false alarms, he would prevail upon Commissioner Kennedy to publish the entire Mad Bomber file. "I guess it has to be done," he said with a shrug.

What happened next would test the credulity of the three officers like nothing else that occurred that afternoon. If the prior four hours had proven nothing else, it had shown that Brussel was prone to making snap judgments. Now, as Finney and his detectives made their way to the door, Brussel once again impulsively verbalized his brazen mind-set.

"Inspector."

"Doctor?"

"One more thing."

A picture of the Mad Bomber pierced though his mind. A meticulous and conservative man of impeccable order. Brussel closed his eyes almost ashamed by the audacity of his own coming words.

"When you catch him—and I have no doubt you will—he'll be wearing a double-breasted suit."

"Jesus!" whispered one of the detectives.

"And it will be buttoned."

# CHRISTMAS IN MANHATTAN

FOR SIXTY-FIVE YEARS THE ELEGANT WHITE SPRUCE HAD FLOURISHED in the open forests of a Dalton, New Hampshire, dairy farm. Its perfectly symmetrical girth and sixty-four-foot stature stood as a majestic tribute to New England's natural beauty. It was, in fact, those very attributes that would make the sprawling evergreen the ideal yuletide offering from New Hampshire's governor, Lane Dwinell, to the city of New York. With typical holiday fanfare, the three-ton softwood had been hoisted into place at the west end of the Rockefeller Center skating rink, draped with two miles of not so carefully concealed wiring, and illuminated with 2,200 seven-watt "firefly" bulbs and 1,200 red, green, and white globes. To the top was wired a four-foot plastic star. The twenty-fourth annual tree lighting at Rockefeller Center had been attended by hundreds, including, according to the *New York Times,* "some of the city's most sophisticated critics," all of whom "acclaimed it as an overwhelming success."

Elsewhere in the city, retail citadels such as Macy's and Gimbels battled hard for holiday shoppers. Department store artisans scurried to complete festive window scenes of marching toy soldiers and snow-covered gingerbread houses, and at each of these popular outlets industrious shop-girls readied decorous displays of winter clothing and holiday wares. Undulating lines of vivacious children wearing leggings and puffy winter coats (and a few bearing apprehensive looks on their faces) snaked past displays of candy canes and frosty angels floating above train set villages ensconced with cotton snowdrifts for a brief moment at the knee of Kris Kringle. It seemed that each year Christmas was coming earlier and earlier.

Though seasonal cheer had spread through the city with its usual commercial regalia, dreams of a white Christmas in the days before the holiday had been dashed with a soaking rain that swept across Manhattan. Umbrellas and yellow rain slickers had taken the place of winter scarves and wool mittens, and a dense fog had intermittently blanketed the area. It was an ominous sign for local merchants hoping for strong last-minute holiday sales, though the changeable weather would prove to be the least of their business concerns. As festive shoppers made last-minute forays into the city's retail districts on the afternoon of Christmas Eve, the piercing sound of police car sirens and the splash of emergency vehicles through puddles along congested city streets once again shattered the otherwise cheerful spirit of the season and seemed to eerily complement the murky gloom that had befallen New York City.

• • •

The day seemed to be creeping by and David Cruz just couldn't keep his mind on the growing stack of books that still needed to be reshelved. College students, most of them home for the holidays, had flocked to the musty reading rooms of the New York Public Library on Forty-second Street, intent on completing some last-minute studies before heading out for some Christmas Eve cheer. Nineteen-year-old Cruz, a page at the library, appeared to be battling against a rising tide of Shakespeare, Browning, and Poe; with every book he returned to the stacks, it seemed three more would appear. He thought the building was more crowded than ever, and that the day would never end.

He had made tentative plans for the evening with his girlfriend, and right now what he wanted to do was to confirm them. It was around 1:30 p.m., and Cruz made his way to one of the two telephone booths on the second floor at the rear of the building. He pulled opened the folding door and fished in his pocket for a dime, which abruptly fell from his hand and onto the corrugated metal floor of the booth. As he knelt to retrieve the coin, Cruz noticed a strange object encased in a maroon wool sock and affixed with a magnet to the bottom of the metal bell box. Paying little attention, he deposited the dime and dialed his girlfriend's phone number. As they spoke, he began to absently examine the object, which appeared to be a five-inch length of iron, capped at both ends and neatly tucked into the sock. Suddenly, his mind flashed to the accounts of the Mad Bomber and the rendering of an unexploded bomb that he had seen in a local tabloid newspaper, and Cruz abruptly ended his call. Holding the object at arm's length, he proceeded to a storage room at the rear of the main reading room, where three other pages examined it and confirmed that, indeed, it appeared to be the work of the Bomber. At that point, Cruz became frightened, opened the casement window in the room, and tossed the device into a patch of ground-ivy vines in Bryant Park, a few feet from the library wall.

Within minutes, more than a dozen emergency vehicles, including patrol and detective cars, the bomb containment vehicle, the mobile laboratory unit, and a fire truck, converged on the scene. More than fifty uniformed officers cordoned off the streets and sidewalks along Forty-second Street, while bomb squad detectives and an array of police brass made their way to the rear of the building, where the device had been thrown. Instantly several thousand Christmas shoppers, curious about the rush of activity, massed along wooden police barriers that stretched across the road at either side of the building. Opposite the library, managers of Stern's department store dialed up the volume of their outdoor public address system to allow the calming sounds of Christmas carols to pervade the confused scene.

Under the anxious eye of Captain Howard Finney, bomb squad detective John O'Brien, donned in a steel helmet and fragment-proof body plating, approached the device and gingerly applied an apparatus that looked like a stethoscope to its outer shell. Unable to detect the pulse of an active timing mechanism, O'Brien guardedly placed the contraption in the usual steel-mesh envelope and attached it by metal chains to the center of a fifteen-foot horizontal bar. Upon his signal that the task was complete, a second similarly adorned detective approached, and with each side of the bar gently resting on their shoulders, the two men slowly made their way around the building to the front of the library grounds and to the massive steel-armored containment vehicle that waited on Forty-second Street. A full police and motorcycle escort blocked traffic at every intersection from Times Square to Fifty-fifth Street along the Hudson as the device was transported to the empty parking lot of a sand and gravel company between piers 92 and 94, where it stayed under guard until the threat of detonation passed. Finally, at Fort Tilden, the bomb was dismantled, examined, and analyzed. From the moment of the initial call to the police, however, there was never a doubt in Finney's mind that he was once again dealing with the work of the Mad Bomber.

. . .

On Christmas morning, an already skittish New York public awoke to the headlines "MAD BOMBER STRIKES AGAIN IN MAIN LIBRARY" and "BOMB IN 5TH AVE. LIBRARY SPURS HUNT FOR PSYCHOTIC," while details of the culprit's "Yuletide gift" unfurled across newspapers and television screens throughout America. Special bulletins interrupted local Christmas broadcasting, and New York radio news programming focused principally on the pervasive threat of the bombings afflicting the city and the status of the ailing police investigation. And in the *New York Times* a front page exposé titled "16-Year Search for Madman" provided enthralled readers with an in-depth revelation of the full police investigation into the case of the Mad Bomber. The article, written with the full cooperation of the New York City Police Department, unveiled in copious detail the clues developed in the case and the arduous pains taken by police detectives to find a suspect. The final section of the article, titled "Psychiatrist Conceives Image," revealed that the police had enlisted the help of a Dr. James A. Brussel, assistant commissioner of the New York State Department of Mental Hygiene, in the hope that the psychiatrist might be able to work "a kind of portrait of the bomb-planter." The article noted that Brussel had "conceived this image":

Single man, between 40 and 50 years old, introvert. Unso-
cial but not anti-social. Skilled mechanic. Cunning. Neat
with tools. Egotistical of mechanical skill. Contemptuous of
other people. Resentful of criticism of his work but probably conceals resentment. Moral. Honest. [Not] interested
in women. High school graduate. Expert in civil or military ordnance. Religious. Might flare up violently at work
when criticized. Possible motive: discharge or reprimand.
Feels superior to critics. Resentment keeps growing. Present or former Consolidated Edison worker. Probably case
of progressive paranoia.

Brussel would later write, "[The *Times* story] didn't contain all my
predictions, but it crystallized the major ones. It told enough to embarrass
me severely if I turned out to be grossly wrong."

XII

# "AN INNOCENT AND ALMOST
# ABSURDLY SIMPLE THING"

SEYMOUR BERKSON WAS NOT PARTICULARLY ENJOYING CHRISTMAS morning. He had risen early and exchanged gifts with his family, but the usual holiday cheer seemed absent from his typically vibrant demeanor. The dynamic publisher of the *New York Journal-American* had been bothered by his paper's handling of the Mad Bomber story, and the events of the past few days had served only to heighten his concerns. He was proud of the urban workingman feel of the *Journal-American* and its reputation for aggressively covering the local news stories of metropolitan New York, but as he began to see highbrow papers like the *Times* and the *Herald Tribune* becoming more active in their reporting on the case, he wondered whether he and his editors had lost their hardnosed competitive edge in the turf war for the world's most vibrant media market. Now, on Christmas morning, with his competitors' version of the Bomber story spread haphazardly across his kitchen table, Berkson's mind began to swim.

He had been a longtime envoy of the Hearst Corporation, coming of age as a special correspondent for the International News Service, Hearst's journalistic "window on the world." Covering stories throughout Europe during the 1930s, he would head the Rome and Paris bureaus and pilot narrative series on Mussolini and other European luminaries. Later, back in New York, he would serve as managing editor of the INS, and in 1945, upon the death of its president, he would be appointed vice president and general manager of the news service, a post he would hold for the next ten years. While serving at the INS in the early 1950s, it was Berkson who was widely credited with coining the legendary phrase "Get it first, but first get it right." In 1955, Berkson was named successor to William Randolph Hearst Jr. as publisher of the *Journal-American,* the New York flagship paper of the Hearst organization. He quickly earned a reputation for hard work, quick wit, and high energy. "To ask Seymour Berkson to relax, really relax," wrote one colleague, "was tantamount to telling him to get out of the news business, or roll over and die."

After sharing an early Christmas brunch with his wife, fashion publicist Eleanor Lambert (who would earn the moniker "Empress of Seventh Avenue"), Berkson retired to the living room in their sprawling East Side penthouse and placed a telephone call to his assistant managing editor, Paul Schoenstein, to discuss the day's news, as he often did on holidays when the editorial staff was away from the office. Schoenstein, who had won the Pulitzer Prize in 1943 for distinguished reporting and for his dramatic personal role in helping to procure penicillin, then rare, for an acutely ill child, had become a staple of the *Journal-American*'s city room and was relied upon by Berkson in most strategic decisions of the paper.

The focus of the conversation immediately turned to the Mad Bomber case and to the latest device found at the public library. It was obvious that the story was going to be the lead for the following day's issue, but Berkson quickly shifted his emphasis to the broader topic of the paper's own disquisitive role in the case. In the early part of December, as the police department began lifting the gag on the flow of information relating to the Bomber, the *Journal-American* had created a special team of investigative reporters specifically assigned to the matter and dedicated to the generation of leads that had, perhaps, been overlooked by the department. As the search for the Bomber heated up, he had been frustrated by the team's lack of results, and he repeatedly pressed Schoenstein on what plans the paper had to further develop the story. Berkson grasped the base of the telephone, rose, and peered through the eleventh-story row of windows to the city streets below. He insisted that the police had developed blind spots in the course of their sixteen-year search, and he was certain that employing the full investigative ingenuity of the paper would result in the disclosure of some unnoticed fact or clue that could lead to fundamental progress. His team of reporters, Berkson persisted, must use all of their creative resources in pursuing the case.

Near the tail end of the conversation, Berkson, shifting his preoccupied gaze between the bustle of Fifth Avenue and the solitude of Central Park, was struck with a thought that he would later describe as a "rather innocent and almost absurdly simple thing." It was, in fact, a proactive "stab in the dark" that would change the entire face of the Mad Bomber investigation.

· · ·

On December 26, 1956, the front page of the *New York Journal-American* brimmed with details of the case and trumpeted the "ALL-OUT SEARCH FOR MAD BOMBER" that was under way by the police. Just below this searing headline in brash prominence lay Seymour Berkson's inventive brainchild:

## AN OPEN LETTER
## TO THE MAD BOMBER
(Prepared in Co-operation with the Police Dept.)

Give yourself up.

For your own welfare and for that of the community, the time has come for you to reveal your identity.

The N.Y. Journal-American guarantees that you will be protected from any illegal action and that you will get a fair trial.

This newspaper also is willing to help you in two other ways.

It will publish all the essential parts of your story as you may choose to make it public.

It will give you the full chance to air whatever grievances you may have as the motive for your acts.

We urge you to accept this offer now not only for your own sake but for the sake of the community.

Time is running out on your prospects of remaining unapprehended.

You can telephone the City Editor of this newspaper at COrtlandt 7-1212, or you can go to any police station or even the policeman on the street and tell him who you are.

In all cases you will be given the benefits of our American system of justice.

Give yourself up now.

# XIII

# "PLENTY OF WHACKS"

COMMISSIONER KENNEDY HAD BEEN DULY IMPRESSED WITH THE REPORT on Dr. Brussel's image of the Mad Bomber and nervously acquiesced to his suggestion to publish the full history of the investigation. "At first we requested that no publicity be given to his acts," the commissioner told reporters, "but this did not deter him. Now we are working on the theory that publicity will enable us to learn something from somebody and thus bring about his arrest." Said another high-ranking police official, "Every hopeful lead has vanished, and the bomber is still as much a mystery as ever." The admission had the feel of desperation and added to the palpable unease settling upon the city.

In late December, as assorted versions of Brussel's psychological amalgam circulated throughout the local newspapers and police department appeals for assistance to the citizens of New York barraged the airwaves, the already glaring media coverage only intensified. With the cooperation of the police, urgent warnings describing the Bomber's handiwork were published together with extensive excerpts of his angry missives, while impassioned pleas for vigilance flooded local editorial pages. "Any one who has any helpful information can help enormously by coming forward with it, for this city will be confronted with a nagging sense of danger until the culprit is caught," wrote the *Herald Tribune*. And the *Journal-American* cajoled, "This then clearly is a case that calls for the fullest cooperation of watchful citizens in working with police to bring the 'Mad Bomber' to justice . . . Let us all then be alert. Only with the capture of this madman will our citizens feel secure once more." Public service notwithstanding, a soaring and inflammatory rhetoric undeniably marked the insatiable reporting of the local media, to the heightened anxiety of the average New Yorker. "For more than 15 years," extolled the *Journal-American*, "a mysterious man has walked the city's streets, threatening the lives of 8,000,000 people. He defies detection and presumably delights in the feeling that he has the power of life and death over all. This man is potentially New York City's most dangerous individual . . ."

It was only a matter of time before a vagarious faction of New York bedlamites would augment, in their own peculiar way, the public anguish generated by the extensive news coverage of the Bomber. Almost from the moment of Commissioner Kennedy's release of information, the feared and inevitable wave of false alarms and bomb scares began to plague the city like a virus. "The hysteria," reported the *New York Times,* "provided a field day for cranks, holiday-season pranksters, lunatic fringers and youths with a perverted sense of humor."

Beginning in early December, a flood of anonymous and malicious telephone calls poured into theaters, department stores, air terminals, office buildings, schools, newspapers, subway stations, police precincts, and even an army base. The calls were placed by a variety of deep-voiced males, harsh-sounding women, and squeaky-pitched teenagers, each informing bewildered call recipients of planted bombs and pending explosions. In many cases, actual lengths of empty pipe, capped on both ends to resemble the widely publicized handiwork of the Bomber, had been placed by the pranksters, and in each instance overtaxed emergency personnel dutifully responded in full crisis mode, expecting the worst and finding either nothing or deviously placed simulations. On December 4, two days after the Brooklyn Paramount bombing, police responded to no fewer than thirteen false warnings, and from December 5 through December 21, fifty separate prank calls were received. As Christmas approached, the hoaxes seemed to subside, but after the highly publicized bomb was found at the New York Public Library, the calls once again surged, and by the end of the year the total had exceeded 160. One New York police officer complained that he had responded to the same movie house on so many occasions that he had seen virtually the entire screen presentation. Another lamented, "Every time we find a real bomb, every whack in New York calls or writes in about imaginary ones. This city has plenty of whacks with a screwball sense of humor."

The heightened sense of awareness caused a tense and jumpy public to misinterpret normally innocuous objects as creations of the Mad Bomber. Throughout New York and beyond, hazardous-looking sights that were in reality nothing more than discarded auto parts or shattered electrical components were reported by concerned citizens and investigated by harried police departments. In Baltimore, a frantic call placed to police headquarters insisted that the Mad Bomber had hit their city and implored police to respond. At the scene, perplexed detectives found the wreckage of a twenty-one-inch television set lying on the sidewalk outside of an apartment house and, upon locating its owner, seventy-year-old John McKnight, were told, "I paid $258 for that durned TV set. I was sitting there watching a program when the thing went blooey. I got so doggone mad, I just picked up the set and threw it out the window. When it hit the pavement, the picture tube exploded." And in Queens, New York, a woman telephoned police headquarters with the clue she was certain would solve the Mad Bomber case once and for all: "He's my husband," she proclaimed. "He's plain crazy. Take my word for it, and don't bother checking. Just arrest him and put him away. It'll be good riddance for everyone."

In the final weeks of 1956, the targets of the hoax calls and imitation pipe bombs included such locations as a crowded-to-capacity Madison Square Garden, a bustling Grand Central Terminal, Yankee Stadium (where 56,836 fans had gathered for the professional football championship game between the New York Giants and the Chicago Bears), the Coliseum, the Waldorf-Astoria Hotel, and even the Egyptian consulate on Park Avenue. Each call and response was carefully documented by eager newspaper reporters and television newsmen, and daily inventories began appearing in local tabloids and broadsheets alike, cataloguing the exact time and location of each bogus report. The highly publicized woes of New York City soon began to spread into surrounding cities and towns and, inevitably, throughout the country and around the world. Bomb scares and homemade devices were reported from Dallas to Wichita, from Philadelphia to St. Paul, and a threat to blow up Albert Hall in London shook England to its core.

The hysteria would reach dramatic proportions. In a *Journal-American* article titled "Siege by Bomber Recalls Terror of 'Jack the Ripper,'" the reporter, Syd Livingston, wrote, "Not since the 'Jack the Ripper' murders in London's teeming East End in 1888–89 has a great city been held in a state of mental siege comparable to what the Mad Bomber has done in New York." On a visit to Hollywood, British filmmaker Alfred Hitchcock was shown a headline of the latest pipe bomb found in New York City and was asked his opinion of the Mad Bomber case. Clearly familiar with the matter, Hitchcock opined in his classically sluggish enunciation,

> The Mad Bomber . . . is a man with a diabolical sense of humor. And he is not a stupid man. You could hardly say that a man who has avoided being caught for 16 years is stupid. Whatever it is that has made this man an enemy of society one can only see a man who is enjoying this thing. He apparently is as much concerned with taunting the police to try and catch him as he is in blowing people up.

And also out of Hollywood, the film studio Twentieth Century-Fox announced that the former head of the company's Movietone News Bureau, Anthony Muto, would soon begin production on a feature film titled *The Mad Bomber of New York City* despite the lack of a writer, script, or, as the *New Yorker* mocked, "a suitably dramatic ending."

With the deluge of hoaxes and false alarms paralyzing the city, Commissioner Kennedy was immediately placed in the position of defending the decision to go public with the details of the investigation. Faced with criticism from the same media that had demanded a more open and forthcoming posture, Kennedy observed that from the time the decision was made to publicize the case, many helpful leads had poured into the department, and though he conceded the "calculated risk" of publicity, he maintained that, on balance, the campaign was succeeding. "The public can cope with the known," he suggested. "It is fear of the unknown that causes apprehension."

Nonetheless, the torrent of pranks and false alarms was clearly taking a toll on the fatigued bomb squad and the department as a whole. Manpower and equipment earmarked for other important investigations had been diverted to round-the-clock bomb scare response duty, prompting the chief of detectives, James Legget, to limit the involvement of the squad and its equipment solely to situations in which an actual device had been uncovered as opposed to the mere receipt of a threatening call. Though defensive of his decision to bring the case public, Kennedy was also angered by the impact of the vexing hoax wave on the actual Mad Bomber investigation and on the already taxed resources of the police department. He publicly warned that all pranksters and hoaxers would be dealt with "firmly," and pointed out that although there was no specific New York law for the prosecution of hoaxers, other provisions such as disorderly conduct and malicious mischief, each of which carried jail terms and heavy fines, could be implemented to end the barrage. "Our policy is to arrest these people and bring them to justice," said Kennedy.

In an authoritative backlash designed to quell the rising tide of hoaxes, a series of well-publicized arrests and prosecutions soon followed. On Long Island, eight boys were arraigned for goading another student to call in a phony bomb scare to gain days off from school, and in Brooklyn two girls who were out for "a little fun" were arrested and held by a night court magistrate on $2,500 bail for phoning in a false bomb threat. A variety of youths throughout New York were arrested for setting off large firecrackers or cherry bombs, and a thirty-seven-year-old fruit store clerk named Morris Rubin, described by his brother as a "low-grade moron," was apprehended at Grand Central Terminal with ninety-two dimes and thousands of private telephone numbers of government officials bulging in his pockets. Arraigned on a charge of disorderly conduct, Rubin admitted to "numerous" fake bomb warnings and was committed to Bellevue Hospital for psychiatric observation. In a nod to Commissioner Kennedy, the presiding magistrate lectured, "If I, or any of my colleagues, get a real prankster . . . he will get the maximum, despite the wails."

In the early morning hours of December 28, amid this wave of hoaxes and public hysteria, an actual device placed by the real Mad Bomber was found embedded deep within the foam cushion of a leather-bound seat in the fifteenth row of the Paramount Theatre at Broadway and Forty-third Street after a showing of Hitchcock's *The Wrong Man*. An ambiguous message had been delivered to the theater earlier that evening, stating that a bomb had either already been found in a seat or had earlier been planted and was set to go off. Police were immediately notified, and fourteen detectives and officers from the West Forty-seventh Street station converged upon the theater. A preliminary flashlight search of the seats and aisles was quietly conducted during the movie presentation and turned up nothing, but a more thorough lights-on check after the 2,500-member audience had departed revealed the bomb. Wrapped in a red wool sock and appearing nearly identical to the Christmas Eve device, police had little difficulty in identifying it as the work of the real Bomber. Bomb squad detectives, clad in the usual metal-armored protective suits, carried the mechanism from the theater in the steel mesh envelope to the waiting transport vehicle, where it was whisked, under motorcycle escort, through the streets of Manhattan to the beachfront of Fort Tilden. Before the watchful eyes of 150 witnesses, including police detectives, army personnel, television and radio news crews, and newspaper reporters from across the city, the device was placed in a hole dug in the sand and detonated upon the clarion announcement, "Fire in the Hole."

Hours after the find at the Times Square Paramount, the New York Board of Estimate unanimously adopted the following resolution offered by Mayor Wagner at the request of Commissioner Kennedy:

> Resolved . . . that the City of New York hereby offer a reward of $25,000 for information leading to the apprehension and conviction of the individual responsible for the placing of infernal machines or bombs in various places in the city during the past several years.
>
> The Police Commissioner shall be the sole judge in determining the person or persons entitled to said reward and the proportionate distribution thereof.
>
> Nothing contained herein shall authorize the payment of such reward or any part thereof, directly or indirectly, to any member of the Police Dept. of the City of New York.

Shortly thereafter, the Police Patrolmen's Benevolent Association augmented the reward by an additional $1,000. It was the first time since the 1940 bombing of the British Pavilion at the New York World's Fair that reward money had been posted by the city or an arm of the police department for the apprehension of a wanted criminal. As the reward was announced, Chief Leggett appealed to members of the public who might have seen anyone carrying any peculiar-looking object into the Paramount on the evening of the twenty-seventh or who otherwise might have appeared suspicious or somehow out of character. Commissioner Kennedy later stated that the Bomber was "of the killer type . . . He is not a mastermind but a mental defective who is under the delusion that he is a superior man . . . He sets the bombs off for a psychic kick. He needs help."

With the announcement of the reward money by the city of New York, the level of hysteria only multiplied. Nervous residents kept suspicious vigil over the movements of their neighbors, and darkened houses and unexplained excursions suddenly became the focal point of rumor and accusation. As published police photographs of lethal devices and abandoned knives joined reports of covert FBI involvement in the case, the already frayed nerves of New Yorkers deteriorated and the general "atmosphere of a siege prevailed."

Police detectives investigated hundreds of tips, leads, and sources provided by a now fully engaged citizenry, but as the bomb hoaxes continued and even increased, the watchful eyes of the public often drew erroneous and unreliable conclusions. The department dealt with the usual rash of serial confessors guilty of nothing but the act of a sham confession, but it was the flawed perceptions of well-intended citizens, and even the police department itself, that would lead to the inevitable flood of bogus leads and false accusations.

Shortly after the public library bomb was discovered and publicized, two scientists recalled a chance encounter they had with a shabbily dressed man at a science and technology exhibit held at the library on Christmas Eve. The man spoke incessantly of the explosive properties of a particular compound and the various strategic uses of chemical-based bombs. Convinced that the individual was nothing more than a sophistic crank, the scientists evaded him and went about their business. Later in the day, when they heard of the explosive device found on the library grounds, they were immediately reminded of their earlier encounter and contacted the police. During two hours of interrogation, the scientists had provided a detailed description of the suspect, and police scurried about in search of a garrulous, dingily dressed man about six feet in height with a bookish interest in explosive substances.

When the Mad Bomber struck the Times Square Paramount Theatre on December 28, movie patrons, eager for a chance at the alluring newly announced reward money, searched their minds for any clue of a suspect. Among them, a couple described a suspicious man sitting two seats away in an area of several otherwise unoccupied rows and in very close proximity to where the bomb was ultimately located. The suspect, according to the couple, was bald, in his early fifties, stood about five foot six or perhaps seven inches in height and spoke in a thick German accent similar to what several police descriptions had attributed to the Bomber. Of particular interest to police was the description of a middle-aged woman who apparently accompanied the suspect, thus furthering the intriguing possibility of a female accomplice. The idea that the Bomber could be a woman disguised in men's clothing had previously been advanced, and now the concept gained momentum with new and seemingly credible evidence.

On the Upper East Side, several jewelry shops reported what seemed at the time to be a promising lead. Each of the jewelers had notified police detectives and journalists that they had been visited on a number of occasions by a "poorly dressed, thin, pale-faced . . . [man], possibly of German or Nordic extraction," who repeatedly asked for particular inexpensive used watch movements that he said he wanted for a collection. After finally being apprehended and enduring no less than eight separate interrogations by different members of the New York City Police Department, each of whom thought that perhaps they had nabbed the Bomber, the "meek and simple" itinerant watch repairman who sought mechanisms from local jewelers for mending and resale was cleared of all suspicion. For his own protection and for the sake of overwrought detectives, the man was gently prodded to drape a small cardboard sign over his chest like a beggar's plea, reading: "I am NOT the Mad Bomber."

Of the thousands of interrogations conducted by police in the sixteen-year search for the Mad Bomber, at least one, at the pinnacle of the 1956–57 holiday histrionics, would turn tragic. On December 28, police detectives, hungry for valid leads, apprehended an elderly "mystery man" who had been suspiciously milling about the telephone booths and washrooms of Grand Central Terminal, where one of many false alarms was being investigated. Intrigued by a pair of red wool socks found in the man's pocket, the officers took the man into custody and transported him to the East Thirty-fifth Street police station for questioning. As the detectives began the process of booking and fingerprinting, the suspect—later identified as George Cermac, a sixty-three-year-old Yugoslavian immigrant living in Bethlehem, Pennsylvania—suddenly clasped his chest and collapsed to the floor. He was dead before the interrogation could begin, though later he was cleared of any suspicion of being the Mad Bomber.

• • •

As 1956 came to a close, FBI director J. Edgar Hoover grimly announced that Americans had committed more major crimes during the year than any previous year in the country's history. Offenses ranging from auto theft to capital murder had shown a stark national increase, and local trends in New York City weren't expected to be dramatically better. Back in Waterbury, Connecticut, George Metesky, undaunted by the feckless statistics of law enforcement, reveled in the spotlight of notoriety that he had at long last achieved, anonymous as it was. Daily, he drove out of town to purchase the New York newspapers that chronicled the trail of havoc he had so skillfully ignited, and he gleefully tracked what he saw as the impotent efforts of a hapless police force. Carefully appraising and assessing every word of the articles, Metesky pondered whether even greater bombs in higher-profile locations would be required to bring Con Ed to justice.

On December 26, 1956, as George Metesky sat in his Daimler automobile with the *New York Journal-American* sprawled across his lap and contemplating his next move, his eye was enticingly drawn to "An Open Letter to the Mad Bomber."

# "THE FOUR FISHERMEN"

Seymour Berkson would be accused by rival newspapers of staging nothing more than a cheap publicity stunt in the publishing of his open letter, but he would staunchly defend his decision as not only a service to the community, but the blazing of an "uncharted course" in journalistic history. "We've heard of people being pulled off ledges by word of mouth," he would later say, "but we didn't know if the printed word would stop acts against society."

In his Christmas morning conversation with Paul Schoenstein, Berkson had casually—almost offhandedly—noted that the Bomber seemed to harbor a deep-seated grievance. Why, he posited, couldn't the paper publish a communiqué to the Bomber urging him to reveal his complaints and accusations and at the same time assure him that he would receive, in Berskson's words, "a fair deal under American justice." Might not such a letter "pique his interest and tempt him to bring his grievance into the open?"

Though the proposition appeared to be reasonably formulated, the risks were enormous. While Berkson maintained a good faith belief that his open letter would be seen and responded to by the Bomber, he also knew that there was a possibility of a boomerang effect against the paper if, in fact, the Bomber reacted to it in a violent or vengeful manner. The angry backlash of the readership could severely harm the paper or even put it out of business. As publisher, Berkson weighed such risks against the obvious and opposite benefits if the Bomber actually took the overture seriously and responded in kind. In the end, Berkson maintained that he never would have exposed the *Journal-American* to the colossal hazards if he hadn't absolutely believed in the soundness of the idea.

The deliberations on the subject were brief indeed. The typically contemplative Schoenstein enthusiastically jumped at the proposal and instantly suggested that it be put into swift action. A flurry of telephone calls ensued to the managing editor of the paper, Sam Day, known for his stalwart crusades on behalf of journalistic freedom, and the burly and flamboyant city editor, Edward Mahar, and within minutes there was a consensus among the four to forge ahead with Berkson's intrepid plan.

From the beginning Berkson insisted that the strategy for the open letter be executed with the full knowledge and cooperation of the New York City Police Department. Commissioner Kennedy had already adopted Dr. Brussel's suggestion that an open provocation of the Bomber might challenge him and force him into a reaction. Here, thought Kennedy, was the perfect opportunity to put Brussel's theory to the test, and, without hesitation, the commissioner endorsed the plan.

Later that Christmas day, Schoenstein drove to the faded sandstone building on the Lower East Side of Manhattan that was home to the *Journal-American* and, with the guidance and assistance of Berkson, Day, and Mahar, began work on the paper's open letter. Together, the *Journal-American*'s "Four Fishermen," as they would come to be known, trawled their lines into uncertain waters, hoping for the ultimate catch.

. . .

Public appeals for information by the *Journal-American* continued unabated. With promises to shield the identity of anyone providing the paper or the police with information relevant to the Mad Bomber case, staff writers and editors beseeched jewelers, plumbers, hardware stores, hunting shops, and the public at large for cooperation. As a steady flow of hoaxes and pranks poured into the paper's city room, most of New York doubted that the real Bomber would ever respond to an open letter. "More than one rival paper, more than one reader of the *Journal-American*, considered the appeal to be a new high in wishful thinking," wrote one Hearst reporter.

Notwithstanding the prevailing skepticism, competing newspapers made similar overtures to the Bomber so as not to be excluded from the frenzy of increased circulation. The news-radio arm of the *New York Daily News,* WNEW, had been transmitting cryptic late-night messages at the end of their hourly news breaks, sympathetically consoling the Bomber and coaxing him to contact *News* reporter Jess Stearn, in an effort to address his concerns and perhaps negotiate a surrender. Stearn had, in fact, received several letters from the Bomber in response to the effort, but as the *Journal-American* seized a more dominant role in the attempted communications, the WNEW campaign turned derogatory toward the Bomber and eventually faltered. A similar plea was made by Walter Winchell in his *Of New York* column in the *Daily Mirror,* wherein he wrote, "To the sick person who has placed bombs in different places for the past 16 years . . . Please inform me of your losses and suffering . . . I want to help you. Tell me how."

Meanwhile, a watchful *Journal-American* city room scrutinized every article of mail that it received in the days after Christmas, hunting for those distinctive-looking block letters and hoping for a response to their alluring open letter.

· · ·

William Randolph Hearst Jr. would describe the *Journal-American* as a "family":

> Reporters, advertising salesmen, secretaries—we had worked there most of our lives. We cared for and helped one another . . . No one had more fun covering the heartache and happy times of the city. That was because most of us were native New Yorkers. We were a wild and often senti-mental bunch who loved New York because it was our town. We wrote about it with affection, anger, and despair . . .

No one covered New York as well as we did in the
1950s . . . not the Times, not the Herald-Tribune, not the
World-Telegram & Sun, Daily Mirror, Daily News, or the
Post. In those days you competed hard for millions of subway readers . . . New York was then the most exciting city
in the world . . .
We were good. At times, magnificent.

In what Hearst would later call the *Journal-American*'s "finest hour,"
at 8:10 p.m. on the night of Friday, December 28, a copy boy dropped a
special delivery envelope on the desk of the *Journal-American*'s assistant
night city editor, Richard Piperno. The letter, postmarked the previous
night at the Mt. Vernon, New York, post office, bore the neatly formed,
pencil-written signature characters of the Mad Bomber—and Piperno,
who had studied previous samples of the distinctive handwriting, knew it.
Within minutes, deputy police commissioner Walter Arm was notified of
the letter and, soon after, he and Commissioner Kennedy converged upon
the *Journal-American*'s sixth-floor offices on the South Street waterfront,
where Berkson and Schoenstein had already gathered.

The city room, where the Bomber's letter would be scrutinized, was
unquestionably the vital pulse of the newspaper, taking up one dominant
area of the floor sectioned off into various departments and haphazardly
furnished with chipped and cigarette-burned filing cabinets. A series of
interconnected steel desks illuminated by wire-hung light fixtures were
manned by reporters and rewrite staff busily verifying leads or tapping
out stories on Remington typewriters. The building itself, constructed
in 1926–27, was set among the soot and grime of abandoned East River
docks and tenements, and had a deteriorated and arcane appearance.
Originally one of Arthur Brisbane's real estate ventures, the building was
purchased by the senior Hearst, who reportedly erupted, after seeing the
moaning structure for the first time after completing the transaction,
"Arthur, you've done it to me again!" The only section of the sixth floor

with separator walls was the executive offices, which ran along a narrow corridor adjacent to the city room. Here, in Berkson's private suite, beneath the fixed leer of a mounted Acapulco sunfish proudly displayed by its conqueror, the team met for the next four hours to discuss the details of the Bomber's response and to create and adopt a joint strategy for moving forward.

In actuality, the *Journal-American* city desk had received two letters, both contained in the same envelope. The first, directed to WNEW and to Jess Stearn of the *Daily News*, began with the terse rebuke, "YOU ARE FINISHED—" The missive, which spoke of betrayal and abuse, claimed that the two bombs found at the public library and the Times Square Paramount during Christmas week had actually been planted months earlier, and accused the paper and the radio station of being "NOTHING MORE THAN THE SLIMY CREATURES THAT YOU ARE." It closed with the menacing warning, "I MAY PAY YOU A VISIT. *F.P.*"

The second letter, written on decorative Christmas paper and adorned with an ornamental snowman at the top, began:

TO JOURNAL-AMERICAN—I READ YOUR PAPER OF DEC.
26—WHERE WERE YOU PEOPLE WHEN I WAS ASKING
FOR HELP? PLACING MYSELF INTO CUSTODY WOULD
BE STUPID—DO NOT INSULT MY INTELLIGENCE—BRING
THE CON. EDISON TO JUSTICE—START WORKING ON
LEHMAN—POLETTI—ANDREWS . . . THESE GENTS
KNOW ALL . . . ALL THE N.Y. PRESS WAS ALSO
INFORMED—


I WILL KEEP MY WORD—NO BOMBS UNTIL AFTER
MID-JANUARY—THE METHOD OF BOMBING WILL THEN
BE—DIFFERENT—

In an attempt to indicate good faith the writer then pointed out the location of several undiscovered bombs at Radio City Music Hall and provided a list of all bombs that he had placed during 1956, should additional devices be located during the period of "truce," as he called it—one of which, at the Empire State Building, has never been found. The letter concluded:

> BEFORE I AM FINISHED—THE CON. EDISON CO. WILL WISH THAT THEY HAD BROUGHT TO ME IN THEIR TEETH—WHAT THEY CHEATED ME OUT OF.
>
> MY DAYS ON EARTH ARE NUMBERED—MOST OF MY ADULT LIFE HAS BEEN SPENT IN BED—MY ONE CONSOLATION IS—THAT I CAN STRIKE BACK—EVEN FROM MY GRAVE—FOR THE DASTARDLY ACTS AGAINST ME. CALLING ME NAMES—IS JUST FRUSTRATED STUPIDITY IN ACTION—
> F.P.

"Unquestionably genuine," said Commissioner Kennedy. Berskon's eyes widened like a child's, his mind formulating the eighty-point boldface banner headline of the next morning's issue. The elation was short-lived. Though the letter had contained good news for anxious New Yorkers— word of a truce—it had also contained a plethora of information, undeniably useful to police analysts, for which time and contemplation would be required. Kennedy thought for a moment and then expressed what Seymour Berkson had already begun to surmise in the pregnant pause of silence: Pending further lab and investigative analysis, the contents of the letter should not, for the time being, be publicized.

The request, one that Berkson found difficult to defy with the stern-faced police commissioner sitting directly opposite him, ran counter to everything he felt as a journalist. Here was a scoop that could easily send readership figures of his paper off the charts, but the risk of alienating his new rapport with the Bomber and the police department itself with an all-out burst of headlines weighed heavily on his mind. The matter was fully discussed between the men, and it was finally agreed, in the spirit of compromise, that the Bomber's letter would not be immediately published so as to give the police time to digest and investigate the new clues presented. A more considered and deliberative approach was called for.

On January 2, 3, and 4, an obscure yet compelling item, composed with the full input and cooperation of the New York City Police Department, appeared hidden in the personals column in the announcements section of the *New York Journal-American*:

> WE RECEIVED YOUR LETTER. WE APPRECIATE TRUCE.
> WHAT WERE YOU DEPRIVED OF? WE WANT TO HEAR
> YOUR VIEWS AND HELP YOU. WE WILL KEEP OUR
> WORD. CONTACT US SAME WAY AS PREVIOUSLY.

The mysterious communication was another daring shot in the dark, open for all to read yet intended only for one set of eyes. Its writers could only hope that the scrutiny of those eyes would find its way to the beseeching message.

As the city of New York said goodbye to one year and intrepidly entered the next, the Four Fishermen and the brain trust of the New York City Police Department anxiously awaited word from the Mad Bomber.

• • •

With the deluge of hoaxes still plaguing the department—130 from Christmas Eve through New Year's alone—and a slew of bogus replies pouring into the *Journal-American* daily, police detectives sifted through every word of the Bomber's curious response to the open letter, searching for any clue as to the identity of its writer. The task of distinguishing the Bomber's genuine communications from the counterfeits was made considerably easier by his idiosyncratic use of pencil rather than ink on a uniquely cut and folded standard stamp-embossed U.S. Post Office envelope with the placement of "N.Y." on a separate line in the address above the words "Journal-American." Though Berkson had agreed not to immediately publish the contents of the Bomber's response or the distinctive characteristics of its mailing, the paper did allude, in a general way, to the leads generated by it and from his prior letters, and the police vigorously pursued each.

The Bomber's reference to Lehman, Poletti, and Andrews as individuals possessing some special knowledge of his grievances had caught the eye of police investigators as suggestive of some tangential political involvement in the matter. Herbert H. Lehman had served as governor of New York from 1933 through 1942, and Charles Poletti served as his lieutenant governor. More specifically, the mention of Elmer Andrews, who was the state industrial commissioner under Governor Lehman, reaffirmed the possibility of a workmen's compensation dispute that had been reviewed, perhaps at the upper levels of state government, as being somehow part of the Bomber's feud.

When contacted by police, Andrews recalled an incident around 1935 in which he was forced to discharge an angry and menacing employee of the compensation board for a continuous string of infractions, and that the same individual had once lost another job at Consolidated Edison under the same set of circumstances. Each of the three politicians, however, police discovered, had routinely received hundreds if not thousands of crank letters from disgruntled citizens, none of which could be specifically recollected by either man or his staff as particularly eye-catching or alarming. As for the specific lead provided by Elmer Andrews, the police investigated and then dismissed it as heading them down a "blind alley."

The spotlight of the investigation then turned to the outskirts of New York City. The telltale Mt. Vernon postmark on the Bomber's letter to the *Journal-American* was from the same general community as his prior letters. Most had come from White Plains or other points north of the city and had led investigators to the conclusion that their perpetrator might reside in or have connections with the affluent suburbs of

Westchester County. Dr. Brussel had suggested that the Bomber lived far-ther north, perhaps in the state of Connecticut, and used the areas outside of the city as a postal way station of sorts, but the supposition reached by the New York police was based upon other compelling evidence uncov-ered by simple, boots-on-the-ground investigative work.

During the first few days of 1957, detectives had begun questioning a number of plumbers and supply house managers throughout the area to bet-ter understand the Bomber's repeated past use of the words "well-coupling" in his letters to describe the lengths of pipe used in the construction of his devices. Investigators had always found the expression somewhat puzzling and foreign, and upon speaking with the local tradesmen, confirmed that the phrase was, in fact, specifically indigenous to the towns in and around Westchester County, as opposed to the term "line pipe coupling," which was commonly used by plumbers and suppliers within the confines of New York City. Combining this revelation with the telling postmarks on the Bomber's various letters, police quickly honed their search for the Bomber and converged in droves upon the quiet northern New York suburbs of Mt. Vernon and White Plains.

On January 3, 1957, New York City police detectives informed a gathering of seventy-five public officials representing thirty-nine separate police departments in Westchester County that the hunt for the Bomber would now focus within their jurisdiction. Samples of the Bomber's distinc-tive block printing were circulated to each of the represented departments, and, before long, detectives, sheriffs' staff, and patrolmen descended upon a variety of Westchester County offices in a round-the-clock check of 357,000 automobile license applications, 26,000 court files, 150,000 jury lists, 20,000 pistol permit requests, and 9,000 county clerk judgments for handwriting matches. To aid in this monumental task, thirty veteran New York detectives in the midst of a refresher course at the police academy were abruptly removed from class to join the newly formed Bomb Inves-tigation Unit, twelve of whom were sent directly to White Plains to sift through documents. Meanwhile, the department, on the direct order of

Commissioner Kennedy, redistributed a circular with a photograph of one of the Bomber's unexploded devices to all 23,000 members of the force, including those serving in White Plains, together with detailed instructions on what to do if such a contraption were to be found.

Within days of commencing the Westchester County investigation, forty-two possible suspects had been developed on the basis of handwriting analysis and were being watched by the finest trailing detectives on the New York force. Hundreds of possible matches had been revealed from the hundreds of thousands of samples reviewed, and each was sent to Captain Finney at the New York City Crime Lab for further paring. The resulting list of forty-two matches was considered close enough, in each case, to be suspicious, and detectives began compiling detailed dossiers on the private and public lives of every man under surveillance.

On the recommendation of Dr. Brussel and pursuant to the Bomber's own statements that his "days on earth are numbered" and that most of his "adult life has been spent in bed," investigators began canvassing hospitals and medical professionals, requesting them to be on the lookout for a man fitting the descriptions generated by and for the police department, in the belief that the Bomber was perhaps under the care of a physician, nurse, or psychiatrist. With every promising suspect or enticing lead, however, came a timely alibi or exculpatory detail that brought police back to the investigative drawing board. On the evening of January 10, however, just as the department had begun to doubt the validity of their own current methods, it seemed that perhaps their luck had changed.

With the investigation targeting individuals in poor states of health, word had come to police that a sixty-seven-year-old widower who lived alone in the Bronx near the border of Westchester County—a former metalworker—had died at Fordham Hospital from bronchial pneumonia. The suspect, Andrew Kleewen, had been born in Latvia and spoke in a thick accent easily confused as German, and he generally fit the published description of the Mad Bomber. Upon a check of the dead man's apartment, police found the premises to be in complete disarray, with piles of newspapers, letters, bills, and receipts massed on the floors, upon most of the surfaces, and stuffed in several bureaus. Many of the letters, copies of which Kleewen had retained, had been addressed to high-ranking public officials such as President Roosevelt, Secretary of State John Dulles, various congressmen, state legislators, and the mayor of New York, and almost all complained of this or that wrong perpetrated against the writer. Initial descriptions of Kleewen's handwriting promisingly seemed to contain indications of a Teutonic style, and when a stack of bills from Consolidated Edison Co. going back twenty-five years was found among his belongings, the bomb squad was called into the investigation.

• • •

During the fragile period of unease while Seymour Berkson and Commissioner Kennedy cautiously nurtured a tenuous relationship with their newfound correspondent, the *Journal-American* had grudgingly fulfilled their promise to the police not to publish the Bomber's letter until a full analysis of its contents could be conducted. With the Bomber's stated deadline looming, investigators worked feverishly to wring whatever evidence they could from the letter without risking further danger to the public by permitting the reckless publication of pertinent and sensitive information. In a matter of days, however, the inquisitive eyes of an editor from the *New York World-Telegram and Sun* had detected the well-concealed personal ad intended solely for the Bomber, confronted an indiscreet police official with the evidence, and wangled an ill-advised confirmation that the *Journal-American* was, in fact, sitting on a letter authored by the Mad Bomber. The following day, Berkson and Kennedy were dismayed to find a page-one article in the *World-Telegram* titled "Mad Bomber's Letter Hints Brief Truce," scooping the story of the Bomber's letter to "a New York newspaper" and brazenly publicizing the clandestine efforts of the unnamed paper to initiate communications with their quarry. Instantly, a variety of other news outlets around the city repeated the story and, before long, the *Journal-American*'s guarded secret had become the talk of the town.

"We were in the awkward position of being honor-bound not to print a line about [the letter]," Berskon later said. Though he had bristled at the *World-Telegram*'s shameless tack of preempting the story and perhaps endangering the police investigation, the *Journal-American* had by no means ceased reporting on the Bomber story during the uneasy truce. They wrote extensively—and responsibly—about the continuing rash of hoaxes and the ongoing investigation in Westchester County, but then, in the first week of January 1957, the paper inexplicably printed a story lambasting the volatile personality with whom they sought a trusting association as a "psychopathic 'enemy of society,'" quoting a New York deputy police inspector. The inflammatory article, ostensibly placed with the authority of the *Journal-American*'s editorial staff, did not miss the eye of the Bomber, and he quickly articulated his displeasure:

TO NEW YORK JOURNAL AMERICAN . . .

YOU PEOPLE HAVE LEARNED NOTHING FROM 'HELL
WEEK'—YOU INSIST UPON POISIONING THE MINDS
OF PEOPLE AGAINST ME—YOU PUT ME IN THE WORST
POSITION—DELIBERATELY—THEN YOU ASK THAT I
CONFIDE IN YOU—I HAVE BEEN BETRAYED ONCE
AGAIN—I DO NOT TRUST YOU—YOU HAVE THE CHOICE OF
PLACING THE MAIN CONTENTS OF THE LETTER I SENT
YOU BEFORE THE PUBLIC—OR YOU HAD BETTER HAVE A
VERY GOOD REASON FOR NOT DOING SO—I HAVE KEPT
MY WORD—I WILL ALSO KEEP MY WORD—YOUR TIME IS
RUNNING OUT—ARE YOU GOING TO TELL THE TRUTH OR
WILL YOU BETRAY THE PEOPLE—I WILL BUY A PAPER
ON THURSDAY—THE RESPONSIBILITY IS YOURS . . .
- F.P.

Compounding Seymour Berkson's ire over the mischief of the *World-Telegram*, the harsh and ominous response had clearly not been the conciliatory gesture they had hoped for. Again confirmed as genuine, the Bomber's letter immediately triggered a flurry of activity among the *Journal-American* and the New York City Police Department in the hope of averting what now looked like an imminent resumption of bombings. Though its very receipt had the effect of clearing as a suspect Andrew Kleewen, it more importantly told police that the time for rumination was over. Unless an appropriate response could be articulated before the Bomber's deadline of Thursday, January 10—not twenty-four hours from then—the worst fears of the paper and the department could be realized. The earlier decision not to publish the Bomber's message had to change.

On the evening of January 9, Commissioner Kennedy and his top brass once again met with Berkson, Schoenstein, Day, and Mahar at the offices of the *Journal-American*. In a spirited, often contentious, meeting that lasted much of the night, it was finally agreed that the Bomber's first letter, received on December 28, would be published by the paper with the exception of certain censored items deemed by the commissioner to be sensitive in nature, which would be expunged from the disclosure. Berkson would finally get his hard-earned scoop.

The following day, just beneath the wailing front page headline "THE MAD BOMBER WRITES!" a full copy of the letter, minus the expiration date of the proposed truce and the actual identities of the public officials Lehman, Poletti, and Andrews, appeared in the Bomber's own distinctive printing. The direct quote "<u>MY DAYS ON EARTH ARE NUMBERED</u>," underlined for accent, lay just above the headline. Also appearing on the front page, in a carefully worded message crafted by Berkson and his staff and scrupulously edited by Commissioner Kennedy, a second open letter to the Mad Bomber was placed just beneath the fold, in hopes of placating the Bomber while subtly drawing additional information from him:

F.P.

We are publishing for you and all to see the main contents of your recent letter.

Study fails to explain what you meant by your reference to L----, P----, and A----.

What questions shall we ask these three prominent men?

Please make yourself clear enough for us to understand. We cannot help you air your grievances unless you help us ascertain what they are.

We repeat our offer to see that your grievances are presented fully and fairly.

We also continue our promise to see that you receive the full benefits of our American system of justice if you will continue your truce and arrange to surrender yourself at the time and place of your choosing.

We realize, too, that time is running out on our chances to be in touch with each other. You will get best results by answering quickly.

We know you kept your word about the truce.

Please write us in the usual way. Make your points clear so that another long delay will not ensue.

City Desk, N.Y. Journal-American

The January 10, 1957, issue of the *New York Journal-American* was purchased by 757,410 enthralled New Yorkers. On that day, the Four Fisherman and the commissioner of the New York City Police Department held their collective breath in the hope that the Mad Bomber was among them.

Their wait was not a long one. At 7:30 p.m. on January 12, the Bomber's response to the second open letter was postmarked in White Plains, New York, and delivered to the *Journal-American* city desk two days later. The dispatch, instantly recognized as containing a treasure trove of information and even the hint of an assuaging tone, was this time regarded as a scrupulously protected secret to prevent a repeat of the *World-Telegram* fiasco and was revealed only to Seymour Berkson's immediate editorial team and the office of the police commissioner. Finally, it appeared that Berkson's perilous dialogue with the Mad Bomber had begun to pay its dividends.

"I WILL EXTEND THIS ONE SIDED 'TRUSE' [*sic*] UNTIL MARCH 1ST—YOUR EFFORT ON MY BEHALF EARNED SAME—NEVER DOUBT MY WORDS—SHOULD I RESUME OPERATIONS AFTER MARCH 1ST I WILL LET YOU KNOW FIRST," wrote the Bomber. The letter claimed that the bomb discovered at the Times Square Paramount Theater on December 28 had been placed months earlier and thus was in no way to be construed as a breach of his first truce. The Bomber then provided a series of technical details about the size of the couplings and potency of the powder used in several of his prior bombings, and suggested that the future course of events depended on what could be done by the paper on his behalf before March 1. Then, in a barrage of disclosures he began to reveal the origins of his grievance. "I WAS INJURED ON JOB AT CONSOLIDATED EDISON PLANT—AS A RESULT I AM ADJUDGED—TOTALLY AND PERMANENTLY DISABLED—I DID NOT RECEIVE 'ANY AID'—OF ANY KIND FROM COMPANY—THAT I DID NOT PAY FOR MYSELF—WHILE FIGHTING FOR MY LIFE—'SECTION 28' CAME UP." He complained that Con Ed recommended that his claim be brought before the Workmen's Compensation Board, and insisted that the company then blocked his every effort to do so. Lehman, Pelotti, and Andrews, the letter continued, had full knowledge of the "perjurers" who interfered with his case, and promised, according to the Bomber, to conduct an investigation that twenty years later still had not occurred. "I DID NOT GET A SINGLE PENNY FOR A LIFETIME OF MISERY AND SUFFERING—JUST ABUSE." And then his anger welled:

WHEN A MOTORIST INJURES A DOG—HE MUST REPORT IT—NOT SO WITH AN INJURED WORKMAN—HE RATES LESS THAN A DOG—I TRIED TO GET MY STORY TO THE PRESS—I TRIED HUNDREDS OF OTHERS—I TYPED TENS OF THOUSANDS OF WORDS (ABOUT 800,000)—NOBODY CARED—I GOT A SAMPLE OF WHAT YOU CALL "OUR AMERICAN SYSTEM OF JUSTICE" AT FIRST HAND— AS YOU CAN SEE—I DO NOT WANT MORE OF IT IF I CAN HELP IT—I [AM] DETERMINED TO MAKE THESE DASTARDLY ACTS KNOWN—I HAVE HAD PLENTY OF TIME TO THINK—I DECIDED ON BOMBS—YOU PEOPLE ASK ME TO SURRENDER MYSELF—WELL SIR—WHO IS REALLY GUILTY—YOU OR I?---

F.P.

The embossed postal cancellation stamped across the outside of the envelope read simply and ironically, "Pray for Peace."

Seymour Berkson was delighted with the letter. The Bomber's own words, directed to his newspaper and exclusively his to exploit, would make rich copy indeed. Commissioner Kennedy's detectives, however, far less fascinated by the commercial value of the letter, now focused their investigation on the New York workmen's compensation system, which plainly seemed to be at the heart of the Bomber's grudge.

Sensing that they were edging ever closer to that critical piece of information that would crack the case and anxious to continue the now escalating dialogue, the *Journal-American*'s editors and the police commissioner once again agreed upon a slightly redacted version of the Bomber's letter to appear in the paper alongside a third open appeal to "F.P.," which appeared in the January 15 issue.

"Can you name the perjurers?" the letter asked. "We are as anxious as you to tell the whole truth about your case. But only you seem to have all the facts."

As James Brussel had informed the police, the Bomber's paranoid and narcissistic personality yearned for attention and respect, and may, in fact, cause him to become frustrated by the safety of long-term anonymity. Here was an opportunity, thought Commissioner Kennedy and his deputies, to play on that egocentric need and to further elicit crucial details through a simple invitation to the Bomber to expand upon his own story. In essence, they hoped to sympathetically massage the Bomber's ego while gently prodding him for particulars. "Your story is convincing," continued the appeal:

> We want to help you, but can only do so if the partial portrait of injustice you have begun to paint is brought into sharper focus. Once it is, we promise to tell your full story to the world. If you have been cheated, as you point out, we will procure the best counsel to aid you . . . If you can give us further details and dates we are assured by competent legal authority that your case **CAN** indeed be reopened with a fair and just hearing of all the evidence you have.
>
> We know you will keep your word. We will keep ours.

The letter concluded with an invitation to "come in and present your case in person."

Behind the scenes, a coordinated effort between the *Journal-American*, Consolidated Edison Company, the New York Labor Department, and the Police Commissioner's Office further sought to cautiously draw out the Bomber. At both the corporate offices of Consolidated Edison and the Workmen's Compensation Division of the New York Labor Department, clerks busily searched their files, comparing handwriting samples and fact patterns against those presented in the Bomber's letters, while the chairwoman of the Workmen's Compensation Board herself, Angela Parisi, personally hunted, often late into the night, through the board's files and records dating back to 1913, in search of a possible match. At the same time, a calculated effort to appease the Bomber was under way within the pages of the *Journal-American*. On January 16, the paper published a full copy of a letter directed to Seymour Berkson and bearing the signature of Harland Forbes, president of Consolidated Edison Company of New York, expressing his deep concern over the plight of the Bomber in light of repeated references to the company's potential involvement in the matter. In a coordinated ploy to cajole further decisive facts from their wayward former comrade, the message, appearing on official Con Ed letterhead, concluded, "We would welcome some further information regarding the case, such as the date or the nature of the incident. We wish to assure 'F.P.' that we will make a thorough and impartial reappraisal if we have some facts to work on." The letter appeared under the bold first-page heading "WE WANT TO HELP."

Meanwhile, the *Journal-American* editors, with the assistance and request of top police brass, secured a statement from Isidor Lubin, the New York Industrial Commissioner, promising that the state labor department could provide the Bomber a review of his case if warranted. "If an injustice has been done to this person by the Department of Labor," declared Lubin, "I will do everything in my power to see it rectified." As with the letter from Con Ed, Lubin's statement appeared prominently on page 1 of the January 16 issue of the paper and bore the headline "State Promises Review of Case." In the followup article, individual photographs of both Forbes and Lubin were respectively placed atop the bolded labels "CONCERNED . . ." and "VOW HELP . . ." The conciliatory message to the Bomber was unmistakable.

In the coming days, as all of New York watched and waited for the Bomber's next communication, the *Journal-American* kept up its campaign of assurances. It pledged, through a variety of articles and headlines, "the most scientific medical care" available, and stated that opinions from lawyers specializing in workmen's compensation cases had already been compiled in preparation for a full rehearing of his case. Perhaps overstepping its journalistic bounds, one article even suggested that Commissioner Kennedy's assurance to the Bomber of the best psychiatric care was tantamount to a pledge of "immunity from prosecution." All of these things, including "top legal counsel," vowed the *Journal-American*, were available to the Bomber should he merely make himself known through a face-to-face meeting or the furnishing of further particular details.

On Saturday, January 19, the awaited reply, mailed from the general post office on Eighth Avenue and Thirty-second Street, arrived at the city desk of the *Journal-American*. From the moment that Seymour Berkson read the opening salutation—"My dear Friends"—he knew that the dramatic climax of the Mad Bomber case was near—and that the *Journal-American* would be the enthusiastic scrivener to the triumphant episode.

The Bomber's response was, in actuality, two rambling letters, one hand-printed per his usual course, and the other typewritten, both of which were immediately poured over by Berkson and Commissioner Kennedy. The handwritten component immediately proclaimed the words that all of New York yearned to hear: "THANKS VERY MUCH FOR YOUR EFFORT," began the note. "THE BOMBINGS WILL NEVER BE RESUMED—COME WHAT MAY—YOU PEOPLE HAVE LET THE PEOPLE KNOW—MY PART OF THE STORY—I CANNOT ASK FOR MUCH MORE."

The typed letter began with the long sought-after revelation coveted by authorities: "I was injured on September 5th, 1931." It was the missing link that New York police had been waiting for and would have the instant effect of focusing and narrowing the search through the compensation files for the Bomber's specific record. The Bomber indicated that, were he free to act without stigmatizing or hurting "the people who deprived themselves so that my life could be sustained," he would consider a meeting or even a surrender without delay. "I THINK THAT A FACE TO FACE MEETING COULD BE FIGURED OUT," continued the Bomber in his handwritten note, "AS THERE ARE SO MANY THINGS THAT COULD THEN BE FREELY DISCUSSED."

And then, in a doff of the hat to Seymour Berkson, the Bomber signed off with the tribute that would both forge and antagonize the bond between journalism and police work forever:

```
        IN ABOUT 3 WEEKS TIME THE N.Y.
    JOURNAL AMERICAN ACCOMPLISHED WHAT THE
    AUTHORITIES COULD NOT DO—IN 16 YEARS—YOU
            STOPPED THE BOMBINGS.
                    F.P.
```

# ALICE KELLY

THE DELIBERATIONS REGARDING AN APPROPRIATE RESPONSE TO THE Bomber's revealing letters took place at the home of Seymour Berkson on Sunday, January 20, mere hours after their delivery to the *Journal-American*. The usual team of editors and police officials was markedly cheered by the bond of trust they had forged with the Bomber, but the question remained as to how best to reel in their prey. They studied and debated the content and tone of the letters and the offers contained in each and, at the behest of Berkson, even consulted with several psychiatrists retained by the newspaper to analyze the psychological implications of the communiqués. Plans were immediately drawn to publish the hand-printed portions of the Bomber's groundbreaking communication, though, at the insistence of Commissioner Kennedy, the typewritten letter, which contained the date and details of the Bomber's injury at Con Ed, would be withheld as the investigation continued. Finally, it was agreed that another open letter would be drafted that would combine an empathic appeal and a shared desire for justice with an insistence that the time had come for the Bomber to avail himself of the opportunities that had been offered to him. "You can decide where, how and when to meet us," the letter coaxed. "Please write us in the same manner as previously, outling [*sic*] the procedure you would like to follow for the face-to-face meeting . . ."

The overture would never appear in the *Journal-American*.

· · ·

As part of the routine investigation of the case, a painstaking search of Con Ed's employee records had been conducted by detectives of the Bomb Investigation Unit and Con Ed clerks alike in the quest for any match of handwriting or other telltale sign of the Mad Bomber. For several years police investigators had independently combed through thousands of the company's employment records, and during the first few weeks of January 1957 they had narrowed their search to the "dead" compensation files kept at a Con Ed warehouse on Hester Street. The search had been limited to the records of past employees who were not expected to further protest their claims or have future dealings with the company, and it was completed by detectives on Friday, January 18, just prior to the *Journal-American*'s receipt of the Bomber's latest revealing missives. Later that afternoon, a call was placed by police to Con Ed headquarters asking whether the company had in its possession any further employee records of compensation cases. Con Ed's widely reported and generally accepted version of what followed next would be the subject of conjecture and heated debate for years to come.

According to Con Ed, at the very moment of the police request for further documents, an administrative task force of company employees was, in fact, hard at work in a second-floor suite of the corporate office building on Irving Street, reviewing a set of 1,000 compensation files that had been labeled "troublesome"—many of which were dated prior to 1940. The mysterious files, all of which were subject to the possibility of future claim or contained some express or implied threat, had been originally housed at Hester Street and were transferred to Con Ed's main facility several years earlier. With the increased level of scrutiny that came as a result of the Bomber's published reference to an unresolved compensation case, however, the task force, made up of four female clerks and a male supervisor, had been assigned, according to the company, to begin an in-depth review of these compensation files as of Tuesday, January 15.

Con Ed reported that in the late afternoon of Friday, January 18—at perhaps the very moment that the Mad Bomber was composing his latest letters to the *Journal-American*—one of the task force members, a tall and trim New York woman by the name of Alice Kelly, came across a startling find. A senior office assistant and twenty-five-year employee of Con Ed, Alice had been assigned to review some of the "troublesome" files contained in several cabinets on the second floor of the company offices, and by close of business on Wednesday, January 16, she was, according to her own estimation, about halfway through the task. Called away to other business the following day, she returned to the assigned file drawers on Friday afternoon, where about two hundred of the original one thousand files assigned to the team remained.

At approximately 4:20 p.m., as Alice later recounted, she reached the third file of the second drawer and casually glanced at its outer cover. Immediately, her blue eyes were drawn to the words "injustice" and "permanent disability," which had been placed at the top of the file in bold italic printing in red ink, as if to key certain corresponding information within.

Armed with a prior sample of the Mad Bomber's handwriting and a mounting sense of anticipation, she opened the file and began examining its contents. At first she noticed nothing unusual. The file contained the same application forms and claim letters that she had seen countless times in the course of her records search. The employee had commenced work at the Hell Gate powerhouse in 1929, earning $30.12 per week, and was injured in a boiler room accident in 1931. He was separated from payroll in 1932 and he filed a claim for compensation in 1934. The claim was disallowed, subsequently appealed several times, and conclusively denied in 1936. There were several typewritten letters in the file addressed to the compensation board, but none appeared to be overly aggressive or indicative of hostility or violence. As Alice continued her examination of the file, however, she noted that the claimant's correspondence after 1936 began to carry a distinctly biting style and an oddly familiar stiff and stilted tone. Suddenly she noticed one particular letter that had been forwarded to Con Ed in which the writer stated his intention to retaliate for certain "injustices" that had been inflicted upon him and to "take justice in my own hands." Instantly, Alice's mind flashed to the articles she had recently read in the *Journal-American*, and to the strange expressions used by the Bomber in his now infamous letters. "The word 'injustices' sort of remained seared in my mind," she would later say.

Her pulse began to quicken as the phrases "dastardly deeds" and "treachery" leapt off the pages of several other letters, and with her widened eyes still firmly fixed on these telltale clues she shrieked to the other members of her team, "I think we have it!" The women gathered around and eagerly flipped through the various letters in the file, quickly agreeing on the significance of the find. As she nervously turned the elusive file over to her supervisor, Alice Kelly barely noticed the typewritten name and address on the lip of the folder: "Metesky, George P., 17 Fourth Street, Waterbury, Connecticut."

Police officials would doubt every word of Con Ed's account.

• • •

George Metesky had seriously considered turning himself in. He had purposefully provided personal details to the *Journal-American* that he knew might lead to his apprehension, and the inner rage that had goaded him for nearly two decades had finally found an outlet. Though his health was again deteriorating—he claimed in one of his recent letters that he spent nearly sixteen hours of each day in bed—he had been energized and even purified by his public dialogue with Seymour Berkson. When he began his violent rampage against Con Ed, he had never intended for it to stop. Indeed, with the ravages of his chronic illness, he never expected to live as long as he had. But finally the relevant parts of his story had begun to come out, and the "kind attitude of the Police Commissioner," as he noted in his latest communication, had provided him with the cathartic gift of an empathetic ear. And now, a milder George Metesky simply figured it was over.

Thoughts of surrender, however, came with many complications and Metesky was justifiably concerned about what an arrest would do to his sisters. "WHAT ABOUT MY PEOPLE—WHO HOUSED ME—FED ME—CLOTHED ME—AND DID EVERYTHING THEY COULD—AND STILL DO—TO SUSTAIN MY LIFE?" his note had questioned. "I WOULD NOT SELL MY PEOPLE OUT FOR ALL [THE] MONEY IN N.Y.C." "Were I alone," the typewritten companion letter assured, "I would accept what is now offered me without a moments delay." Perhaps, thought Metesky, if he sought the refuge of his friends at the *Journal,* his family could be protected and he would finally be given the opportunity to air the full details of his grievances against Con Ed. Conceivably, he mused, a surrender could be the only way for his nemesis to be brought to justice.

• • •

As directed, when dealing with a file of interest, Herbert Schrank, the Con Ed task force supervisor, promptly telephoned the presiding detective at the Hester Street warehouse and informed him of the Metesky file purportedly unearthed by Alice Kelly. He read aloud each of the relevant letters and provided the name and address listed on the folder, and though the information appeared to be of interest to the detective, he had no confirmation that the discovery was of any real value. It would be several hours before receipt of the Bomber's most recent dispatches containing the stunning revelation of the injury date, and thus there was no immediate suggestion that the file necessarily contained any vital clues. The supervisor was simply thanked for his good work and told that someone would come by to pick up the file.

• • •

On the following morning, Saturday, January 19, detectives from the New York City Bomb Investigation Unit, acting on the information provided by Herbert Schrank, forwarded a teletype query to the Waterbury Police Department, requesting a "discreet check" on George Metesky of 17 Fourth Street in Waterbury. At the same time a message was forwarded to the Connecticut State Motor Vehicle Bureau in Hartford requesting a photostatic copy of any automobile registration held by Metesky. At first, the local police could find no public record of their suspect. The town clerk's office indicated a registered owner of 17 Fourth Street by the name of George Milauskas, however, and Captain Ernest Pakul decided that a further check was warranted. Pakul, a veteran officer of the Waterbury Police Department and a longtime resident of the Brass City, was familiar with the tousled neighborhood along the Naugatuck River, and he knew that it was not uncommon for the first- and second-generation immigrant families in the area to informally adopt undocumented or unofficial surnames without reporting the change to local authorities. Pakul thought that perhaps the name "Milauskas" had, at some point, been informally changed to "Metesky," and, though he had not been informed by New York Police of the purpose for their requested check, he sent one of his detectives into the area to discreetly investigate further. Under the pretext of a fact-finding mission in connection with an automobile accident, the officer conducted a detailed canvassing of the neighborhood in a cloaked effort to uncover as much information as possible about 17 Fourth Street and its occupants.

At 4:37 that afternoon Captain Pakul forwarded a detailed teletype reply to the New York City Police Department, confirming that a well-proportioned, chronically ill, unmarried man by the name of George P. Metesky, a/k/a George P. Milauskas, described by neighbors as "strange" and "aloof," did, in fact, reside alone with his two sisters at 17 Fourth Street, Waterbury, Connecticut. Unsure of the significance of his officer's findings, Pakul promised to keep the property under surveillance.

• • •

That Saturday night at approximately eight o'clock, the Bomber's letters arrived at the *Journal-American* city desk, and though Commissioner Kennedy and his immediate circle was directly advised of the important revelations contained in the letters, the team had previously agreed upon a protective posture of silence to thwart any unauthorized publication of the sensitive disclosures. The pivotal date of injury that could, in the right hands, solve the case thus remained haplessly concealed for the next thirty-six hours.

Whether the result of overcautious restraint or simple gaffe, a series of investigative missteps had conspired against the police. Commissioner Kennedy would later protest that the Metesky file was simply "one of a number" of promising leads the police had been working on, but he knew that the department's failure to immediately retrieve the record would be viewed as a monumental blunder at the pinnacle of a long and frustrating investigation. Though a full explanation was never formally provided, it is evident that after his meeting with the *Journal-American* editors on Sunday, January 20, either Kennedy had failed to communicate to his detectives the critical information contained in the Bomber's letters or, armed with such information, the detectives had failed to appreciate the need to match it to the promising Con Ed file. Either way, two separate and decisive pieces of evidence that together would have likely lead to an arrest remained overlooked for the better part of that cold winter weekend.

. . .

At 9:00 a.m. on Monday, January 21, Detective Bertram Scott was finally directed to take the ten-minute ride from police headquarters to the Irving Street offices of Con Ed to retrieve the compensation file of one George P. Metesky. In the patrol car, Detective Scott read through the file with mounting interest and, whether he was aware at that time of the September 5, 1931, date of Metesky's fateful injury or he learned of it shortly thereafter, Scott hurriedly put a call into his commanding officer, Deputy Chief Inspector Edward Byrnes, and exclaimed, "This sounds an awful lot like our man."

## XVI

# "THE PRICE OF PEACE"

THOUGH DWIGHT DAVID EISENHOWER HAD BEEN ACCUSED OF HAVING A fervent belief in a "very vague religion," he would follow conviction and perhaps a modicum of political judgment in holding the events of his second inauguration not on Sunday, January 20, as mandated by the twentieth amendment to the U.S. Constitution, but on the following day so as not to offend the public conscience. The official oath of office had been administered on Sunday morning in a quiet ceremony in the East Room of the White House, but the formal observance at the U.S. Capitol would be delayed so as not to run afoul of the traditional day of rest.

To a gathering of more than 750,000 citizens amassed before the East Portico on January 21, 1957, Eisenhower warned that "[n]ew forces . . . stir across the earth, with power to bring, by their fate, great good or great evil to the free world's future." With hope and determination, he proclaimed, ". . . we can help to heal this divided world. Thus may the nations cease to live in trembling before the menace of force. Thus may the weight of fear and the weight of arms be taken from the burdened shoulders of mankind." And in a concluding appeal to the better angels of mankind, the thirty-fourth president implored, "May the turbulence of our age yield to a true time of peace, when men and nations shall share a life that honors the dignity of each, the brotherhood of all."

As President Eisenhower boldly implored the nation to grant his clarion "Price of Peace," as the speech was titled, a chilling fog had begun to gather along the inclines of the Naugatuck Valley and into the decaying crevices of Waterbury, Connecticut.

• • •

By Monday morning, the connections between the injury date contained in the Bomber's letters and the Con Ed file on George Metesky had been made. The description compiled by Waterbury police had squared closely with the profile drawn by Dr. Brussel, and the evidence finally seemed to point to one suspect.

At 3:00 p.m. the first of several waves of New York bomb squad detectives began their trek out of the city and into Waterbury's Brooklyn district. Under the direction of Chief Edward Byrnes, detectives Michael Lynch, Richard Rowan, Edward Lehane, and James Martin converged upon the Waterbury Police Department and began compiling further evidence on George Metesky. In conjunction with local officers, the New York detectives searched city directories to again confirm Metesky's address, checked motor vehicle bureau records for possible handwriting samples, and began discussion on the logistics of a possible confrontation and arrest. As evening approached, the detectives drove to the Fourth Street neighborhood to case the area and plan their approach.

Back at the Waterbury Police headquarters, Captain Pakul had been conducting his own investigation. He called a relative who lived across the street from Metesky, and, though he had been interviewed earlier in the day by another officer, Pakul asked him to once again describe his neighbor. "Queer," came the response. The relative further recommended that Pakul consult with a former tenant in the Metesky home—Miles Kelly—if he needed further verification. Pakul telephoned Kelly and, together with the four New York detectives, went to his home to conduct an interview. Kelly, recollecting his prior rancorous dealings with Metesky, portrayed the man as "unstable" and described the strange and vindictive behavior that began in 1942 with Metesky's enlistment rejection at the draft board and continued through their time at the Waterbury Tool Company. Kelly had endured complaint after bitter complaint from Metesky to the company owners and had been the subject of letters to the draft board and even the president of the United States, petitioning for Kelly's induction into the armed service. Now, as Kelly huddled with the officers and learned of Metesky's possible involvement in the Mad Bomber case, he was only too pleased to draw a diagram of the Metesky home for the men.

By the time the group returned to Waterbury headquarters, there had been broad agreement that the threshold probable cause requirements for a search warrant had been met, and Captain Pakul telephoned the local district attorney and presiding judge, informing both of the evolving state of the investigation. By 10:30 p.m., the warrant had been executed and Detective Lynch telephoned Chief Byrnes for authorization to proceed. Byrnes informed the detective that on the basis of a preliminary comparison of handwriting conducted earlier that day, a match of George Metesky appeared to be "a good bet."

Byrnes directed Detective Lynch and his team to move in.

• • •

As the four New York detectives accompanied by Captain Pakul and three of his own men stealthily pulled their unmarked vehicles up the steep incline of Fourth Street, the murky fog that had shrouded the region now roiled in their headlights like a ubiquitous ashen spirit. The mood was tense and the huddled men repeatedly reviewed the logistics of their expected confrontation and the possible contingencies they may face. Satisfied with the soundness of their plan, they eased to a halt in front of the gray, weather-beaten home, emerged from their cars, and silently advanced into the midnight gloom.

Several of the detectives scurried to the back of the structure to guard any rear exits, while one remained at the unkempt front yard. The remaining contingent climbed the groaning steps of the wooden porch and knocked solidly at the front door, hands firmly clasping loaded service revolvers stowed within the side pockets of their overcoats. The men stiffened with anticipation as instantly—almost expectantly—a small threshold light went on, and the front door creaked open. There, revealed by the dim light, stood a stocky yet inoffensive-looking middle-aged man dressed in claret-colored pajamas smartly buttoned to the collar, a bathrobe, and slippers. "It was almost like the guy was waiting for us," Detective Lehane would later remark. "His hair was neatly combed; his eyeglasses were spotless, sparkling."

"George Metesky?" asked Captain Pakul.

"Yes."

"These gentlemen are New York City Detectives." Metesky glanced down at the badges that each now flashed before him, his sunken chin innocuously receding into the folds of his neck. He regarded the officers with an unconcerned, almost amused look etched across his face.

"We're checking on an auto accident. Do you own an automobile?"

"Yes I do," said Metesky. "A Daimler." The men exchanged furtive glances, aware of the corresponding registration documents obtained earlier from the Connecticut Motor Vehicle Bureau.

"We'd like to come in and have a look around. We have a search warrant, Mr. Metesky," said Detective Lynch. "Would you like to see it?" Metesky flashed an amiable grin, his blue eyes sparkling in the muted light.

"Oh that won't be necessary. If you say so I believe you. Come in."

The men filed past the small parlor and peered at the worn furniture and faded wallpaper of the first floor apartment. Lace curtains trimmed the windows and the hallway contained photographs of small children and a print of the baby Jesus. Metesky notified the officers that his sisters were asleep and he asked that they not be disturbed. Agreeing, Detective Lynch suggested that they begin the search with Metesky's bedroom.

The room was small but meticulously ordered. Clothing, folded to military precision, was placed according to style and type in even rows within an oak dresser, and, like in the hallway, several children's photographs and a religious image hung neatly on the wall. The carefully made bed with its brass frame was squarely positioned in the room, and to the left, a wooden Zenith radio sat atop a table within arm's reach. The detectives immediately spotted two New York City subway tokens and some flashlight bulbs sitting on the dresser, and in the closet was a loaded .38-caliber revolver, the possession of which, Captain Pakul notified the group, was not a crime in Connecticut.

"Have you ever driven to New York City, George?" one of the detectives asked. Metesky said that he had, and when asked if he had routed his trips through White Plains, he admitted it to be the case.

In a bedside drawer, Detective Rowan discovered a notebook with the name "George P. Metesky" boldly printed on the cover and containing some hand-printed pages within. The men flipped through the book and instantly recognized the distinctive lettering and staccato phrases used by the writer. At that point Metesky was given a pen and a sheet of yellow paper and asked to write his name. The officers watched intently as each disjoined letter appeared on the page like plucked notes on a violin, and from the characteristic double bars of the first letter *G*, they knew they had their man.

With bespectacled eyes peering up at the detectives, Metesky politely asked, "This is not then about an auto accident?" The men exchanged glances, and Detective Lynch responded, "Why don't you go ahead and get dressed, George. We'd like to see the garage."

A moment later, George Metesky walked out of his bedroom. He was wearing freshly shined brown shoes, a brown cardigan sweater, a red dotted necktie—and a double-breasted blue suit with narrow pinstripes. It was neatly buttoned.

• • •

He led the group outside along a muddy, gravel-strewn driveway, and, as the icy fog glistened in the dancing flashlight beams, he unlocked the door and guided the men into his garage. The black Daimler sedan sat silently in the darkness. As Metesky flicked on the lights, the broom-swept and well-ordered workshop came into view. Rows of methodically placed tools appeared along the walls, and at the back of the structure lay a spotless workbench and a box of more tools underneath. At once, Detective Lynch's attention was drawn to a manually controlled metalworking lathe resting atop the bench. As he began to investigate, Metesky again solicited, "This is not then about an auto accident?"

Detective Lynch studied Metesky momentarily and said, "You know why we're here, don't you, George?"

Metesky grimaced slightly and shrugged his shoulders.

"Come on, George," persisted the detective. "You know."

The officers drew closer in a tightening ring around their suspect. "Perhaps I had better consult an attorney," stammered Metesky.

Sensing a possible confession, Lynch persevered, "Never mind an attorney, George. Why are we here?"

Metesky's eyes narrowed and his breathing became quick and uneven. "Maybe you suspect that I'm the Mad Bomber," he offered.

"Maybe you are not so *mad*," Detective Lynch responded with a grin. "Tell me. George, what does F.P. stand for?"

The trepidation seemed to melt away from Metesky's mind and his demeanor instantly transformed to one of purpose and self-assurance. He looked around the garage at each of the men and haughtily adjusted the knot of his tie.

"Fair Play," came the answer, his blue eyes wide with defiance.

• • •

By the time the handcuffed Metesky had been led back down the unpaved driveway and into the waiting cars, Anna and Mae Milauskas had awoken and huddled at the front doorstep. Shivering in the cold and bewildered by what was unfolding, they sobbed and pleaded with the men. "George couldn't hurt anybody. Don't worry about him. He couldn't hurt anybody." As the entourage sped away into the night, Metesky gazed plaintively at his gaunt sisters through the fogged rear window of the unmarked patrol car.

Within minutes of arriving at Waterbury Police headquarters, Detective Lynch telephoned Chief Byrnes back in New York and informed him that Metesky had been taken into custody. They reviewed the evidence compiled at the home and Byrnes directed that Detective Lynch begin a preliminary interrogation. In the meantime, Byrnes and other high officials of the department, including chief of detectives James Leggett, Captain Howard Finney, and deputy commissioners Walter Arm and Aloysius Melia, together with representatives of the bomb squad and the police laboratory, piled into multiple official-use vehicles and sped north through the darkness to Waterbury, Connecticut.

At 1:30 a.m., Metesky was taken to one of several interrogation rooms on the second floor of the Waterbury detective bureau, where he was seated opposite Detective Lynch and the entire New York–Waterbury arresting team. Metesky peered at the officers with a pleasant and cooperative calm and, for the better part of the questioning, smiled affably. It was, according to one television report, "an innocent, happy, strange smile." He spoke in soft and courteous tones, and though he had no foreign accent, as had been predicated by some on the force and in the press, he frequently resorted to double negatives and grammatical lapses of speech.

Using a prepared chronological chart of events and furiously scribbling notes on a yellow tablet as he listened, Detective Lynch began his questioning with the earliest bombings and letters, and slowly moved forward in time. Though Metesky appeared hazy about some of the dates and particulars of several events, he worked closely with the detective and willingly made a full admission of responsibility for each of the units, as he called them, providing technical details known only to police. Metesky explained that he "got a bum deal" from Con Ed after being gassed on the job in 1931. Having contracted tuberculosis and having received little compensation from his employer, Metesky continued, he was left with no alternative but to take matters into his own hands.

• • •

Almost as soon as it happened, word of Metesky's apprehension had begun to spread, and all through the night hordes of media began to converge on Waterbury. Radio-equipped cars from New York and all over New England transported news reporters and equipment crews to the beleaguered police department, and soon representatives from the national wire services as well as major television networks began to appear on the scene. An ecstatic *Waterbury Republican-American* would brag, "Waterbury went coast-to-coast this morning as the first news of the arrest of a suspect in New York's 16-year hunt for the man New York police dubbed the 'Mad Bomber' leaked out."

At 3:00 a.m., the officers took a break from their inquiry and placed Metesky in a holding cell. Hearing a ruckus downstairs, Captain Pakul hurried to the department's first-floor booking area and was immediately accosted by a slew of early arriving local news reporters. "There is absolutely no question of it," declared Pakul to the swelling crowd. "He's the guy." The Captain identified Metesky as a fifty-four-year-old resident of Waterbury and confirmed that he had made admissions covering approximately sixty different bombs. Pakul commended Metesky's "remarkable memory" in readily recalling pertinent details of each event, and confirmed recently published statements that the suspect had suffered from tuberculosis.

As Pakul spoke with members of the news media, officials from the New York City Police Department finally arrived at Waterbury headquarters and proceeded without public comment to the upstairs interrogation room, where the other detectives were hopelessly attempting to gain a few moments of sleep. Detective Lynch composed himself and proceeded to brief the men on the admissions that had been made by their suspect. At 4:40 a.m., Metesky was roused from his holding cell and once again led to the interrogation room. Though he had had little if any sleep, his cheerful demeanor dimmed not the slightest, and as the questioning commenced he once again remained smiling and cooperative.

The inquiry, now conducted by Chief Leggett in the presence of the other police officials as well as a stenographer, began with much of the same ground covered by Detective Lynch. He inquired as to Metesky's motive for the bombings and his injury at the Hell Gate power station, and he elicited a detailed description of his subsequent illness and his attempts to obtain satisfaction through the workmen's compensation system. One by one, Metesky was then taken through all of the bombings from 1940 through 1956 and asked to explain, describe, and corroborate the techniques used to carry them out. Again, Metesky admitted to each and every bombing.

With the assistance of Detective William Schmitt, who joined the officers in the interrogation room, the questioning became much more technical in nature. Schmitt, who for years had been assigned the task of analyzing the various fragments and inner components of Metesky's bombs, understood, perhaps better than any other person, the detailed machinations of the infernal machines and their construction, and he periodically interposed questions for the chief to ask. Metesky obligingly offered explicit details regarding the design and inner workings of his various bombs, removing any remaining doubt that the Mad Bomber had finally been captured. When the discussion turned to the early fusing mechanisms, however, even Schmitt was amazed by Metesky's ingenuity. Their dialogue was captured by the stenographer:

Q. What was the means used to explode that bomb [at Grand Central Station]?
A. It was a wafer.
Q. What do you mean a wafer?
A. The wafer was a Parke-Davis throat disc which would be affected by the moisture in the bomb housing. I would put about three drops of water in it.

Leggett turned to Schmitt with wide eyes and a slackened jaw. The department had been puzzled for years about some of the timers utilized by the Bomber and suddenly the remarkable technique had been revealed by its creator.

Q. How did it work?
A. It would compress the disc releasing the pressure on the ball bearing.

George Metesky, the Mad Bomber of New York.

17 Fourth Street, Waterbury, Connecticut—the Metesky home. "The house was not loved," wrote one observer. "It was only maintained."

The 10×14 sheet metal and iron garage in which Metesky constructed each of his "units." One police officer commented that it was "as clean and orderly as a hospital operating room."

Fully armored bomb squad detectives carefully remove an unexploded pipe bomb from the Paramount Theatre Times Square on December 28, 1956.

Porter Lloyd Hill receives emergency treatment for his injuries following the February 21, 1956, bombing of Penn Station.

Police detectives gather in the aftermath of a blast in the lower level washroom of Grand Central Terminal on March 16, 1954. The Bomber timed the device to detonate precisely at the start of rush hour.

The Pyke-LaGuardia Carrier exits Grand Central Terminal on December 27, 1956, carrying an unexploded pipe bomb. The carrier was fashioned from a fifteen-ton semitrailer flatbed truck outfitted with woven steel cable left over from construction of the Brooklyn Bridge.

Courtesy Library of Congress, Prints & Photographs Division, *New York World Telegram & Sun* Newspaper Photograph Collection, United Press.

Police lab samples of the Mad Bomber's handwriting.

Courtesy Library of Congress, Prints & Photographs Division, *New York World Telegram & Sun* Newspaper Photograph Collection, United Press.

POLICE DEPARTMENT
CITY OF NEW YORK
NEW YORK 13, N. Y.

January 4, 1957

# PIPE BOMB

The object illustrated below is a PIPE BOMB of a type that has been detonated in a number of places in the city in the past several years. IT IS EXTREMELY DANGEROUS AND MUST NOT BE DISTURBED UNDER ANY CIRCUMSTANCES.

When any such mechanism resembling this construction come to your attention, you should forthwith clear the surrounding area of people within a radius of 300 feet and you are to immediately notify the New York City Police Department at CAnal 6-2000 or SPring 7-3100.

MODUS OPERANDI: On prior occasions the perpetrator has inserted the pipe bomb in a man's sock, apparently to camouflage it. Bombs of this type have been found in various public places including telephone booths (attached to bell box or inserted in the fan casing), theatre seats, public lockers, men's lavatories, and subway cars and stations.

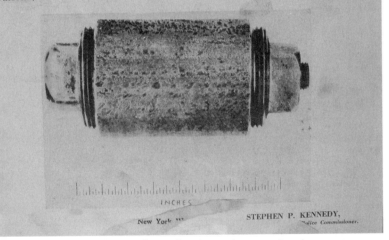

INCHES

New York                                STEPHEN P. KENNEDY,
                                         Police Commissioner.

NYPD notice circulated throughout the city and among local newspapers warning the public of the Mad Bomber's handiwork.

Courtesy Library of Congress, Prints & Photographs Division, *New York World Telegram & Sun* Newspaper Photograph Collection.

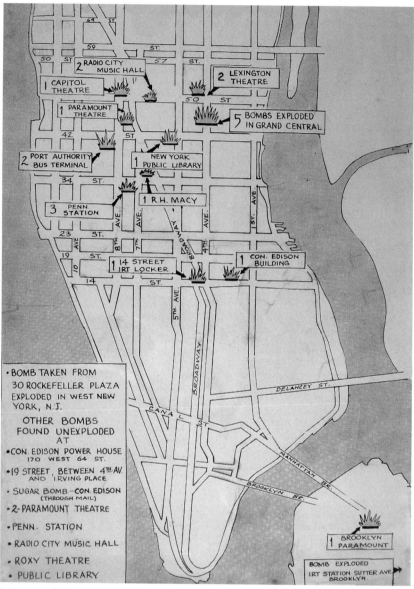

Maps tracking the Mad Bomber's exploits appeared in newspapers throughout the city.

Courtesy Library of Congress, Prints & Photographs Division, *New York World Telegram & Sun* Newspaper Photograph Collection.

Police Commissioner Stephen P. Kennedy. He would declare the Mad Bomber case to be "the greatest manhunt in the history of the Police Department."

Dr. James A. Brussel, remembered by some as the father of criminal profiling.

Courtesy *New York Daily News*.

Seymour Berkson. He and his "Four Fishermen" devised the ingenious plan of an Open Letter to the Mad Bomber.

Courtesy Bill Berkson.

Alice Kelly, a twenty-five-year employee of Con-Ed, had been assigned to review the company compensation files labeled "troublesome." She would stumble upon a find that would give police the first major break in the Mad Bomber investigation.

Courtesy Library of Congress, Prints & Photographs Division, *New York World Telegram & Sun* Newspaper Photograph Collection, United Press.

Metesky is led by arresting officer Michael Lynch (left) and Captain Ernest Pakul (right) from the second floor interrogation room of the Waterbury Police Department for booking.

Courtesy Library of Congress, Prints & Photographs Division, *New York World Telegram & Sun* Newspaper Photograph Collection.

Metesky arrives at police headquarters in New York following his apprehension in Waterbury, Connecticut.

A crowd of curious onlookers hopeful for a look at the Mad Bomber is restrained outside of police headquarters as Metesky arrives for booking.

Courtesy Library of Congress, Prints & Photographs Division, *New York World Telegram & Sun* Newspaper Photograph Collection, United Press.

Metesky beams before the cameras outside of a New York City courthouse.

Courtesy Library of Congress, Prints & Photographs Division, *New York World Telegram & Sun* Newspaper Photograph Collection, United Press.

Metesky proudly displays the *New York Journal-American* as he is led into police headquarters in New York City.

Courtesy Library of Congress, Prints & Photographs Division, *New York World Telegram & Sun* Newspaper Photograph Collection.

A cache of bomb-making materials found in Metesky's home following his arrest.

Courtesy Library of Congress, Prints & Photographs Division, *New York World Telegram & Sun* Newspaper Photograph Collection.

The Mad Bomber behind bars at the Waterbury Police Station. One of his lawyers would later say that Metesky could "easily pass as a person who could be your next-door neighbor."

Leggett took a deep breath and exhaled loudly, signaling a break in the questioning. "Would you like a cup of coffee and a sandwich?" he asked. Metesky smiled broadly and cleared his throat. "I would like some throat discs."

. . .

Though the search of 17 Fourth Street had included the basement of the home and the confessed workshop of the accused, detectives had failed to uncover any bomb components or other corroborating physical evidence of Metesky's menacing endeavor. It had been assumed that the materials used for each bomb had been separately purchased just prior to construction in an effort to keep stockpiled incriminating evidence to a minimum, but the police weren't sure. Following the formal interrogation, Detective Schmitt entered the small holding cell where Metesky lay on a canvas-blanketed bunk and asked, "George do you recognize my name?" Metesky smiled and responded that he did. In an effort to establish a rapport, Schmitt then asked whether he had any thoughts or concerns, knowing that Metesky must have been aware from published reports that he, Schmitt, had been taking apart and analyzing many of the bomb units at the police lab.

"Oh yes," replied Metesky. "I worried about you." He hesitated, and then continued sternly, "But those monsters at 4 Irving Place were to blame."

Schmitt peered intently at Metesky, realizing that his attempts at reasoning were futile. "George," he began, "We know you made the bombs. Are there any more in the house? Your sisters are still there and if anything happens to them, it will be on your head."

Metesky's smile transformed into a deep frown. "You didn't find them, did you?" he said.

"Find what, George?"

Then, like a child playfully giving himself up in a game of hide-and-seek, Metesky calmly explained to Detective Schmitt where his cache of bomb-making materials could be found.

A short time later Schmitt and four other New York detectives were on their backs in the basement of Metesky's Waterbury home, peering with flashlights into the dark recess behind two soapstone set tubs and the gray concrete wall. Anna and Mae had continued to protest their brother's innocence to several reporters who had called on them earlier that morning, and now with the two sisters prattling in his ear, one of the detectives reached a bare arm into the space, probed the area with his hand, and seconds later murmured, in a straining voice, that he had found something. Then, one by one, like the birth of a litter, he produced red wool sock after red wool sock—four in all—stuffed with four pipe couplings of various lengths with corresponding plugs, three shock-resistant wristwatches, five flashlight bulbs, two springs, three containers of smokeless powder, and a horde of various other bomb-making supplies. Detective Schmitt would later certify to Captain Finney and eventually to the criminal courts of New York City that "the items [taken from the Metesky home] are the component parts used in the construction of an infernal machine known as, 'Pipe Bomb.' Further examination and comparison of these items and the workmanship and tools involved causes [me] to form the opinion that they are similar to the component parts recovered at various locations in New York City . . . between March 16, 1954 to December 27, 1956, inclusive."

. . .

At daybreak, Metesky was led by a bevy of detectives downstairs to the headquarters booking desk, where he signed a stenographic transcript of his interrogation and was formally booked and arrested for violation of Connecticut's explosives statute, pending possible extradition and further charges from New York City. He was greeted at the desk with a barrage of cameramen and news reporters from state, metropolitan, and national papers and wire services, who clamored for a photograph of the Mad Bomber. That afternoon, the smiling face of George Metesky appeared on television screens and the front pages of newspapers from New York to San Francisco. "[T]he face might have been that of a successful political candidate or a winner of a Nobel Prize," later reflected Dr. Brussel, who delighted at news of the arrest. "Metesky was smiling . . . No, not smiling: *beaming* . . . He shouted cheerful greetings to the crowds who gathered . . . Under one arm he carried a neatly wrapped brown-paper parcel containing a change of underwear. It was as though he were going on a vacation. He seemed to be enjoying every minute of it."

For Commissioner Kennedy and the New York City Police Department, however, the controversy was just beginning.

## XVII

# "YOUR NEXT DOOR NEIGHBOR"

THE POLICE HAD PRIVATELY FEARED THAT THE BOMBER HAD BEEN PLAN-
ning a "last laugh" of sorts by placing a booby trap or a time bomb
in the garage set to detonate upon the prowling of unwelcome guests.
Word that the authorities had been conducting an investigation in the
neighborhood early on the day of his arrest could surely have reached
Metesky, and the possibility that he may have prepared a violent surprise
loomed in their minds. There was no avoiding, however, a more detailed
search of the dreary garage at the back of 17 Fourth Street. Shortly
before Metesky's revelation to Detective Schmitt about the supply of
bomb-making materials hidden in his basement, investigators from
Waterbury and New York once again descended upon the Bomber's
clandestine workshop.

Clearing away the scores of newsmen and photographers that had
gathered on and around the property, the detectives warily entered the
garage and began the process of accumulating and cataloguing evidence. The metalworking lathe that Metesky had used to fashion each
of his creations was once again examined and, when deemed safe to do
so, disconnected from the conduit wire which led from the cellar of the
home. Fine metal shavings on the bench surrounding the machine were
brushed into manila envelopes, and a variety of drills and other tools
were inspected for relevance and incrimination. Boxes of evidence and
the lathe itself were carried to waiting police cars for transport to the
New York City police lab. A Remington typewriter used by Metesky to
compose many of his earlier communications, as well as his most recent,

had already been removed from the home, and initial tests matched it to the Bomber's typed letters. The case against George Metesky was growing by the minute.

Later that morning an army of police officials led the accused from Waterbury headquarters to a city court special session for arraignment. "This is the man," said Deputy Commissioner Walter Arm to a reporter as he climbed into the lead car. "We know him by his admissions. Secondly, we know him by a check of his handwriting." Metesky waved to the crowd of reporters as the procession of vehicles sped from the department to the downtown courthouse.

• • •

A surprisingly spry-looking George Metesky stood at attention before Judge Hugh McGill, surrounded by a slew of brawny patrolmen and court officers. His eyes glimmered with amiable cheer despite the stressful events of the previous night and the attendant lack of sleep. The usually tranquil and dignified courthouse had been transformed with a rush of nearly two hundred spectators and journalists who had come to witness and record the occasion. The crackle of news camera bulbs echoing through the courtroom and strategically mounted television film tripods throughout the hall imparted a theatrical feel to the event. For the first time in the history of the Waterbury city court, a sitting judge had permitted news photographers and cameramen into the courtroom to memorialize the proceedings, to the surprise of many veteran observers. "It is a bit unusual," admitted Judge McGill after the hearing, "but I believe that much more time was saved, and much confusion avoided by allowing photographers to get their pictures, than to order the courtroom cleared and limited to seating capacity and reasonable standing room . . . I believe that, in all fairness no harm was done to anyone concerned."

As the courtroom was called to order, the prosecutor, James Shea, informed the judge that a warrant had been issued against Metesky, and he briefly outlined the local charges against him. He explained that additional warrants were in transport from New York City and that, based upon a conversation he had with Metesky prior to the hearing, the accused intended to waive extradition and face those warrants directly in New York City.

"Do you understand these proceedings?" asked Judge McGill, turning to the handcuffed Metesky. A burst of camera light flashed against the white pillars that extended floor to ceiling behind the elongated bench.

"I have a pretty good idea."

"And do you understand your rights?"

Metesky smiled and softly responded that he did.

McGill then explained the ramifications of a waiver of extradition and asked Metesky if he consented to a return to the jurisdiction of New York City, to which Metesky nodded affirmatively. He was directed to execute the formal waiver dispensing with the lengthy extradition proceedings that would otherwise have been required, and bail was set at $100,000, pending arrival of the New York warrants.

Anna and Mae, who had somberly watched the proceedings from the gallery, asked one of the court officers for permission to visit their brother before he was taken to New York. The request had been granted and the two women were brought downstairs to the holding cell at the basement level of the courthouse where their brother had been taken after the hearing. As they approached the steel bars Metesky rose silently and the sisters, each dabbing tissues at their dampened eyes, plaintively asked if the charges against him were true. He hesitatingly admitted that they were, and, though devastated by the confession, Anna and Mae gathered their fortitude and promised to secure competent legal counsel to fight the case as best they could. Earlier that day, the women had begged a crowd of news reporters who had gathered at their home not to believe the allegations that had been levied against their brother. "George couldn't possibly be the 'Mad Bomber,'" they urged. "He just isn't the type." They explained in detail that an accident in 1931 had resulted in their brother's prolonged illness and that his former employer, Con Ed, had ignored his pleas for assistance. "Sometimes," Anna said, "George remains in bed 17 hours a day. He can't breathe on damp days, and sometimes he can't eat." And in later statements to the press, John Metesky, George's older brother said, "His arrest is ridiculous and outrageous. We'll get the best lawyers in the country to defend him." Describing his brother as a devout and religious man, John continued, "He is a gentleman in every way." Now, as George Metesky's unabashed admission that he was in fact the Mad Bomber echoed through the news media, his siblings grappled with the sobering prospect that it was true.

Prior to Metesky's departure from the Waterbury City Court, the self-proclaimed "on-the-street-reporter" John Tillman, working for television station WPIX, was granted a five-minute filmed interview with the Mad Bomber. Asked how he felt, Metesky replied, "Well it's a little confusing. Much too confusing." He expressed sympathy for his two sisters who, he insisted, knew nothing of his activities, and he professed a dislike of all the hoopla surrounding his apprehension, claiming, "I try to live quietly. I get on with as little confusion as possible." When asked why he resorted to bombs, Metesky explained matter-of-factly that he "had no other choice." He related years of frustration in attempting to have his compensation claim heard, and he explained that all of his letter writing had gotten him nowhere, thus forcing him to engage in the bomb-planting campaign. In a coincidental quirk of fate, the interview would appear later that evening on a news program sponsored by the Consolidated Edison Company. The name of the show was the "Con-Ed 3-Star News."

By noon, "The story of the century," as the local papers were calling it, was drawing to a close for the city of Waterbury, Connecticut. A New York City magistrate had signed a hastily prepared warrant for Metesky's arrest that was limited to the February 21, 1956, bombing of the Penn Station washroom that injured porter Lloyd Hill, and Assistant District Attorney Karl Grebow sped north to deliver the document to the Waterbury authorities. Though some in the Naugatuck Valley took a curious pride in their newfound notoriety, city officials and the police department in particular were jubilant to see George Metesky hurried into the center car of a police motorcade, whisked out of the Brass City, and bound for New York.

• • •

Many of the same media crews that covered Metesky's arrest, booking, and arraignment in Waterbury followed the entourage to Manhattan and joined scores of others to greet the jovial Mad Bomber. In distinct contrast to the malicious image conjured up during his sixteen-year reign of terror, the descriptions of George Metesky at various points in the criminal process evoked thoughts of a docile, almost sympathetic, figure. One newspaper noted:

> The man police arrested today as the "Mad Bomber" looks like a man who has never been mad at anything in his life. His little blue eyes stare aimlessly from his gold-rimmed glasses. His face is almost unlined despite his 53 years, and his receding chin and inoffensive manner belie the fact that he was the object of one of the biggest manhunts in New York police history.

He "could well have passed for a school teacher," wrote another reporter, while the *New York Times* suggested that "[t]he prisoner resembled a beaming church deacon . . . His somber blue suit with pencil stripe, his neat shirt and tie, his shoes, all bespoke the neat, careful citizen."

As word spread that the Bomber was in transport to the Fifth Precinct headquarters, a mob of curious onlookers flocked to the narrow ways surrounding Centre Street for a closer look at the notorious suspect. The copper-domed, Baroque-style police building stood on its full triangular city block like a grand European watchtower meant, as local folklore would have it, to "impress both the officer and the prisoner with the majesty of the law." With dusk falling upon the raucous taverns and old-world shops that lined the area surrounding the building, the motorcade weaved its way through the congested streets of Little Italy and stopped at police headquarters, and the handcuffed Metesky was ushered from the car. Flanked on either side by the displeased Detectives Lynch and Martin, Metesky smiled widely and raised his arms to the bloated crowd that now jostled against the barriers erected by police on both sides of the cluttered street. Like a conquering warrior returning home from battle, Metesky hailed his greetings to the swarm and happily acquiesced as clamoring news photographers, some precariously perched on nearby rooftops, shouted, "This way, George. This way."

With camera bulbs flashing like lightning, a reporter shouted, "You glad it's over, George?"

"Yes," came the answer in a burst of laughter.

"Are you sorry you hurt the people?" barked another journalist.

"Yes, I'm sorry I hurt the people." Reflecting for a moment, he added, "but I'm not sorry I did it."

As the assemblage made its way through the booking room door, Metesky proudly raised in his hands that day's issue of the *New York Journal-American*, which prominently displayed on page 1 a photograph of his own smiling face beneath the bold headline "Letters to *Journal* Trap the Mad Bomber."

At 4:40 p.m., before a horde of police officers and journalists, George Metesky was photographed, fingerprinted, and formally charged with violations of New York State Penal Code sections 1895 and 1897, the so called Sullivan Law, alleging malicious mischief and felonious assault. The initial charges alone, which encompassed only one of the thirty-two recorded bombings, carried a possible sentence of forty-two years. Throughout the booking, Metesky's jovial smile didn't falter for a moment.

• • •

Later that evening Metesky was transported to the felony court for the Borough of Manhattan for arraignment on the charges against him. A large crowd of television, radio, and newspaper journalists who had gathered in and about the courtroom stirred as Metesky was led into the dimly lit chamber in handcuffs. Still attired in the same blue double-breasted suit, he remained calm and confident throughout the hearing despite the gravity of his situation.

City Magistrate Reuben Levy listened to the court officer announce the official statement of allegations concerning the Penn Station bombing of February 21, 1956, and upon a finding that Metesky was not yet represented by counsel to defend him on the charge, appointed Benjamin Schmier from the Legal Aid Society of New York to act as Metesky's lawyer free of charge. Schmier, a pragmatic and flamboyant defender of indigent rights, had ironically won the acquittal in 1951 for Frederick Eberhardt on the charge of sending a sugar-laden bomb to Con Ed through the mails—a crime that had actually been committed by George Metesky. Through a lengthy career at Legal Aid, Schmier would represent more than 50,000 defendants and distinguish himself as "the poor man's legal representative."

After a short recess to allow the lawyer to consult with his client, the session was once again called to order and Schmier rose to address the court. Without hesitation, he requested that Metesky be committed to the psychiatric division of Bellevue Hospital for observation. "I must however state publically," Schmier hesitatingly continued, "that the defendant is very interested in the newspaper *The Journal American*, which has offered to supply counsel for him for his compensation case . . . and he wishes for me to tell you that while he may not be able to communicate with them he would like *The Journal American* to send its lawyer for . . . [that] part of the case." Knowing that Judge Levy was, of course, powerless to facilitate any such communication, Schmier had made the statement to pacify the fervent demands of his client, who would have to be satisfied with the simple placement of the matter on the record.

"Now getting to the legal application," continued Schmier, "the defendant tells me a story of how he comes to stand before your Honor."

Noting that the case against Metesky was already a matter of well-known public record, Schmier elected not to burden the court with a recitation of the obvious and instead began to lay the foundation for what his well versed legal mind told him would almost certainly become an insanity defense. "Apparently," observed Schmier:

> He is a man who in speaking to any member of the community could easily pass for a person who could be your next-door neighbor. But with all my thousands of cases behind me, your Honor, I get to see through the defendant as I talk to him a man who is laboring under a terrific psychosis, a persecution complex, something which had bothered him for years, and he says that he finds all of his aggrievement against the public satiated by the bombings because the public treated him so poorly in his desires to . . . get his compensation case heard. So that from this compensation case, which has its incept many, many years ago, the defendant justifies himself against the general public, which is the very basis of a schizophrenic personality, your Honor . . .

> You are asking me to act for this defendant and before I can act, I must be convinced in my legal mind that this defendant understands the nature of the charges against him and is able to differentiate between right and wrong. I am not sure of that. As a matter of fact, if I were forced to make a statement for the record on that score, I would say it is my humble belief at this time that this defendant is of such a state of mind as not to understand the nature of the charges against him. I would like to be fortified with a psychiatric report and I think the interest of justice would be served if your Honor would grant my application.

Judge Levy listened intently to Schmier's plea and turned to George Metesky, who was absently listening to the proceedings. "My feeling," began Levy,

> is that the manner in which Mr. Metesky gave expression to the real or fancied grievances are, well, to say the least, indicative of a deranged mind . . . and I think it is proper at this point to commit him for observation, so before he is asked to meet this charge it can be determined by experts that he is in a condition to understand the nature and quality of his acts and make a defense to the charge.

The judge paused and searched Metesky's eyes for any indication of comprehension. "Committed to Bellevue for observation," he said with a rap of the gavel.

Metesky smiled politely and, when prompted by the officers, serenely shuffled out of the courtroom, still clinging to the *New York Journal-American.*

## XVIII

# REWARDS, ACCOLADES, AND ACCUSATIONS

FROM THE MOMENT OF GEORGE METESKY'S ARREST, ALICE KELLY HAD been considered the most logical recipient of the $26,000 reward offered by the city and the Patrolmen's Benevolent Association. The newspapers touted her as the girl with the "rare photographic memory" and offers of congratulations for her fine public service poured in from all corners of the city. Admiration for Alice Kelly was so high in the days following the arrest that it was suggested by some that she be invited to the reviewing stand at the annual St. Patrick's Day parade, while one vocal shareholder of Con Ed even demanded that she be considered to fill an open seat on the company's board of directors. As the City of New York unanimously sung the praises of Alice Kelly and her employer, however, some members of the police department bristled with anger.

". . . [W]e say it's not so," said Deputy Commissioner Walter Arm upon his return from Waterbury at a hastily convened press conference held at the Centre Street police headquarters. His voice quivered with emphatic emphasis. "The physical act of picking . . . out [the file] was done at the request of the Police Department." Arm explained that on Friday night, January 18, detectives from the Bomb Investigation Unit had finished their work at the Hester Street warehouse and then continued their search at the Con Ed main offices upon being advised of the existence of the so-called troublesome company files. Later that evening or early Saturday morning, he insisted, his officer, Detective Bertram Scott, came upon the Metesky file and recognized the characteristic handwriting and use of language. Though Arm acknowledged that he did not yet have a full report on the issue and that there still existed a "difference of opinion" as to who actually located the revered file, he insisted that "[a]s far as we know now it was one of our men." As if to emphasize the pivotal role of the department in the apprehension and arrest of the Bomber, the next morning Commissioner Kennedy called the entire membership of the BIU into his office to thank and congratulate them for their part in tracking the man down. Kennedy made special public mention of Bertram Scott as well as the four New York detectives who made the arrest in Waterbury, and promised that as a result of their "excellent work" promotions of both grade and assignment would be forthcoming. There was no mention of Con Ed at the commissioner's meeting.

The tiff over who actually found the Metesky file at Con Ed's main offices was, in reality, one of form rather than substance. A simple interview of the detectives assigned to the matter would quickly reveal that the department, in fact, had no direct role in locating the file, and on January 23 Commissioner Kennedy reluctantly conceded the point to a gathering of twenty feisty reporters who had persistently demanded a meeting while posted outside of his door. Seated at the same mahogany desk used by Theodore Roosevelt during his term as commissioner sixty years earlier, Kennedy explained that Arm's statements as to who had found the so-called "hot" file had been made on the basis of incomplete information supplied by tired and overworked detectives, and though they were made in good faith, the assertions were, in fact, mistaken. In making the admission, however, Kennedy had opened an inevitable firestorm of controversy. Noting that detectives had been notified of the Metesky file on Friday evening and had communicated with Waterbury police on Saturday, the gritty reporters pointedly inquired why the department had waited until Monday to make the arrest in Waterbury. The befuddled commissioner could only stammer that detectives were working hard on other similarly promising leads at the time. "The main thing is that we got the man," he said with a feigned grin.

"This was not good police work, was it, Commissioner?" asked one of the reporters sharply.

"A man has been arrested who was at liberty for sixteen years," he defensively responded. "His dangerous potentialities have been nullified. Yes."

The reporters persisted on the point, arguing that the commissioner could not possibly have been satisfied with his department's slow reaction to Con Ed's recovery of the Metesky file. Kennedy hesitated for a pregnant moment and then, feeling cornered, responded with the true crux of his anger. Slowly he began, "Police were working for five or six years and did not know of such a file." He folded his hands in front of his breast, restraining a bitter tone that now enveloped his voice. The reporters furiously scribbled their notes on pads of tousled yellow paper. "We have no power over Con-Ed to force them to give over their files—to know that there was such a file." What Commissioner Kennedy did not tell reporters was that a growing suspicion had taken root among police brass and BIU detectives implicating Con Ed personnel in a years-long, systematic scheme to fraudulently withhold the Metesky file from their view.

· · ·

For years, despite persistent requests from police investigators, Con Ed lawyers and administrators had consistently maintained that all employee files dated prior to 1940 were no longer in existence. Frustrated, but understanding of the company's policy of records retention and destruction, detectives limited their search to what was known and available. On January 14, 1957, however, just days prior to Alice Kelly's find, detectives received what they called a "confidential tip" that Con Ed did, in fact, possess those earlier files and had purposely withheld them for more than two years of the investigation. Though the identity of the informant was never disclosed, later facts would bear out its reliability.

The explosive allegations did not remain secret for long. By Friday, January 25, fierce charges and arrogant denials were publically exchanged through the New York media. Statements from unnamed police sources were published accusing Con Ed of obstructing the search for employee records and charging that if the relevant files had been produced by Con Ed upon their original request, Metesky would, in all likelihood, have been apprehended sooner. As specific files of interest did emerge, police alleged that Con Ed protested and stalled at every instance, claiming that the records contained sensitive legal matters that would have to be reviewed by company lawyers prior to their release.

The Con Ed response to the allegations was swift and indignant. "Our employees have worked around the clock going into files and making information available to the police," erupted William Brady, a Con Ed public relations official at a hastily arranged press conference. "If any charge is to be made, let them take off their masks. Let the man making the charges identify himself and tell us what the charges are . . . We are not police. We sell electricity," he hissed. "When the police asked for information or names, or access to files, we gave it." Harland Forbes, the president of Con Ed, announced simply, "As far as I know, they had complete access to our files and went through them many times."

Commissioner Kennedy chafed with anger at Con Ed's statements but remained characteristically understated to the reporters who raced to police headquarters for a response. "The complete investigation showed that our men had checked through all available files of Con Edison," Kennedy responded diplomatically. "My impression is that we were told that 1940 was the earliest record."

As the relationship between Con Ed and the New York Police Department disintegrated into a cynical rift of mystery and suspicion regarding access to the company files, the underlying question of entitlement to the reward money became the talk of the town. With accusations being hurled in every direction it appeared that no one was willing to come forward and lay claim to the prize. Though Con Ed and the public at large appeared to favor Alice Kelly as the leading entrant, the police privately seethed at the thought of any Con Ed employee collecting the reward, and Alice herself had soured at all the attention and appeared reluctant to make a claim.

Police investigators had quickly concluded that not only had Con Ed obstructed their search for files, but also, in an effort to protect themselves, they had concocted the story of how Metesky's file had actually been located. Edward Lehane, one of Metesky's arresting officers, later disclosed in a magazine interview:

[Alice] was like an executive secretary, some type of highly rated job in Con Edison.

[The Metesky file] was in a file in a vice president's or somebody's office. They knew that file was there. There was a whole file cabinet full of cases that they felt were sensitive cases, cases that may have brought embarrassment to Con-Ed. They knew that we had detectives in Albany looking over all the old compensation files. There was some indication, I believe, that we were getting close . . . So they knew that the goddamn net was closing. That's when Con-Ed suddenly came up with it.

For his part, Commissioner Kennedy, whose charge it was to determine eligibility for the reward, had considered the politically unpopular decision of withholding the prize altogether on the technical legal ground that a "conviction," as required by the Board of Estimates posting, would never be attained if the Bomber were to be held incompetent to stand trial or otherwise committed to a psychiatric institution. Though the department appeared ready to use every available tool to prevent Con Ed or its employees from profiting by the reward, Kennedy declared, perhaps untruthfully, that "[a]nybody who files a just claim will get consideration from me."

On January 25, Harland Forbes contacted Commissioner Kennedy and requested a meeting between the two men in an effort to resolve the simmering conflict between Con Ed and the police force. After an hour-long conference, it was announced that a formal investigation headed by Deputy Police Commissioner Aloysius Melia, who was in charge of the department's legal affairs, would be held to determine exactly who should be given credit for trapping the Mad Bomber. The pressure on Kennedy to take the focus off the police investigation and to place it upon the swift prosecution of George Metesky, however, was mounting with each passing day. That weekend, as Melia prepared the details of his fact-finding probe, the *New York Times* posed the larger question that all of New York seemed to be asking: "Why, with all the available clues, did it take more than fifteen years to track down the Bomber?" Kennedy couldn't wait to change the subject.

During the first week of February, Deputy Commissioner Melia interviewed twenty-five detectives and officers of the New York City Police Department involved in the Bomber investigation, and formally deposed multiple employees of Con Ed, including Alice Kelly herself. Alice had consistently indicated that her role in finding the Metesky file was nothing more than a routine part of her job and that she accordingly intended to make no claim for the reward money. "I have no more right to [the reward]," testified Alice, "than the man in the moon."

With Alice Kelly out of the reward picture, and no other legitimate claimants willing to enter the fracas, the Federation of Women Shareholders, led by its outspoken president, Wilma Soss, sensed another battleground for her feminist crusade. A longtime advocate of minority shareholder rights and more particularly women's causes in the corporate arena, Soss demanded that Con Ed make claim for the reward on behalf of Alice Kelly and, if awarded, distribute the monies evenly amongst Con Ed Employees, the Mutual Aid Association, the Police Welfare Fund, and the New York Newspaper Reporters Association. Con Ed refused Soss's entreaties, citing complete neutrality in the matter, and Alice, feeling somewhat manipulated, forwarded a stern statement to Soss explaining that her refusal to make application for the reward was based upon her own "long and serious consideration," made without influence. The decision, she stated, was "irrevocable." Confirming her consistent posture of privacy, Alice informed Soss, "I realize of course, that I cannot prevent any action your organization sees fit to take as stockholders of Consolidated Edison, but I must, in all fairness, inform you that I, personally, object to any action which may involve me in a controversy of which I want no part."

Alice's pleadings were ignored, and on February 13, 1957, a formal application was made with the commissioner's office by the Federation of Women Shareholders on behalf of Alice Kelly for consideration of the reward money. It would be the only official claim for the reward filed with the commissioner's office.

• • •

Among the clamor and conversation regarding rewards and compensation, Thomas Dorney, the security guard at the RCA Building at Rockefeller Center who had, in August 1956, unwittingly taken home one of the Mad Bomber's creations, now threatened to bring suit against Metesky for $500 in damages sustained to his kitchen when the pipe bomb exploded in his home.

Frederick Eberhardt, who had been wrongfully arrested in 1951 as a prime suspect in the Mad Bomber case, filed a claim with the New York City controller, seeking redress for the loss of forty days work, the expenses of seven trips to New York, and the return of his bail money.

Lloyd Hill, the Penn Station porter who spent two months in St. Vincent's Hospital recovering from eighteen fractures of the right foot suffered in the Bomber's washroom explosion of February 1956, had been unable to work since the incident but contemplated no claims for further recompense beyond the $15 per week he received from the state Workmen's Compensation Board. "I haven't had any ill feeling toward him," said Hill regarding the Bomber. "Most people can work their way out of difficulties; some have to resort to such means; it's not their fault."

And in a letter to the Editor of the *New York Times,* Ruth S. Jackson of Norwalk, Connecticut wrote: "Why not contribute the reward money offered for the identification of George Metesky to the National Association for Mental Health? It might be used there to prevent some similar maladjustment to society. Then we would all be rewarded."

. . .

The official report of Aloysius Melia's inquiry into the circumstances surrounding the location of Metesky's Con Ed file conceded full credit for the find to Alice Kelly. It explained that Walter Arm had innocently misconstrued a police statement alluding to Detective Bertram Scott's Monday morning retrieval of the file to mean that Scott had been the one to actually locate the file, and insisted that at no time during the investigation had Scott or any other member of the department actually taken credit for the find.

Notwithstanding the acknowledged credit given to Alice Kelly, she steadfastly refused to lay claim to the reward. It remains unpaid to this day.

. . .

The mystery of Con Ed's role in withholding files and obstructing the search remained even after Melia's inquiry. While general counsel for Con Ed admitted that he had informed police that some company files dated before 1940 had been destroyed, he insisted that he was referring only to "litigation files" and that the remaining compensation files existed and were never withheld from police. Harland Forbes called the matter a "misunderstanding," and by then Commissioner Kennedy just wanted to put the matter to rest.

Though the formal inquiry was officially closed without sufficient evidence to implicate Con Ed personnel in any type of criminal misconduct resulting from the search for the Metesky file, the department privately and evermore maintained its suspicions against the power company. When asked why Alice Kelly didn't take the $26,000 reward money, a member of the BIU, Detective William Schmitt, simply said, "You tell me."

· · ·

As the New York City police feuded with Con Ed over files and rewards, the staff of the *Journal-American* city room drank away the days following Metesky's arrest at a former longshoreman's watering hole on the South Street docks called Moochie's Saloon. There, among the stench of stale beer and decaying plaster, pressmen, reporters, editors, and secretaries celebrated the tributes of New York and awaited the Pulitzer prize that each knew they deserved. Though the Pulitzer would never come, accolades and messages of congratulations from all over the state poured into the offices of the *Journal-American* like ale from Moochie's spigots for their role in the capture of the Mad Bomber.

The governor, Averell Harriman, forwarded a telegram to Seymour Berkson that read: "I congratulate the *Journal-American* for its part in the evident solution of the 'Mad Bomber' case. This is in the finest tradition of American journalism in the cooperation of a newspaper with the police and other authorities."

Similarly, Mayor Wagner lauded the *Journal-American*'s efforts in the case and officially wrote:

The *New York Journal-American* is to be heartily congratulated on the splendid public service it has performed in this matter.

In close cooperation with our own Police Department, the *Journal-American* has once again demonstrated how a newspaper can be of great service to the community.

Speaking for all New Yorkers I want to extend our grateful thanks for the *Journal-American's* unselfish devotion to the good principles of government.

Again my heartfelt congratulation to all members of the *Journal-American* staff who contributed toward ending this menace to the community.

By unanimous vote of the New York City Council, a resolution of appreciation for the *Journal-American*'s "outstanding public service" in bringing about the Bomber's arrest was read into the public record, praising the paper's "exceptional vision and dedication to the safety of the city by devoting unlimited space to stories and appeals aimed at discovering the identity of this elusive terrorist."

And from Washington, D.C., came a telegram from the FBI addressed to Seymour Berkson that read:

I know you and your staff can take great satisfaction in your most recent cooperative efforts which have led to the identification and apprehension of the quote Mad Bomber unquote. This is another graphic illustration of how the press on a day to day basis cooperates with law enforcement agencies. Law enforcement can very well look upon the press as an ally and the developments in the quote Mad Bomber unquote case conclusively prove the point.

Congratulations on a job well done.

John Edgar Hoover.

Perhaps the most meaningful tribute of all to the *Journal-American*, however, came directly from the desk of Commissioner Stephen Kennedy. In a congratulatory letter of thanks, Kennedy wrote:

The capture of the Mad Bomber was the direct result of information furnished by the *N.Y. Journal-American* and developed by the police. The close cooperation in turning over to us promptly all letters received from the Mad Bomber made this outstanding arrest possible. I wish to congratulate the publisher and all those staff members of the *Journal-American* who spent many tireless hours aiding us in ending this menace. The *Journal-American* deserves the gratitude of all citizens of New York for outstanding public service.

In the coming days and weeks, the *Journal-American* and its "Four Fishermen" would receive awards from the Newspaper Reporters Association of New York City, the local chapter of Sigma Delta Chi (a national journalism fraternity), the Women's Press Club of New York, and the National Broadcasting Company. And in a bath of self-adulation William Randolph Hearst Jr. wrote in his syndicated "Editor's Report" that his *Journal-American's* work on the Mad Bomber case was "one of the great journalistic coups of the past generation"—a "Milestone in Press-Civic Understanding."

With the flood of praise and honors pouring into the *Journal-American*, it appeared obvious to some that the paper would, in fact, lay claim to the offered reward. In a January 25 editorial, however, the *Journal-American* removed itself from the conversation. Noting that the paper's name had been raised as a possible recipient, the editorial made their position clear. "Under no circumstances," the *Journal-American* declared, "would this newspaper claim or accept any monetary reward for performing a public service . . . [W]e feel the *Journal-American* has been richly rewarded by the expressions of praise from high public officials and the many warm-hearted letters of congratulations from our readers."

Though the *Journal-American* excluded itself from consideration of the reward, by no means had it modestly accepted the accolades of the city without thought of profit. During its dialogue with the Mad Bomber, the paper experienced what Berkson called a "modest rise" in readership. Upon the arrest, however, daily circulation skyrocketed by 100,000 readers and profits correspondingly rose. Berkson himself appeared on radio and television news programs and was interviewed by the likes of Mike Wallace on the WABD-TV news program *Night Beat*. A dramatization of Berkson's role in the Mad Bomber case even became the focus of an episode of the television program *The Big Story* that aired in April 1957.

As the public tributes flowed into the paper, Berkson and his staff of editors made certain that every word was visibly printed, and at times the self-exultation became insufferable. On January 24, a cartoon rendering appeared in the paper depicting a proud-looking member of the New York Police Department standing side by side with an animated copy of the *Journal-American* that bore the headline "Mad Bomber Captured." An arm from the human-like newspaper was raised in unity with that of the police officer, and both held high a torch labeled "Public Safety." The drawing was named "Partners in Public Service."

For the most part, commentary among rival newspapers regarding the *Journal-American*'s good fortune remained cordial if not outright congratulatory. Recognizing that they had simply been beaten at their own game, the *New York World-Telegram and Sun* extended through their editorial pages congratulations to their "esteemed compeers at the *New York Journal-American* for some first-class newspaper work." The *Journal-American* reprinted every word of the editorial in its next day's edition. Other papers from across the country recognized the *Journal-American*'s work with an editorial tip of the hat, and most recognized the paper's efforts as innovative and groundbreaking. The January 21 issue of *Time* magazine, however, carried a haughtily composed piece titled "Bombs Away," in which the *Journal-American* was accused of withholding from the police vital information contained in one the Bomber's letters in an effort to hold out, in essence, for the "jackpot"—the surrender of the Mad Bomber. An outraged Seymour Berkson promptly sued Time Incorporated for libel.

The suit against *Time* meandered its way through the court system of New York, and, though the statement made in the article was patently untrue, it did not rise to the level of the legal standard for libel. On June 25, 1959, a decision was rendered by the appellate court in favor of the magazine.

Seymour Berkson, who had died earlier that year of a heart attack at the age of fifty-three, did not outlive the case, but, as always, he had made his point.

# A QUESTION OF COMPETENCY

THE NINE-STORY BRICK AND LIMESTONE STRUCTURE THAT HOUSED THE cheerless if not gruesome psychiatric division of the Bellevue Hospital stood against the gray winter skies of Manhattan like a dismal shadow—a harbinger of stormy weather. The fetid East River quietly flowed at the rear of the building while its decaying piers clung tenuously to wooden retention walls along its banks. Though Bellevue Hospital Center—said to be the oldest general public hospital in the United States—was a cluster of hospital pavilions extending four city blocks along First Avenue and interconnected by a labyrinth of foreboding underground tunnels, the epithet "Bellevue" was often used to denote only its infamous and gloomy psychiatric division.

The red brick and wrought iron gates of the Bellevue asylum had, by the 1950s, been firmly ensconced in the public imagination. A temporary (and often longer) home to the wretched and the poor, the facility also hosted notables such as Charlie Parker, Norman Mailer, and Eugene O'Neill for observation following crimes or activities that defied sanity. None other than Kris Kringle himself found himself behind the spiked fences of Bellevue, in the 1947 classic *Miracle on 34th Street*, enduring the probes of psychiatric analysis as he awaited his day in court. In stark contrast to the tortured souls that vacantly roamed the halls of the First Avenue asylum, George Metesky freely traded his neatly buttoned double-breasted suit for the institutional garb of gray wool pajamas, a faded bathrobe tied at the waist, and cotton slippers. He appeared like a man beginning the first day of a holiday retreat.

The city guards who deposited Metesky on the second floor prison ward at Bellevue, occupied by murderers, rapists, and other violent offenders, described their prisoner as a "most happy fellow." "He mingles freely with the other 25 male patients in Ward No. 2 talking 'small talk' about the weather, breakfast and radio and TV shows," wrote one newspaper in the early days of his confinement. "He smiles almost constantly." He was crowned the checkers champion of the ward and became popular with the staff and inmates alike. He cheerfully reminded the nurses and guards when it was time for another patient's medication, and he dutifully informed them when anyone was sick or in need of assistance. "He's always smiling and willing to help," said one attendant.

Metesky's ward consisted of two rooms that formed the corner of the building: one long and narrow and lined on either side with rows of white steel-framed cots, and the other a common area "day room" containing several wooden tables and benches, a television, and a radio. The windows were barred with steel, and three separate iron-gated doors at various exit points of the ward with guards stationed on either side made thoughts of escape a futile endeavor. Within the rooms themselves, many of which smelled of a potent disinfectant-urine combination, four white-coated male attendants joined three corrections officers and a charge nurse to attend to patients' needs and prevent hostilities. Though he had spent the last sixteen years in a most violent endeavor, Metesky showed not the slightest inclination toward violence and spoke not a word to inmate nor staff of why he found himself imprisoned in the dreary confines of Bellevue Hospital.

. . .

The notorious and oft quoted phrase "remanded to Bellevue for observation" was decreed by New York judges more than 1,500 times each year by the late 1950s. Criminal defendants whose mental capacity was in question would be dispatched to the prison ward of the psychiatric division as a way station between the courts and freedom, prison, or final commitment in other institutions. The innocuous "observation" was, in reality, a detailed inquiry required by statute to determine whether the accused was "in such a state of idiocy, imbecility, lunacy or insanity as to be incapable of understanding the charge, indictment, or proceedings or of making his defense."

In earlier years the process of such determination had been left in the hands of a so-called lunacy commission comprising political henchmen haphazardly appointed by the courts through graft and nepotism. With New York's enactment of the Desmond Act in 1939, however, judicial assessments as to the mental capacity of criminal offenders shifted to the examination of capable and licensed psychiatrists within the state or municipal hospital systems. Since the settled law in New York and across most of the country was that one could not be tried, convicted, or sentenced for a crime if his mental condition prevented him from understanding the proceedings or assisting in his defense, the considered judgments of qualified experts expressed through full and detailed reports would often become the deciding factor in a judicial determination of competence or incompetence to stand trial. As George Metesky blissfully adjusted to his new surroundings in the prison ward of Bellevue Hospital, the eyes of multiple psychiatric professionals followed his every move.

$\bullet \ \bullet \ \bullet$

Prior to the adjournment of Metesky's January 22 arraignment, Assistant District Attorney Grebow pointed out that, while Metesky may have been supported by his two sisters, he did, in fact, have $500 on his person and approximately $11,000 in the bank. Though the judge refused to engage the issue of Metesky's finances at that time, his court appointed attorney, Benjamin Schmier, did make inquiry and quickly determined that his client's finances went well beyond the level of destitution required for assistance from the Legal Aid Society. As Schmier prepared to withdraw from Metesky's representation, Anna and Mae were hard at work to secure the best lawyer that they could afford for their brother.

. . .

The *New York Journal-American* kept its word to the Mad Bomber. Within hours of his arrest, the Hearst Corporation had retained, on behalf of George Metesky, the services of the city's foremost authority on workmen's compensation law. Bart J. O'Rourke, a sixty-two-year-old attorney specifically licensed by the state to represent claimants in compensation matters, had pioneered the early development of the field going as far back as the passage of the Workmen's Compensation Act itself in 1914. His knowledge of the law was absolute, and Metesky was overjoyed at news that he had been retained. Finally, Metesky mused, he would get the hearing that had been denied him so long ago.

O'Rourke's first course of action was to review the files of the Workmen's Compensation Board that had been retrieved from Albany upon Metesky's arrest. The board's chairwoman, Angela Parisi, had pledged the full cooperation of her offices and had herself studied Metesky's file and claim history. "[T]here is no question," Parisi revealed to reporters, "that the previous Board was within the scope of its rights" in denying Metesky's claims. The matter had, in her words, been "properly disallowed" by the one-year statute of limitations that applied at that time. At first blush O'Rourke had to agree with the assessment. For whatever reason, Metesky had delayed in the actual filing of his compensation claim. As O'Rourke probed the files, however, his mind searched for a legal technicality or loophole that could bypass the time restrictions and revive his client's fateful claim.

On the day following Metesky's arrival at Bellevue, O'Rourke paid his client a visit. Still clad in blue pajamas and appearing somewhat less poised than he had during the prior several days, Metesky warmly greeted the lawyer. As the two sat opposite one another outside the doors of ward 2, Metesky recounted, in a torrent of memory, the details of his claim for compensation beginning with his September 5, 1931, accident at the Hell Gate power station. Following the conversation O'Rourke explained that he was still in the process of a complete review of the compensation board files but that he could promise nothing in terms of a result. "I understand," said Metesky. "[A] man can only do his best. If the *New York Journal-American* sent you, then you must *be* the best."

Though O'Rourke gave very few details of his intended legal strategy following his meeting with Metesky, he did tell a reporter, "I believe a new claim for compensation may hinge a great deal on the determination in the criminal action and the facts brought out in his trial or at Bellevue." O'Rourke was clearly hinting that his client's sanity, or lack thereof, may determine whether or not an untimely filing of claim could be excused in the eyes of the law.

. . .

James D. C. Murray extracted the black horn-rimmed glasses from his eyes and rubbed his temples, which now throbbed with demonic pain. His typically neatly parted and meticulously combed thinning white hair now hung in tousled shards across his head, disheveled by the desperate passes of his opened and probing fingers. Migraines had plagued him for much of his professional career, and now, as he peered out over the glimmering East River from his upper-floor office of the Woolworth Building, he struggled to regain the poised composure that his standing and responsibility relentlessly demanded. Renowned as a "champion of lost causes," the brooding and introspective seventy-four-year-old had, during the last half-century, built a reputation as an eloquent and disarming advocate of the law and had become one of New York's most sought-after criminal attorneys.

A product of an all-Irish ethnic upbringing, Murray was known for rich expression and thorough preparation, and though he could boil with rage or ooze with sarcasm, he would always retain a simple and unassuming professional decorum in the face of hardship. "He's very much the fox," a colleague would later say. "You have to watch him closely every minute or he'll catch you off guard." In the courtroom, Murray was aided by an incomparable memory for facts and details, seldom resorting to files or notes of any kind and only occasionally even carrying a briefcase.

An incessant smoker and an eloquent orator, Murray had maintained an overriding ethic that emphasized the right of every citizen to a vigorous defense under the law regardless of the charge against him. Despite his representation of some of the city's most abhorrent criminals and the withering disdain of the public that resulted, Murray's genteel demeanor and zealous protection of offenders' rights never faltered for a moment. "I guess I was born with a constitutional pity for those in trouble," Murray would later tell a writer in a rare interview. "When I go to the grave, ten thousand secrets will be buried with me."

The fermenting tensions of his calling had taken their grueling toll, and the curse of relentless and ongoing headaches had been the price extracted for a long and often punishing career. On this day, however, as the pounding began to subside and Murray regained his equanimity, he was finally able to lend focus to the primary cause of his most recent bout of pain.

Murray was a native of Waterbury, Connecticut, and had earlier received a call from another Waterbury attorney by the name of Harry Spellman, who had been retained by none other than Anna and Mae Milauskas on behalf of their beleaguered brother. Though a former New Haven County prosecutor and a respected Connecticut lawyer, Spellman was a bit out of his jurisdiction and comfort zone in the matter of the Mad Bomber, and he asked Murray to join him in the case. He knew that the soft-spoken New York attorney would never turn him down, for his legal philosophy was known to Spellman: "To me, the man on trial is always the underdog, regardless of his background," Murray had been quoted as saying. "He is but an individual, and opposing him is the organized might of society. The forces of law are set in motion to destroy the defendant; the only one who can stand between him and destruction is his lawyer."

. . .

At Bellevue, Metesky was initially given a complete medical evaluation with particular attention to pulmonary function, and though no evidence of active tuberculosis was found, clear indications of the prior existence of the disease were present. Lab tests were ordered, periodic chest X-rays were recommended, and Metesky was submitted to the care and evaluation of the psychiatric division. "He is as jovial and gay today as he was the day they put him in there," said Harry Spellman following one of his meetings with Metesky and James Murray at the institution. "He seems to be doing very well." Metesky's presumed good health, however, would soon come to an end.

· · ·

As Metesky began a rigorous battery of psychological testing and examination at Bellevue, the district attorney's office, headed by Frank Hogan, another Waterbury native, announced plans to immediately begin presenting evidence to a New York County grand jury in an effort to obtain an indictment against him. Prosecutors had earlier stated that if convicted on each of the thirty-two separate bombings, Metesky faced the prospect of life in prison. He would indeed require the best lawyers available.

· · ·

As required by the Desmond Act, the director in charge of Bellevue's Psychiatric Division designated three "qualified psychiatrists" to examine and report upon Metesky's mental condition. The question of sanity, as determined by the psychiatrists, was only part of the story; the law in New York at the time would allow a defendant to stand trial *even if insane* if he was nonetheless able to understand the charges against him and assist in his own defense by conferring with his lawyer. But if the defendant's insanity rose to such a level as to prevent such understanding and assistance, he would be found incompetent and thus be committed to a state institution pending any change in mental capacity. The inquiry and assessment were, accordingly, of narrow construction as prescribed by statute.

In the days and weeks following his commitment, Metesky was meticulously observed and exhaustively questioned by doctors John Cassity,

Theodore Weiss, and Albert LaVerne in an effort to understand their patient's psychological deficiencies as well as capabilities and to assess his mental capacity to stand trial. Throughout the extensive array of interrogations Metesky was noted by the psychiatrists to be "alert, cooperative, and eager to oblige in answering questions." His behavior was described as "exemplary."

Metesky's sisters were interviewed to gain a historical perspective on his life and an understanding of any family issues that may have contributed to his current mental state. Though Anna had staunchly defended her brother in the face of reporters' questioning, she admitted to the psychiatrists that George had "exhibited abnormal thinking and acting since childhood" and described him as "reclusive and aloof" and, even in his early years, "unable to relate to people." The sisters provided a detailed medical history and described the meager employment record of their brother, all of which was independently investigated, verified, and documented by the Bellevue staff.

Metesky himself provided the psychiatrists with a complete and thorough history of his life, including the specific details of his accident at Hell Gate, his efforts to obtain compensation, and his decision to ultimately resort to a bombing campaign. The psychiatrists were provided with many of the numerous notes and letters written by Metesky through the years to government officials, private concerns, and, of course, Con Ed, together with copies of his more recent dispatches to the *Journal-American*. Metesky seemed particularly angry and vindictive toward the three Con Ed employees who he still maintained had perjured themselves against him in his compensation hearing, and he expressed to the doctors a fantasy in which each of the three employees was murdered by gruesome dismemberment. He voiced his desire to exterminate the president of the company with an explosive bullet, and he revealed his ultimate plan to one day sabotage the power centers of New York, throwing the entire city into darkness.

With regard to the bombings themselves, Metesky cheerfully described each event in detail and seemed to exalt in the grandiosity of it all. "I figured I wasn't the forgotten man," he told them. With a "glow of ecstatic fervor," as noted by the psychiatrists, Metesky explained that he had felt absolutely justified in his mission, which he believed saved thousands from the injustices of the evil power company. He seemed utterly proud of what he called his "martyrdom." "I have performed society a great service," he said. In a later transcribed exchange with Dr. LaVerne, Metesky's state of mind regarding the bombings was further revealed:

Q. Have you committed a crime?

A. No, of course not. How can I have committed a crime if I performed society a great service?

Q. Do you feel that you should be punished?

A. No, of course not. When two nations have a dispute they write notes to each other. When the notes are ineffective then they have to use force, they send over bombers, blow up cities, kill and maim many innocent women and children and [w]hen the bombers return from their mission, society pins a medal upon their breast for their good deeds and for services rendered.

Q. Do you feel that you should be similarly rewarded?

A. Certainly.

Q. You learned from newspaper reports that innocent people were hurt by the bomb explosions, did you not?

A. Yes, that's what I heard over the radio and I felt bad about it because if the police were not criminally negligent in their duties they would have gotten those people out of the area.

Q. If you felt bad about innocent people getting hurt, then why did you continue laying many more bombs that exploded?

A. Because I had a great mission to carry out and it was my duty to continue in my efforts to attract attention of the world to expose Con Ed. This was my great service to society . . .

Q. What are you guilty of, if anything?

A. The only thing that I am guilty of is making a loud noise in a public place.

• • •

On January 28, Assistant District Attorney Karl Grebow began presenting evidence to a New York County grand jury on further and more serious charges against George Metesky. Among thirty-five separate witnesses examined by the prosecutor in the Court of General Sessions were eight individuals who had suffered injuries as a result of Metesky's explosives, as well as a slew of bomb squad and police laboratory detectives who linked the physical evidence and writing samples to one man: the Mad Bomber.

Two days later the grand jury returned a forty-seven-count indictment against George Metesky on charges ranging from possession of a bomb to attempted murder in the first degree, acts that, according to the indictment itself, were "imminently dangerous to others and evincing a depraved mind, regardless of human life . . ." The charges, which covered twenty separate incidents, included only those bombings from March 1952 forward in light of the applicable five-year statute of limitations and carried a maximum combined sentence of 815 years in prison.

On January 31, Metesky was brought under heavy guard to the General Sessions courthouse on Centre Street in Manhattan for arraignment under the new charges against him. James Murray, standing next to his shackled client, made the perfunctory request that Metesky be recommitted to Bellevue, where psychological testing and examination was ongoing, on the grounds that he did not have the requisite mental capacity to understand the charges levied against him. Judge Louis Capozzoli cordially agreed without objection from the assistant district attorney, and the matter was put over to February 21 for further review pending completion of the psychiatric reports. It would be the last time that the criminal courts of New York County would look favorably upon George Metesky.

• • •

Meanwhile, in Brooklyn, New York, Kings County district attorney Edward Silver announced plans to seek similar charges against Metesky for his calamitous bombing of the Brooklyn Paramount Theatre on

December 2, 1956. In the coming days, Silver's office convened another grand jury, submitted evidence through twenty-six separate witnesses, and was granted its own multiple-count indictment against the Mad Bomber.

On February 19, a pale and worn though still smiling Metesky was once again loaded into a prison van and transported to the Kings County Courthouse in Brooklyn, where he stood silently handcuffed to a corrections officer before Judge Hyman Barshay. Again James Murray informed that court that his client was in the process of undergoing psychiatric evaluation at Bellevue and requested that the proceedings be postponed pending the results of that evaluation. As with the New York County proceedings, Judge Barshay consented and recommitted Metesky until the final reports as to his competency were available.

In compliance with the technical provisions of the law, Metesky was taken to a police precinct in Kings County for rebooking before returning to Bellevue. After the usual front and side view mug shots were taken, he jovially exclaimed, "Gee whizz! I thought I'd get a Manhattan cocktail after this was all over. Boys I need one bad!"

Clearly not the indulgence requested, the "Manhattan cocktail" that would ultimately be served to George Metesky was, in fact, a looming battle between courts of competing jurisdiction with nothing short of his legal fate hanging in the balance.

· · ·

The average stay in the Bellevue prison ward for psychiatric observation and assessment was about twenty-one days, and though the law actually permitted sixty days for the psychiatrists to draw their report, a growing impatience seemed to permeate the public and the press as the final weeks in the short month of February 1957 passed. "This fellow is smarter than a Supreme Court Justice," commented James Murray when asked about the lengthy deliberations of the Bellevue psychiatric team. "If a blithering idiot gets into the psychopathic ward the doctors can report on him in 10 days or so. But there is probably no limit as to disagreements on

Metesky." On February 21, the rescheduled date of arraignment in the New York County Court of General Sessions, the final psychiatric report was still not available and the matter was further continued until such time that the report was complete. By the end of February, however, the new presiding judge in the court's revolving docket, John A. Mullen, had had enough.

Ruddy faced and Tammany connected, Judge Mullen had gained a reputation over seventeen years of service on the bench as a tough but fair-minded jurist whose angry glower often signaled a harsh sentence. During the 1955 murder trial of Elmer (Trigger) Burke, a notorious killer with organized crime connections, Burke peered up at Judge Mullen, who had presided over the case, and politely said, "I won't answer the question you just directed to me, but I want you to know that I respect you as a judge and I like you as a man." Well after Burke's execution Mullen would reflect that it was perhaps the nicest compliment he had ever received.

On February 28, though the final typed report on the psychiatric evaluation of George Metesky had still not been completed, an angry Judge Mullen, in a fit of judicial irritability, demanded that the defendant be brought before him in an unscheduled and impromptu hearing to answer to the charges of the lengthy indictment. Mullen further ordered that at least one of the three psychiatrists who had been chosen to assess and report on Metesky's mental condition appear together with the prosecutor and counsel for the accused. As the order made its way through the halls of Bellevue and to the law offices of James D. C. Murray, an air of confusion if not panic began to rise. The impetuous command had caught everyone quite by surprise.

George Metesky was quickly dressed and hustled from Bellevue to the New York County Courthouse with the usual entourage of patrolmen and prison guards. Dr. John Cassity, one of Metesky's psychiatric evaluators, met Assistant District Attorney Grebow, who had been summoned from another courtroom, and the pair rushed before Judge Mullen's bench, where they stood in puzzlement. James Murray, who was that day actively engaged in another criminal trial at the Bronx County Court, quickly arranged to have his associate, Irving Greenberg, appear in his stead in an effort to cajole from the judge a postponement of the matter.

As the court was gaveled to order, Greenberg informed Judge Mullen of Murray's unavailability and implored him to reschedule the arraignment to a future date. He argued that Metesky was the client of his law partner and that he, Greenberg, was neither suitably conversant with the facts nor sufficiently competent to offer effective representation to the defendant. Finally, Greenberg made clear to Judge Mullen that the final report on Metesky's mental condition, though very near, was not yet complete.

Unmoved, the scarlet-cheeked jurist curtly inquired whether Greenberg had anything further to add. As the befuddled lawyer stood in silence, Mullen instructed the clerk to swear in Dr. Cassity and he began interrogating the witness.

There had been general agreement among the Bellevue psychiatrists that Metesky was, indeed, incompetent to stand trial, and the final report, when complete, would bear this out. As one of the lead analysts on the case, Dr. Cassity had interviewed and observed Metesky on many occasions and was intimately familiar with the salient provisions of the report that was to come. Thus, when questioned as to the mental condition of his patient, Cassity did not hesitate. He explained to Judge Mullen that though Metesky's general behavior was agreeable, it was evident to the psychiatric team from the start that he was mentally ill. In detailing Metesky's "mission" against Con Ed, Cassity described his gruesome fantasies of murder and his grandiose delusions of providing a service to mankind through his bombing campaign.

"Did he indicate to you at all times that he knew the quality of his actions that he was doing?" asked Mullen.

"I do not think that he knew the nature and quality or significance," Cassity responded without hesitation.

Mullen narrowed his eyes; his thumb and forefinger caressed his chin. "Did it appear to you that he knew the nature of the act that he did or was contemplating doing? Did he know that he was, let us say, exploding a bomb?"

"To my opinion," answered the doctor, "I do not think that he knew the nature and quality of his acts."

"Did he know, in your opinion, that exploding a bomb is exploding a bomb?"

"Yes, I think he knew that."

Mullen's voice grew louder as he peered down at the witness from the ornate oaken bench. "Do you think that he knew that that was against the accepted rules of conduct in the society in which he lived?"

"No I don't think so," he responded.

As the testimony concluded Judge Mullen cast an accusatory eye at George Metesky, who stood serenely to the side of the courtroom, accompanied by several officers. Mullen then shifted his gaze to Irving Greenberg and, despite Dr. Cassity's unambiguous testimony as to Metesky's marginalized mental condition, demanded that a plea to the indictment be entered on behalf of the defendant. A now angry Greenberg sprung to his feet and again objected pointing out that the psychiatric report had not been finalized or distributed to counsel as required by statute, and thus a plea short of an appropriate and fully informed competency hearing would be a legal nullity and a miscarriage of justice. When pressed, the indignant attorney refused to enter a plea, knowing that to do so would move Metesky one step closer to a trial that, with a proper finding of legal incompetency, should never take place. Undeterred, Judge Mullen entered a plea by proxy of not guilty, reserving a later defense of insanity, and ordered Metesky to stand trial for his crimes. "What the doctors say about sanity is one thing," snorted Mullen. "I have formed an opinion. The report is no deterrent at this stage of the game."

Dr. Cassity silently implored Greenberg with insistent eyes, then frowned and bowed his head in frustration.

"All delays in cases of this sort are unwise," continued the judge. "No

harm will be done to the defendant until he is properly tried and convicted by a jury of his peers. A great deal of disservice to the community
can be done by dragging this case along."

With Mullen's coerced and involuntary entry he had effectively escalated the case against George Metesky from one involving psychiatric care
and evaluation to a matter of sterile crime and punishment, and within
moments of the close of the proceedings Metesky was on his way to the
bleak catacombs of the Manhattan City Prison—notoriously known as
the Tombs.

· · ·

When later asked how he felt about the events of February 28, George
Metesky calmly explained, "I have thought about it very carefully and I
have decided that Judge Mullen is conspiring with Con-Ed . . . He is obviously being paid off by them in his public office in some manner."

# "AS PLAIN AS THE NOSE ON YOUR FACE"

On the day following the hotly disputed arraignment in General Sessions, the official typewritten psychiatric report on George Metesky was hand delivered to Judge Mullen. Unanimously approved and executed by the three qualified psychiatrists required by the law, the report stated:

> While generally compliant in his demeanor, both on the ward and in our examinations, it is our feeling that this is merely a façade and that his inner feelings are smoldering with intense hostility based upon definite delusional ideas. While it is true that there might be some foundation in fact for his feelings of having receive[d] unjust treatment, the psychotic ideation is shown here unequivocally by the delusional ideas dominating his thought processes so extensively as to exclude other reality interests. The diagnosis is Schizophrenic Reaction of the Paranoid Type, and the examiners are of the opinion that he is a suitable case for commitment to a mental hospital for the mentally ill.

Dismissing the report as nothing more than a nonbinding consulting opinion, Judge Mullen defended his order compelling Metesky to stand trial, stating, "I don't believe in letting people hibernate in the psychopathic ward, or be used as guinea pigs by psychiatrists when they may be menaces to the public and more properly confined in penal institutions."

• • •

Though there appeared to be no inclination toward self-inflicted harm, Metesky was placed under twenty-four-hour suicide watch at the Tombs. The cell was constantly lighted, and his necktie, belt, and shoes were removed and taken from sight. City officials were taking no chances with the notorious Mad Bomber.

Anna Kross, the progressive corrections commissioner of the New York City prison system, however, was ill at ease with the notion of housing a man who was by most accounts hopelessly insane in a largely non-rehabilitative penal environment. As a former lawyer and judge, Kross had developed a keen interest in the sociological aspects of detention and abhorred the mistreatment of the psychologically impaired. Within hours of Metesky's arrival at the Tombs, Kross telephoned officials at Bellevue, who confirmed that her new prisoner was of doubtful mental competence and clearly belonged in the therapeutic confines of the psychiatric ward. That afternoon, over the voluble objections of Judge Mullen, Kross unilaterally ordered that Metesky be transferred from his prison cell back to Bellevue. "We cannot keep a man who is mentally unsound in a detention institution," she told reporters. "I am going to do what I think is right as commissioner." Irate over Kross's blatant violation of his order of confinement, Judge Mullen threatened to seek a judicial determination of the powers of the commissioner's office. "I don't know what [those powers] are," declared Mullen, "but to repeat, I hope she does . . ."

• • •

From the moment of Judge Mullen's forced entry of plea on February 28, an incensed James Murray began the process of having it vacated. Not only had Mullen conducted a hearing without the benefit of the final psychiatric report on Metesky, but, according to Murray, he had focused his inquiry on the wrong legal standard. Instead of making a determination as to whether Metesky was capable of understanding the proceedings and assisting in his defense—the threshold legal requirement for competency to stand trial—Mullen had, in fact, focused on the defendant's awareness of the nature and quality of his actions and if he could appreciate them as wrong—a standard reserved for trial to determine innocence by reason of insanity. Accordingly, Murray postulated, Metesky had been denied the competency hearing required by law as a precondition to the entry of a plea. On March 22 the awaited showdown between James Murray and Judge Mullen took place in a crowded Manhattan courtroom.

"The law is right there," protested Murray, his blue eyes piercing through the thick lenses of his black-rimmed glasses. "[I]t's as plain as the nose on your . . . face." Charging that the appropriate provisions of the statute had been ignored, Murray argued that no proceedings should have been held until the formal Bellevue report had been received, and he offered his opinion that Metesky was quite obviously incompetent to stand trial.

Blazing with anger, an indignant Judge Mullen retorted that he was uninterested in Murray's opinion and on several occasions he contemptuously referred to the lawyer by his last name only. Pointing out that more than fifty years of legal experience entitled him to certain opinions, Murray persisted that never in his experience had a judge required a competency hearing prior to receipt of the final written Bellevue report.

"I'm not interested in how long you've been around," roared Mullen. He pointed an accusatory finger at the lawyer and angrily reminded him that the report as to the mental condition of the defendant was intended by statute to be no more than an aid to the court and was not required to be followed. He explained that, indeed, a man could be technically insane and still able to defend himself in court.

Infuriated, Murray demanded that Mullen recuse himself from sitting on the case since he had already reached a conclusion as to Metesky's ultimate sanity. "You had no authority to do what you did," charged Murray.

The judge scoffed at the idea, but despite his recalcitrant anger in the matter, had little choice but to abide by the logic of Murray's main argument. A hearing *had* been conducted without the benefit of the full formal psychiatric report, and he knew that his decision would undoubtedly be reversed on appeal. Searching for a face-saving device, Mullen refused to vacate the proceedings themselves as void or contrary to law, but granted the motion to vacate the plea entered on February 28. It was a meaning-less distinction. Despite the very public acrimony, Murray had succeeded in his primary goal: The plea had at least been delayed and a new date of March 29 had been set for a full and legally compliant inquiry on the issue of competency to stand trial.

As the contentious hearing came to a close, George Metesky, sitting in a box reserved for the accused, had to be jostled from a sound sleep.

. . .

As the case in New York County wound through General Sessions, similar proceedings in Brooklyn, Kings County, were also independently being conducted against Metesky. Since he was under indictment in both coun-ties, pursuant to the law, each was bound to make its own determination as to competency, and the judgment of neither court was binding on the other. The potential of what James Murray called "a rather bizarre con-flict" if each court were to reach an opposite decision on the issue loomed on the horizon. On March 27 proceedings as to Metesky's competency to stand trial were begun before Judge Samuel Leibowitz in Brooklyn, and Murray, in his unique fustian eloquence, aptly framed the issue: "one county is looking for the torso and the other county is looking for the head . . ."

Judge Leibowitz wanted no part of the conflict. His long and ambi-tious legal career, which had included the representation of such diverse clients as Al Capone, "Bugsy" Siegel, and the Scottsboro Boys, had taught him to choose his battles wisely, and though he knew that the potential for inter-county strife was high in the Metesky case, he would do every-thing in his power to avoid it for the time being. In a nod of judicial def-erence, Leibowitz adjourned the Kings County inquiry "out of courtesy and respect" pending the next step taken by Judge Mullen in New York County. Prior to the close of the hearing, however, he acknowledged the conclusions of the Bellevue report on Metesky's current mental state and cautioned that following Mullen's decision—whatever that decision may be—"we will proceed in the manner provided by law." Leibowitz turned to Metesky and added, "The law compels us to do that, and that is your constitutional right and your legal right to have such a hearing."

It was clear to all in the room where Judge Leibowitz stood on the issue of the defendant's competency to stand trial.

. . .

On March 29 Metesky was back in General Sessions before Judge Mullen for a formal inquiry to confirm or reject the Bellevue psychiatric report and to determine his competency to stand trial in New York County. In a full-day hearing the three authors of the report unanimously testified that Metesky was incapable of understanding the proceedings against him or to meaningfully assist in his own defense, and at the conclusion of the hearing James Murray rose and requested that the report be confirmed. Though Mullen had been uncharacteristically reserved throughout most of the hearing, he now peered at the lawyer with a look of disdain in his eyes and shouted, almost cheerfully, "Your motion is denied!" The judge then turned his gaze to Metesky, who appeared rather bored with the proceedings, and directed him to enter a plea. Murray interjected loudly, "not guilty, Your Honor," but Mullen, still transfixed on the hapless defendant, ordered Metesky to speak for himself. Appearing baffled and somewhat confused, Metesky turned wide-eyed to his lawyer for direction. Murray nodded in approval and Metesky hesitatingly rose to his feet and muttered "I plead not guilty."

Unsurprised by Mullen's ruling but hoping to keep his client out of the Tombs, Murray reminded the judge that the Kings County order of commitment remained and that Bellevue was the proper facility for Metesky pending resolution of proceedings in Brooklyn. After a brief moment of contemplation, Mullen agreed, grateful to avoid another confrontation with the rather feisty corrections commissioner.

• • •

As the fight over the "head" and "torso" of George Metesky ensued, the lawyer retained by the *Journal-American* to consider Metesky's workmen's compensation claim announced that he had filed an application with the compensation board for reconsideration of the original denial of his client's claim. Bart O'Rourke explained to reporters that since it was the unanimous conclusion of three qualified Bellevue psychiatrists that Metesky suffered from schizophrenia of the paranoid type, and since it appeared that such condition existed during the time in which he was required to file his compensation claim, the time limitations of section 28 that originally barred his claim should be ignored. "I am claiming," said O'Rourke, "that shortly after his final discharge from the Marine Corps in 1929, and prior to his accident in 1931 he was psychotic, delusional and hallucinating . . . If this is true, it is a reasonable hypothesis that during the time he was required to file a claim . . . he was psychotic."

# "HIS DAYS ON EARTH ARE NUMBERED"

WITH THE EYES OF THE LEGAL PROCESS FOCUSED SOLELY UPON THE MENTAL health of George Metesky, it would soon be his physical health that would take center stage. As the tension between New York County and Kings County simmered on the issue of legal competency, Metesky suffered a severe relapse of his ongoing pulmonary tuberculosis and on April 6 hemorrhaged nearly a pint of blood from his lungs. For hours he lay alone on his prison ward cot, convinced that he was dying yet telling not a soul of his condition. Finally, an attendant discovered that Metesky was ill and he was given immediate medical treatment. When his condition was finally stabilized he was asked why he hadn't notified a nurse of his sufferings. "Well it's no use living," he responded.

"This man could at any time develop a ravaging disease," Dr. Albert LaVerne informed members of the press. "This means it might spread to all parts of his body . . . Tuberculosis of this type is a killer." Fully aware that Judge Mullen intended to expose Metesky to the rigors of trial and opposed to even the thought, LaVerne lectured to anyone who would listen that the emotional strain of a trial could likely bring on a fatal pulmonary hemorrhage.

Though Metesky's condition improved little in the coming days, James Murray found himself in a race against time to save his client from the trial that Dr. LaVerne so readily feared. Provisions to empanel a special jury in New York County were well under way, and Judge Mullen, though aware of Metesky's failing condition, had provided no indication that a stay of the proceedings was in the works. Murray knew that the only chance to save his client—both physically and legally—lay in the hands of Judge Leibowitz.

The Kings County hearing on Metesky's competency to stand trial had been rescheduled to April 8. On that day James Murray conferred with Judge Leibowitz in his Brooklyn courtroom chambers, and, with the full approval and consent of the assistant district attorney, they jointly formulated a plan to expedite the competency hearing and thus preempt, at least temporarily, the New York County trial. Aware that the Kings County inquiry could not proceed in Metesky's absence and further that a Kings County judge could not conduct a hearing within the confines of Bellevue, which lay in New York County, the group agreed that as soon as his condition stabilized, Metesky would be transferred out of Bellevue and into Kings County Hospital, where Judge Leibowitz could conduct the competency hearing.

On April 10, a small improvised courtroom was created in a wing off the Kings County Hospital prison ward, where the judge, lawyers, and psychiatrists convened to begin their inquiry. The gathering settled into the sterile and unpleasant surroundings and an uncomfortable silence fell over the room as a barely conscious George Metesky, strapped to a stainless steel hospital gurney and wearing pajamas, a robe, and a gauze hospital mask over his mouth, was wheeled through the door. His skin appeared almost gray in tone and his breathing was rapid and labored, interrupted only by prolonged spells of fleshy and productive coughing. An oxygen tank dangled from the bottom of the mattress, and a bottle of intravenous fluid hung by his side on one branch of what looked like a rolling metal tree. Those in attendance shifted uneasily in their chairs and exchanged furtive glances until Judge Leibowitz called for attention and finally brought the proceedings to order.

In contrast to Judge Mullen's quarrelsome and controversial hearing, the focus of the Kings County inquiry was entirely non-confrontational and dedicated solely to the determination of the defendant's ability to understand the proceedings and to confer with counsel in his defense as required by the law. James Murray began the proceedings by passing copies of the written Bellevue report to all participants, and he called Dr. LaVerne as his first witness. As a preliminary matter, Murray sought to establish LaVerne as a qualified expert and competent psychiatrist intimately familiar with Metesky's case. As the questioning ensued, however, Judge Leibowitz, sensing an opportunity to level a blunt admonition of Judge Mullen, interjected, "How many reports would you say you have signed for the Court of General Sessions where you have made investigations pursuant to the order of the court, approximately?"

LaVerne turned his eyes upward in contemplation. "I would say two or three thousand."

"How many of those two or three thousand reports have been rejected by the Court of General Sessions . . . ," continued Leibowitz.

"I can't recall a single one at this time."

· · ·

"After a very intensive and careful evaluation," Dr. LaVerne testified, "I have come to the inevitable conclusion that he is suffering from a serious mental disease diagnosed as schizophrenia, paranoid type, severely incapacitating." LaVerne spent the better part of the afternoon illuminating his opinion to Judge Leibowitz, with a description of Metesky's long decent into the world of delusion and psychopathology. He illustrated, event by event, how Metesky's conspiratorial and hyper-suspicious mind touched every aspect of his life until finally his delusional thinking crystallized into a crusade to rid the world of a great evil—Con Ed.

"Doesn't he ever come to a point where he realizes that all his actions are futile . . . ?" asked Leibowitz.

"It is not possible for him to shut off the spigot of fury and hatred. He is so obsessed with this emotion that he cannot control it . . ."

Leibowitz glanced at Metesky and asked, "As the man lies there today, if he were set free, he would be a dangerous man, wouldn't he?

"Undoubtedly."

"A homicidal maniac?" the judge persisted.

"I would say, your Honor, of the thousands of schizophrenics that I have had the opportunity of examining and seen, in my opinion he's one of the most dangerous to society, and one of the most psychotic that I have ever seen."

Leibowitz drew an uneven breath, leaned forward, and massaged his pulsing temples. "Is it your opinion that this man is now mentally capable of understanding the nature of the charge against him and making a defense to that charge?"

"In my opinion," responded LaVerne, "he is not capable of understanding the charge or of making—or of conferring with his attorney for the purpose of conducting his defense."

The judge thought for a moment and said, "In other words, it is your position, doctor, and if I am wrong you say so, that if Mr. Murray was to consult with this man in preparing his defense he would be talking to a crazy man, an insane man?"

"That is correct your Honor . . . In the back of his mind is the feeling that Mr. Murray is aiding and abetting the great conspiracy to frustrate him from exposing Con-Ed."

• • •

In his final volley of letters to the *Journal-American* Metesky had ominously professed, "my days on earth are numbered." As the competency hearing reconvened before Judge Leibowitz in the Kings County Hospital on April 15 after a four-day adjournment, it seemed more than ever that the prediction of the court's ailing ward was nearing fruition. Within fifteen minutes of the start of the hearing, Metesky burst into a spell of uncontrolled coughing. His medical doctors rushed to his side and, noting that the initial flare of scarlet in his cheeks had begun to shade blue, administered an oxygen mask and attempted to calm his shuddering body. Gradually the coughing subsided and Metesky began to settle. "It is my feeling," Dr. LaVerne lamented, "that if these proceedings are prolonged too much longer, it is quite possible that your Honor may have a corpse rather than a defendant upon which to make a decision."

The futility of requiring the defendant's continued presence at the hearing was lost on no one in the room, and Leibowitz suggested that Metesky be returned to the ward for treatment while the inquiry proceeded. "I don't think any purpose will be served by having this desperately ill man being tortured here."

With Metesky out of the room, a frank yet on the record conversation between Dr. LaVerne and Judge Leibowitz ensued regarding Metesky's medical condition. LaVerne was not only a psychiatrist but also a medical doctor of some note and was intimately familiar with his patient's tubercular case. Though Metesky's physical condition was irrelevant to the law on the question of competency, it was, however, practically relevant from the standpoint of logistics. A trial simply could not take place while the defendant was medically unavailable to attend the proceedings. After Dr. LaVerne provided a detailed account of Metesky's medical diagnosis and current condition, Leibowitz cut to the ultimate issue, asking, "What is the prognosis, doctor, in this case?"

LaVerne looked sternly at the judge and without hesitation said," The prognosis in a case of this type, with a history of tuberculosis, with many relapses, with several severe hemorrhages, with the extensive advance of the disease which has occurred in the past several weeks, the prognosis is extremely poor."

"Meaning what?"

"Meaning that this defendant will, in my opinion, die from tuberculosis. It's a question of how and when, whether he will bleed to death or suffocate to death."

The judge sighed and asked, "Can you venture any opinion with any reasonable certainty as to just about how long this man is going to live?"

LaVerne responded with the obligatory "That, your Honor, is a question which no doctor could answer," but when pressed on the issue, he offered, "[H]e doesn't have too much more to go . . . I imagine it is a question of weeks."

. . .

On April 18, 1957, before a crowded Brooklyn courtroom, Judge Leibowitz delivered his opinion as to the competency of George Metesky to stand trial. With the proceedings summoned to order with a rap of the gavel, the assistant district attorney rose and stated as a preliminary matter that his office wished to withdraw any objection to the confirmation of the Bellevue psychiatric report. Leibowitz recognized the action as a signal of unanimity in the decision he was about to convey.

Clamoring news reporters eager to gain their particular angle on the headline of the day furiously scribbled notes upon rustling yellow tablets, and as the judge began to speak, an audible hum of anticipation filled the gallery. "The decision of this Court," began Leibowitz in a quiet yet assured tone, "is based solely on the report of the Bellevue Hospital psychiatrists and the evidence adduced upon the hearings concerning Metesky's mental state at the present time."

He breathed deeply and set his eyes upon the prepared text of the decision.

The court finds as follows:

(1) Metesky is now and has been for many years suffering from the mental illness of schizophrenia of the paranoid type. This disease is progressive and deteriorating in character.

(2) Although Metesky has some superficial awareness of the charges made against him, he nonetheless does not properly comprehend the gravity of the offenses and their true significance.

(3) Metesky is incapable of properly conferring with his lawyer on a lawyer and client basis in the preparation of his defense. Thus by reason of his insanity, he is incapable of making his defense.

Pursuant, therefore, . . . the Court is constrained to commit Metesky to the Matteawan State Hospital for the Criminal Insane, there to remain until he is no longer in such a state of insanity as to be incapable of understanding the charge made against him and making his defense thereto . . .

Judge Leibowitz remained fully aware that, notwithstanding his decision, the New York County Court of General Sessions retained jurisdiction over Metesky and could at any time opt to remove him from Matteawan and put him on trial for his crimes. He accordingly asserted an emotional, albeit indirect, plea to Judge Mullen and District Attorney Hogan, in the hope that Metesky's desperate circumstances would dissuade them from further action in the matter.

"The law does not concern itself, in this proceeding, with the prognosis by the physicians concerning Metesky's tubercular condition," observed Leibowitz. He raised his eyes from the text of his prepared remarks and peered silently into the transfixed assembly as if to emphasize the heartfelt import of his words. "However," he continued, "one would be less than human not to be sympathetically moved by the pitiful condition of this hopelessly incurable man—incurable both mentally and physically. The physicians have told the Court that his days on earth are numbered."

# THE BIRTH OF CRIMINAL PROFILING

DR. JAMES BRUSSEL AND HIS NOVEL FORM OF CRIME PSYCHIATRY HAD begun a meteoric rise to mythical status from nearly the moment of Metesky's arrest. Though his psychological profile of the Mad Bomber played little if any direct role in the actual apprehension of the man, the approach had been widely publicized and heavily touted as a successful and innovative new tool available to law enforcement. In February 1957, *Newsweek* magazine described Brussel's image of the Bomber as "amazingly accurate" in a piece titled "Proven Profile," and shortly after Metesky's arrest, the *New York Times* stated that the authorities "had not done badly in getting a theoretical portrait of the man they were seeking." Brussel himself quickly became a public sensation. He granted a deluge of interview requests from nationally syndicated radio, television, and newspapers outlets, and in each instance was quick to point out that George Metesky did, in fact, fit the description that he had so aptly provided to police prior to the arrest. Brussel reveled in the notoriety, offering incisive opinions regarding the origin of Metesky's disorder, and, though he had never actually met and examined the man, he had little hesitation in labeling his condition a "textbook case of paranoia."

As for the police department itself, the validity and usefulness of Dr. Brussel's profile depended wholly upon who was asked. Captain Howard Finney and those of a similar mind-set in the technical divisions and scientific laboratories of the department regarded Dr. Brussel's work in high esteem, while the rank and file "boots-on-the-ground" bomb squad detectives had little use for what they viewed as the arrogant and theoretical world of psychiatry. Detective William Schmitt, one of the skeptical plain-clothes officers present on the afternoon of Brussel's famous postulation, maintained that the "word picture" that miraculously developed before his eyes "could fit anyone in the world." He had little regard for Brussel or the other "scientific types," who weren't involved in the day-to-day dangers of crime fighting and he doubted whether any unproven psychiatric method could ever assist in the apprehension of unknown criminals.

It is perhaps difficult to assess the accuracy and usefulness of Dr. Brussel's profile in the Mad Bomber case. Attributes and predictions regarding the Bomber had been offered and publicized by so many different police technicians, psychiatrists, and newspapers that the actual content of Brussel's specific profile is rather allusive. Brussel himself had been accused of placing a somewhat sanitized version of the profile in his memoir, omitting, it was argued, certain predictions that would later prove to be inaccurate. Indeed, some of the publicized character portraits of the Bomber at the time suggested that he would have a facial scar and others opined that he was of German extraction, and though Brussel would later be criticized for these inaccuracies, there is little evidence that his actual profile contained either of those items. In point of fact the only publicized accounts of the profile during the search for the Mad Bomber and just beyond that specifically named Dr. Brussel as the author made no mention of a facial scar or of the culprit being of German descent.

To be sure, several of the characteristics uncontrovertibly formulated by Dr. Brussel fell short of accuracy. His profile had predicted that the Bomber would be a high school graduate, between forty and fifty years of age, living in Bridgeport, Connecticut, and suffering from heart disease. Though each of these items was close to the descriptive mark, Metesky was in actuality a high school dropout, age fifty-three at the time of his arrest, living in Waterbury, and suffering from tuberculosis. And regarding Brussel's astounding prediction that the Bomber would be attired in a buttoned double-breasted suit at time of apprehension, his critics would point out that Metesky was, in fact, wearing pajamas when police knocked at his door—at midnight. In summarizing the criticism of Dr. Brussel's conclusions, Malcolm Gladwell wrote in his 2007 *New Yorker* essay "Dangerous Minds," "A profile isn't a test, where you pass if you get most of the answers right. It's a portrait, and all the details have to cohere in some way if the image is to be helpful."

Despite the critical commentary, as a whole, Dr. Brussel's Mad Bomber profile was viewed as a remarkable success and was greeted with broad praise. His work on the case was recognized as the first formal application of psychiatric principles to crime scene investigation in the United States, and would gain wide acceptance as an innovative milestone in the creation of a new crime-fighting medium. In some circles Dr. Brussel would come to be known quite simply as the founding father of criminal profiling.

In the years following the arrest of the Bomber, Brussel would be called upon by various law enforcement agencies to duplicate his astounding profiling method. In April 1964 the assistant attorney general of Massachusetts, who was at the time caught in the throes of an exasperatingly fruitless Boston Strangler investigation, sought out and met with the New York psychiatrist and nervously asked, "I hope you can do your Mad Bomber trick for us here, Dr. Brussel." Participating in a committee of mental health professionals who were actively engaged in the investigation, Brussel would take the minority position that the Strangler was in fact a sole perpetrator, an opinion that would be borne out as fact with the ultimate arrest of Albert DeSalvo.

In 1968 Brussel reached the pinnacle of his notoriety with the publication of his memoir, *Casebook of a Crime Psychiatrist.* In the book, he highlighted his work on various high-profile cases, including that of the Mad Bomber, the Boston Strangler, and several others that had confounded police for years, and he expounded upon his "private blend of science, intuition, and hope" that would become the basis of modern criminal profiling. Portions of the book were syndicated in newspapers throughout the country, and soon others were taking notice of Dr. Brussel's innovative methods. *Casebook of a Crime Psychiatrist* would shine the light of awareness and credibility upon this new combination of psychology and law enforcement and become, according to one former acting director of the FBI, "the first crude manual in criminal profiling for police use."

In March 1969, Dr. Brussel's book received an avalanche of publicity from an unexpected source. *Casebook* had been out for less than a year when Sirhan Sirhan was placed on trial in Los Angeles for the murder of Robert Kennedy. As the courtroom drama unfolded, daily reports of the testimony dominated media outlets and detailed accounts of the prosecution and defense themes were revealed and analyzed by laymen and law enforcement at every level. As part of the defense strategy that Sirhan was functioning under a diminished mental capacity at the time of the murder, a California psychiatrist named Martin M. Schorr was called upon to interview and examine Sirhan and offer a professional opinion based upon his findings. Schorr testified that Sirhan suffered from paranoid schizophrenia stemming, in part, from his relationship with his father, and the defense offered as evidence a report that Schorr had prepared in support of his conclusions. Portions of Schorr's report, however, contained extensive and verbatim quotes from *Casebook of a Crime Psychiatrist* regarding Brussel's similar analysis of the Mad Bomber. The problem was that Schorr adapted Brussel's language to his own analysis of Sirhan but used no quotation marks and made no effort to attribute his statements to the true author. "I am not the best writer in the world," testified Dr. Schorr in a grueling cross-examination. "He tells his story in vivid, illustrative language. It's an exciting kind of writing and he is an exciting author." Needless to say, Schorr's overall testimony was discredited by his attempt to elucidate his own report with the unauthorized words of another. Though Brussel contemplated legal action for plagiarism, Schorr's blunder would provide *Casebook* with the literary approbation that few other sources could.

. . .

The technique of modern criminal profiling would undergo its evolutionary development in an FBI Academy lecture course titled "Applied Criminology" that was taught and developed beginning in 1970 by Special Agent Howard Teten. A good-natured and intellectually oriented criminologist who would come to be known as "the Gentle Titan" among his colleagues for both his physical and professional stature, Teten had developed his own method of crime scene analysis in the early 1960s as an officer at the San Leandro Police Department in California. Upon joining the FBI and ultimately becoming an academy training instructor, Teten was provided the opportunity to refine his theories and soon began testing his approach on a variety of solved and eventually unsolved cases. As word of Teten's work and mounting successes spread, his course was expanded and soon he took on a partner, a special agent from New York named Pat Mullany, whose credentials included an advanced degree in psychology as well as classroom experience. Teten himself would later acquire several advanced degrees and complete the coursework for a PhD in criminal justice, but in the early 1970s the team taught and applied their newly developed profiling concepts to FBI agents and law enforcement officers across the country. When the FBI opened its new academy in Quantico, Virginia, in 1972, Teten and Mullany were invited as instructors to the groundbreaking Behavioral Science Unit (BSU), which was dedicated to bringing the science of psychology to the study of criminal behavior, and their national reputation for breathing life into unsolved cases steadily grew.

In 1973 Teten became aware of Dr. Brussel's memoirs and, recognizing his pioneering contribution to the discipline of profiling, sought him out in an effort to compare and contrast methodologies. In a series of meetings in Brussel's Manhattan apartment the two men cordially and intellectually debated the focal points of both approaches and examined the pros and cons of each. Teten would later write:

He was a wonderful old gentleman and certainly experienced in his brand of profiling . . . I was so impressed I asked if he would teach me his technique. I said that I would be happy to pay whatever he charged. His reply was that neither I nor the FBI could afford his charges, and since it was against his policy to offer reduced rates, he would have to donate his time. I . . . learned a great deal, but I disagreed with some of the assumptions contained in his approach.

Teten recognized that Dr. Brussel's method of profiling relied heavily upon Freudian principles and ethnic preferences to analyze specific crime scene elements and to combine these with his findings to form a psychological impression of an offender. "In what might be termed a three tier approach," wrote Dr. Teten,

Dr. Brussel first focused on those parts of the crime scene which may contain psychologically relevant data. Upon identifying those parts, he then examined each one individually for their possible meaning and impact. Once this was accomplished, he combined the information derived from each part to form a detailed profile of the offender's mental state at the time of the crime.

Dr. Brussel had an exhaustive, almost encyclopedic knowledge of the manner in which the characteristics of mentally abnormal people affected their behavior. Using this knowledge, he identified the various mental abnormalities observed in terms of known mental disorders. This approach enabled Dr. Brussel to not only identify any major mental disorder affecting the perpetrator, but also to visualize any secondary disorder contributing to or modifying his or her behavior. He then developed detailed profiles of the perpetrators and their lifestyles using the common characteristics and behaviors associated with the mental disorders identified.

Though Brussel employed what Dr. Teten admitted was a "comprehensive and probing level of analysis," there were fundamental differences in the way the two men approached the issue. Unlike Dr. Brussel, Teten did not believe, for the most part, that Freudian theory could readily produce consistently reliable data as to an offender's psychological tendencies. Further, he felt that Brussel's methods were overly dependent upon an uncontaminated crime scene—an assumption that could not be universally made with confidence. Finally, Teten believed that ethnicity could not be relied upon as an accurate indicator of weapons choice or criminal behavior. Though the two men generally agreed that Brussel's approach was the more comprehensive and discriminating of the two, they recognized that it also had the greater likelihood of leading to biased or erroneous results. Conversely, Teten's approach, while less capable of producing specific and usable data, was less subject to bias and misinterpretation. "I would much rather offer only general information that is accurate, than a detailed but possibly misleading profile," wrote Dr. Teten.

Though they would agree to disagree on methodology, Teten studied the basic principles of Dr. Brussel's work, contrasted them with his own, and used them in his lecture course at the BSU in Quantico as a historic example of a successful profile. In the years that followed, he would team with and inspire other law enforcement professionals such as Roger Depue, Robert Ressler, Dick Ault, and John Douglas, each of whom would contribute to the expansion of the FBI training program and the development of criminal profiling as a practiced law enforcement technique.

The pioneering work of Howard Teten as revealed in the classrooms and laboratories of the BSU has been immortalized in recent years in books and motion pictures such as *The Alienist*, *The Silence of the Lambs*, and *Kiss the Girls*. Strange and eerie accounts of unsolved crimes and ingenious methods of profiling continue to fascinate the public and provide entertainment through the annals of real-life mystery. It was, however, the inventive achievement of Dr. James Brussel that provided the critical turning point—the magical coming of age moment—that would lend awareness and credibility to this fledgling and untried technical process. What began in the winter of 1956 as the impulsive postulates of a Manhattan psychiatrist born of the frustration of an overtaxed and fatigued police department, would become, through the efforts and research of an innovative progeny, a scientifically recognized and generally respected law enforcement tool.

"He was an innovator," wrote Howard Teten regarding Dr. Brussel. "[A]n individualist who was not content with the status quo, choosing instead to seek new approaches and methods in his dedication to the betterment of man—and he found a way to fulfill that dream. Who could ask for an opportunity to do or accomplish more?"

# RIGHT FROM WRONG

During Judge Leibowitz's open-court ruling that Metesky was psychologically unfit to stand trial, he had accurately explained that, according to New York law, Kings County would retain jurisdiction over the case even during Metesky's period of commitment at Matteawan State Hospital. Accordingly, if, in the opinion of the Matteawan psychiatrists, Metesky ever regained his sanity, he could be brought back to court and tried for his crimes. Leibowitz had contrasted the situation with a ruling of not guilty by reason of insanity after an actual trial on the merits, in which case a defendant would be similarly committed but could be released if found sane rather than sent back to the courts for trial.

Noting the similar retention of jurisdiction in New York County, Judge Leibowitz used the occasion of his ruling to blast the legislature in allowing the anomalous situation of two courts in neighboring counties to arrive at separate and inconsistent judgments as to competency to stand trial. His conflict with Judge Mullen had proven frustrating and fruitless and, despite his order of commitment, remained largely unresolved. "To the layman and the lawyer alike this seems indefensible on the basis of just plain common sense," lectured Judge Liebowitz.

Though Metesky had not stood trial and therefore had never formally asserted the insanity defense, the proceedings to test his competency delved into many of the same general issues and principles and elements of proof that such a defense would normally have examined.

The high-profile case against Metesky would, accordingly, focus the spotlight of controversy upon the insanity defense in New York and become a springboard for change in the system.

At the time, insanity laws in the United States were undergoing a period of flux and instability. By the mid 1950s, the McNaughton rule, the long-standing law in New York and in most other jurisdictions that excused a defendant from criminal responsibility if he did not know the nature and quality of the act or that the act itself was wrong, was under attack by judges and many state legislatures. In some states the rule had been abandoned in favor of the Irresistible Impulse rule, which stated that even if the defendant cognitively understood the difference between right and wrong, he would nonetheless be excused if mental disease had caused him to lose the power to choose between right and wrong. And in 1954 the United States Court of Appeals expanded both rules in the famous *Durham* case, which held that "an accused is not criminally responsible if his unlawful act was the product of mental disease or mental defect."

Using the bully pulpit of his high-profile ruling in the Metesky case, Judge Leibowitz admonished the New York legislature to adopt changes in current insanity laws to bring the state into accord with modern advances of scientific knowledge. "I trust that the State of New York will not remain in the tail end of the procession and cling to the McNaughton rule that was born back in the middle of the last century, when little or nothing was known about psychiatry." To bolster his sermon on the issue, Leibowitz called upon Dr. LaVerne to expound upon the need for legislative changes in the realm of insanity as a legal defense. In a prearranged complement to Leibowitz's ruling, the judge garrulously congratulated LaVerne as "a fine example of what a psychiatrist should be," and invited him to step forward before the bar to offer whatever recommendations he may have on the issue.

"Metesky may have had a delusional mission which compelled him to explode bombs in order to arouse public interest," began LaVerne, "but unwittingly he has performed a useful mission to society in focusing the spot-light upon a dire need of reform in legislation." The doctor provided a brief history of the laws of insanity and cautioned that the current standards originated at a time when psychiatry was in its infancy and little was known of the workings of the human mind. With clinical advances in the field, and recognition of psychiatry as a credible adjunct of medicine, LaVerne stated that it was time for the law to catch up to the science. "The Metesky case poses a challenge in that it will expose the entire field of law . . . to a thorough re-evaluation. The present laws of our state that determine the question of sanity are cumbersome, obsolete, time-consuming, costly and may even harm an already mentally ill defendant."

Criticism of New York's statutory version of the McNaughton rule had actually begun shortly after its initial enactment in 1879 and reached a crescendo shortly after the Metesky case. Essentially, it was the dichotomy between medical insanity and legal insanity that drove the effort toward legislative reform. Modern psychiatry had shown that an individual could possess the requisite mental faculties to be aware of the nature and quality of his acts and to know that they are wrong, while at the same time suffer from a psychiatric disorder that removed the normal powers of self-restraint. Stated another way, one could technically know what he was doing yet still be utterly unable to stop it. The law, it was argued, did not account for this anomaly.

In October 1957, no doubt inspired in part by the controversy of the Metesky case, the first practical step in the reconsideration of New York's insanity laws took place in the form of a conference sponsored by the State Department of Mental Hygiene with the cooperation of the Governor's Council. In support of the reform effort, Governor Harriman stated at the conference:

Application of [the McNaughton Rule] results in the law treating an individual as sane even though he may suffer

from mental defects which affect his otherwise rational activities . . . At present, criminal trials in which a
defense of insanity is raised are marked by a conflict
in testimony between psychiatrists who rely on the one
hand on the McNaughton rule and on the other upon the
standards set by medical and psychiatric science.

In the coming years specific proposals for legislative change were
sponsored, and several advanced through committee and even to a
vote of the New York Assembly, but each time the political sensitivity
of the issue resulted in either withdrawal of the bill or outright rejection. Finally, in 1965, after consultation with the District Attorney's
Association, New York prosecutors, and prominent psychiatrists, a
revision to the arcane McNaughton rule was proposed that seemed
palatable to the critics. Though most supporters of reform had advo-
cated adoption of a more liberal approach to the problem—a defense
based upon the inability to conform one's conduct to the requirements of the law—a compromise position was agreed upon and a
newly revised standard for insanity in New York criminal cases was
adopted by the state legislature.

With the enactment of section 30.05 of the New York Penal Law,
the originally codified McNaughton rule was amended to prevent criminal responsibility for one's conduct "if at the time of such conduct, as a
result of mental disease or defect, he lacks *substantial capacity* to know
or appreciate either: (a) the nature and consequences of such conduct;
or (b) that such conduct was wrong." The intent and effect of the new
statutory provision was to relax the stringent requirements of the old rule
and to allow the defense of insanity even when the defendant possessed
some rudimentary understanding of the nature and quality of his act
or that such act was indeed wrong. Though the statute was amended in
1984 to shift the burden of proof to the accused, the legal standard by
which insanity was determined in New York remains to this day. The

impassioned pleas of Judge Leibowitz and Dr. LaVerne had added to the chorus of change that would affect perhaps the most controversial issue in American criminal law.

As George Metesky lay helplessly in the tuberculosis ward of Matteawan State Hospital fighting for his life, however, he knew little of the dramatic changes in law, politics, and psychiatry his case would one day help to inspire.

He cared only for each struggling breath that he drew.

# MATTEAWAN

IF BELLEVUE WAS THE MENTAL HEALTH EQUIVALENT OF PURGATORY, Matteawan State Hospital stood as the hopeless embodiment of the blazing abyss itself. Behind the confused sprawl of interconnected redbrick chambers, the dazed and tormented souls that populated the human "storage bin" that was Matteawan endlessly roamed sterile corridors lacking purpose, lacking hope. The physical structure stood as a gloomy metaphor for insanity. Jutting dormers and stilted bastions formed the uneven roofline of each segmented wing of the complex and hauntingly coalesced into a taller main structure, the central focus of which was an extended crowned vertex lined with steel-barred windows. The foreboding arched entryway at the base of the main building might just as well have borne Dante's ominous inscription to the gates of hell, "Abandon hope, all ye who enter here."

Prior to the age of reform that would give birth to institutionalized care for the mentally ill, horrific as many of those institutions may have been, the diagnosed insane were treated as criminals and were subject to torturous "treatments" typically aimed at exorcising evil spirits deemed to be at the root of the deviant behavior. Indeed, prior to the mid-nineteenth century little distinction had been drawn in New York between the criminally insane and the less dangerous non-criminal element suffering from mental illness. Both were universally and jointly treated in the New York State Lunatic Asylum in Utica—the first state hospital in New York.

As enlightened thought crept into the world of psychopathology, however, it became readily apparent to mental health professionals that integration of the two distinct populations presented dramatic and unjust dangers to the civilly, as opposed to criminally, committed patients. In 1855 the New York Legislature, in recognition of these dangers, moved to segregate criminally insane inmates to institutions falling under the jurisdiction of the Department of Correction, and in 1859 the first State Lunatic Asylum for Insane Convicts was opened on the grounds of Auburn Prison. Those "twice cursed" with the stigma of mental illness and criminality would now be housed in hybrid institutions that would come to be known as "mental prisons."

As the asylum at Auburn gradually reached capacity and then became overcrowded, legislative appropriation was made for a larger, more accessible facility in Beacon, New York. The nine-hundred-acre estate of John J. Scanlon, a locally famous race horse owner, was purchased and in 1892 the newly constructed, 450-bed asylum for insane criminals at Matteawan was unveiled among the placid backdrop of the Fishkill Mountains.

The stated purpose of Matteawan was to provide for the "isolation of dangerous and vicious patients." According to one New York judge later reviewing an application for commitment to Matteawan, the internment function of the institution "gives primacy to the problems of security and custody and little or no recognition to the need of the patient for care and treatment."

Through the years, the emphasis on mere confinement of the criminally insane, as opposed to recovery, would inevitably lead to allegations of maltreatment and abuse. Sadistic beatings and involuntary medication at the hands of unqualified and unlicensed staff would send a lifeless and tormented population into a vortex of physical and psychological hardship. Unlike the more benign conditions of the civil institutions operated by the Department of Mental Hygiene, the close confinement, inadequate staffing, and poorly equipped facilities of Matteawan regularly deprived patients of opportunities for treatments and therapies sorely demanded by their pathetic psychological circumstances. The dangers, restraints, and poor conditions to which the criminally insane were routinely exposed extended far beyond what they would endure even at some of New York's harshest prisons. Grievous overcrowding and a gravely distressed atmosphere would contribute to a general environment of indignity and frustration that, according to one observer, would make Matteawan "a place more likely to drive men mad than to cure the insane."

Into this hopeless and malevolent environment entered a legislative dereliction that often made commitment to Matteawan tantamount to a life sentence. Denied any effective therapeutic measures, patients often remained on the wards of the institution for years without care or improvement, and the self-fulfilling prophecy of prolonged hospitalization kept them sick. Until the mid-1960s, when reform would take hold, state hospitals for the criminally insane operated under a loose regulatory scheme that permitted the superintendent and internal staff of each institution to arbitrarily decide on the fate of each patient. Without the constitutional safeguards of due process that would eventually penetrate the system, patients were left to flounder on the stark wards of Matteawan and other state hospitals with little possibility of recovery or release. In 1965, prior to the introduction of reform measures, 703 patients of Matteawan had been confined for at least ten years, 306 for at least twenty years, 119 for at least thirty years, 29 for at least forty years, 4 for at least fifty years, and 1 for an astonishing sixty-four years. Many of these forgotten souls had become, in the words of one judge, "marooned and forsaken."

As the sallow and haggard George Metesky was wheeled into the tuberculosis ward of Matteawan State Hospital in the early spring of 1957, it appeared unlikely that he would survive long enough to add to the facility's grim longevity statistics.

. . .

Despite the abysmal record of treatment of the psychological needs of its residents, Matteawan ironically fared well in the physical care of its medically ill patients. With the development of modern multi-drug therapies for tuberculosis, many afflicted with the condition were stabilized and often improved at the facility and on hospital wards across the country. Though Metesky was administered the appropriate therapeutic remedies at Matteawan for his grave illness, it initially appeared that any recovery was in doubt. He had lost more than twenty pounds and remained confined to bed, struggling for every breath and suffering from fevers and night sweats.

In the months following his arrival, the New York County district attorney's office hovered like a vulture, repeatedly writing to the superintendent of the facility inquiring as to the condition of their indicted defendant, and in each case the prosecutor was informed that Metesky continued to suffer the debilitative effects of the disease and remained on the tuberculosis ward of the hospital, receiving treatment. As the months passed, however, though the doctors had predicted an imminent death, Metesky's physical condition gradually began to stabilize, and by December 1958 he had even begun to shown signs of improvement. The Matteawan staff was quick to point out, however, that his psychological condition had shown no signs of change, and soon the letters from New York County trickled to a halt. A prosecution of George Metesky, it seemed, would depend on the whims of a mental health system slow to relinquish its own.

· · ·

As Metesky began his slow convalescence, word came from Albany that the state Workmen's Compensation Board had rejected Bart O'Rourke's bid to reopen his client's original claim for benefits. In rejecting the appeal the board stated that no conclusive proof had been offered to show that Metesky was mentally incompetent at the time of his 1931 accident at Hell Gate, and thus there had been no excuse for the late filing of claim. Following his mandate from the *Journal-American*, O'Rourke filed an appeal of the decision with the Appellate Division of the New York Supreme Court, but on December 4, 1958, the court sided with the board and once again firmly and irrevocably denied the claim.

The life work—the vast crusade of George Metesky—had finally come to an end.

. . .

At Matteawan the Mad Bomber seemed to be anything but. By 1961 his tubercular condition had fallen into remission, and he was transferred to a psychiatric ward of the hospital. He associated with few and was, by most accounts, a model inmate who troubled neither the staff nor the inmate population. He received no treatment, medication, or therapy of any kind relating to his adjudicated mental illness, and he was, subject to the limits of his broad confinement, left to his own devices for activity and recreation. For the most part he passed his hours calmly reading books, writing in his tablet, and listening placidly to radio programs that he eagerly anticipated throughout the day.

As Metesky's health improved, however, his anger and bitterness once again began to brew. While on the tuberculosis ward he had witnessed an inmate named Paul Simulick being repeatedly beaten by two night shift guards, and he quickly developed a deep resentment for the staff of Matteawan and the institution itself. "They used to take him out around midnight and beat him up," wrote Metesky. "They would do this almost every night. It terrorized the other patients . . . Six months after I got off [the tuberculosis ward], Paul died. He just couldn't take it anymore."

By 1962, fueled by the horrors of Matteawan, Metesky was back to his old cantankerous ways. He began an angry letter-writing campaign to anyone who would listen regarding the horrid conditions at the institution and the poor treatment of its patients. Rambling dispatches began arriving at the desks of New York judges, including that of Judge Leibowitz and others, in which Metesky complained bitterly about Matteawan itself and the process by which he found himself confined there. He accused James Murray and Harry Spellman of bungling his case and stealing his money, and he claimed that they purposely engineered and contrived his insanity so as to relieve him of his assets. "I became fully convinced that I was betrayed and abandoned by my attorneys," wrote Metesky in one letter.

Soon, like so many others on the wards of Matteawan, he began to protest his continued institutionalization at the facility, and in November 1963, just two days after the assassination of President John F. Kennedy, Metesky sent a confused and irate letter to New York County District Attorney Frank Hogan demanding that he, Metesky, either be put on trial for his crimes or that all charges against him be dropped. The slow or nonexistent responses to his letters only served to further infuriate him and instigated what would become the new crusade in George Metesky's life—a bid to personally secure his release from Matteawan.

For the next ten years Metesky dedicated nearly every waking hour to the complicated and thorny legal questions surrounding the confinement of the criminally insane. He educated himself as to the constitutional issues of his case and he meticulously researched and hand-drafted a storm of legal documents designed to gain a new hearing as to his sanity and to eventually advance his case to trial in New York and Kings County. "So many injustices have been done to me," Metesky told a Matteawan psychiatrist. "[T]hat is why I want to go to court, to straighten them out, and to question all these people. I was never mentally ill, but I was sent to a mental institution. All this was concocted and contrived."

In January 1964 Metesky brought a petition to the Supreme Court of New York in Dutchess County for a writ of habeas corpus. His statement alleged that his civil rights had been violated by his imprisonment at Matteawan, and it requested that he be discharged from the facility in order to face trial on the criminal charges pending against him. At a short hearing held a month later before a county judge behind the walls of Matteawan, Metesky testified, "I made this application in order to tell the Court that I am sane, that I understand the nature of my charges, and that I am able to confer with counsel." Upon the perfunctory statement of a state psychiatrist that Metesky remained in a mentally impaired condition, unable to assist in any defense, however, the petition was summarily dismissed.

Angry and undeterred, Metesky immediately drew and filed a carefully handwritten appeal of the dismissal with an accompanying brief to the Appellate Division of the New York Supreme Court, alleging that he was denied a hearing in the true sense of the word since he was not permitted to cross-examine the psychiatrist who testified against him. Two years later, a five-judge panel of the Appellate Court unanimously agreed. The dismissal of Metesky's habeas corpus petition was reversed and the matter was sent back to the county court for a further hearing as to his competency to stand trial.

On December 15, 1966, Metesky, now represented by an attorney familiar with the perilous landscape of Matteawan, was provided his long-awaited hearing in a Poughkeepsie, New York, courtroom. In an often contentious examination, several Matteawan psychiatrists testified that their patient had exhibited no perceptible psychological improvement since 1957, when he was originally committed to the institution. When asked to describe some of the symptoms still displayed by Metesky, one of the witnesses stated, "Inappropriate emotional reaction, expressed delusional ideas. Illogical thinking. Misrepresentation of real occurrences. Impaired judgment and lack of insight. I may add, grandiosity, autistic thinking. Suspiciousness. Distrust." When another psychiatrist was asked whether Metesky appreciated the possibility of his losing should he be released from the hospital and advanced to trial, he informed the court, "He doesn't pay much attention to the charges. That's [not] what's important. The importance is to bring out to this Court injustices, and that's what I feel would also prevent him from really defending himself and discussing with his counsel." According to the Matteawan psychiatrists, Metesky was still looking for a forum to expose his old nemesis, Con Ed.

Despite lucid and coherent testimony from Metesky himself at the hearing that he had personally and independently navigated the intricate waters of a habeas corpus petition and the even more complex matter of an appeal from its denial, two months later, the Dutchess County judge again dismissed the petition. "In our opinion," wrote the court, "[Metesky] has failed to establish that he possesses the requisite appreciation of the nature of the crimes with which he is charged. We further hold that he remains incapable of adequately assisting and contributing to [his] defense."

Now sixty-three years old, George Metesky was once again remanded to the custody of Matteawan State Hospital "for further care and treatment." Though never brought to trial or convicted on any criminal charge, it seemed that he was destined to remain institutionalized for the rest of his life.

• • •

Beginning in the mid-1960s a wave of court decisions, some from the United States Supreme Court itself, swept through the area of mental health and confinement. An enlightened age of reform began to ascend and a recognition of the constitutional rights of the accused—even those committed and long forgotten in state mental institutions—emerged. With specific regard to Matteawan and other similar institutions operated under the control of the Department of Corrections, a series of cases from 1966 through the end of that decade established that the criminally insane who were subjected to the harsh confinement of so called "mental prisons" were entitled to the same procedural rights and safeguards as those provided to civilly committed non-criminals. "We have, thankfully, come a long way from the days when ignorance induced fear of the mentally ill," wrote federal circuit judge Irving R. Kaufman in 1969. "As great strides in psychiatric knowledge have been paralleled by evolving concepts of due process, humane procedures for the commitment and treatment of the mentally ill have replaced snake pits and witch hunts."

Buttressed by these and other court decisions that recognized the limitations of state-run facilities to indefinitely intern the criminally insane without the provision of certain procedural safeguards, George Metesky once again took on the system—this time in an all-out effort to gain his freedom. In November 1970, Metesky personally and without the benefit of counsel filed a petition with the Supreme Court of New York in New

York County against District Attorney Frank Hogan, seeking a dismissal of the pending 1957 indictment against him. In a long and often incoherent handwritten plea, Metesky again berated his lawyers, Matteawan, and the entire court system for his mistreatment and unjust confinement. He accused the district attorney of perpetuating "a tacit working agreement with Matteawan" to keep its patients perpetually institutionalized, and he accused the facility's psychiatrists of being insane themselves. Arguing that he possessed the "sanity, intelligence and fortitude" to fight the charges against him, but noting that New York County had made no attempt to bring him to trial in the thirteen years since his indictment, Metesky stated that "elemental decency" required the dismissal of the charges. In essence, he attempted to force the prosecutor's hand.

The district attorney's office filed an opposition statement claiming that it was Metesky's own incompetence to stand trial that prevented them from logically proceeding on the indictment, and in reliance the court quickly denied Metesky's petition. Metesky promptly filed a supplement to his petition that claimed that District Attorney Hogan had engaged in forgery of documents and other unspecified criminal acts. Again, he implored the judge to dismiss the indictment against him. "The laws are explicit," scolded Metesky. "[A]ll that is needed—is honest enforcement." When the supplement was ignored by the court, Metesky again brought the matter to the attention of the Appellate Division, which this time refused to hear the matter.

In the coming months Metesky continued his legal battles against Matteawan, Frank Hogan, and the entire New York penal system with a flurry of claims and petitions, filed in the Federal District Court. In each of these cases he spewed his angry and conspiratorial diatribe in letters and pleadings that, for the most part, accomplished nothing in the way of persuasive factual or legal argument. Institutionalized and clearly unrecovered, Metesky, now sixty-eight years old, seemed to be floundering in a sea of legal frustration and ill will, while moving not one step closer to freedom.

. . .

In the winter of 1971 the cause of George Metesky and nearly five hundred other indicted but never tried inmates of Matteawan State Hospital drew the attention of a young and idealistic lawyer by the name of Kristin Booth Glen. For several years Glen had eyed New York's statutory scheme of institutionalized detention of the criminally insane with skepticism and concern. She researched the conditions at Matteawan and waited for the right opportunity to challenge what she viewed as an unconstitutionally applied system of confinement. Working with the progressive minded law firm of Rabinowitz, Boudin & Standard in association with the National Lawyers Guild and the Bill of Rights Foundation, both left-leaning civil rights advocacy organizations, Glen recognized that in George Metesky and others like him at Matteawan she had found the appropriate representatives to challenge the system.

In a class action suit filed in the Federal District Court in New York City, Glen, buttressed by lawyers from the American Civil Liberties Union, argued that the New York statutes allowing Metesky and the other similarly situated inmates to be confined at the whim of the institution without the right to a jury trial on the question of whether they were in fact dangerous amounted to a violation of the equal protection clause of the United States Constitution. The case would be the first step in a journey that would ultimately change the face of mental health facilities in New York and beyond.

. . .

Shortly after the filing of the federal class action, the director of Matteawan, in a separate and unrelated but legally required exercise, filed a notice with the Supreme Court of New York in Kings County stating that, though Metesky had been incarcerated at the facility for nearly fifteen years, he intended to retain custody of Metesky as a "dangerous incapacitated person" as that classification was defined under newly enacted and applicable New York statutes. Under the new law, which was designed to provide some measure of procedural safeguard to institutionalized inmates, Metesky was given ten days to file a request for a hearing before a judge on the issues raised in the notice. The filing would set into motion a flurry of legal activity that would go to the very essence of Matteawan's system of retention.

Immediately, Metesky responded with a ten-page, bold-lettered seething denunciation of Matteawan and its staff. "AS THE COURT WELL KNOWS," wrote Metesky, "MATTEAWAN STATE HOSP-TIAL WHICH IS UNIVERSALLY DAMMED—NEVER PRAISED BY ANY FAIR-MINDED JUDGE, HAS NO REASON FOR ITS HYPOCRITICAL EXISTENCE." As to the merits of the actual notice, Metesky responded, "I AM FULLY COMPETENT TO STAND TRIAL AND HAVE BEEN COMPETENT TO DO SO FOR YEARS. I HAVE BEEN PREVENTED FROM ESTABLISHING MY SAN-ITY THROUGH THE USE OF CRIMINAL AND UNCONSTITU-TIONAL MEANS . . . I DISPUTE DR. JOHNSTON'S CLAIM TO BEING A DANGEROUS INCAPACITATED PERSON AND ASK . . . THAT A JURY TRIAL BE GIVEN ME ON THIS MATTER." Metesky's document, rambling and accusatory as it was, satisfied the min-imum requirements for a judicial hearing on whether or not he was, in fact, a "dangerous incapacitated person," and on January 25 a New York Supreme Court judge ordered that Metesky be transferred to the Kings County Hospital for the purpose of a future hearing on this issue within the court's jurisdiction.

. . .

On April 14, 1972, word came from the Federal District Court that a three-judge panel led by Judge Morris Lasker had ruled in favor of Metesky and the other class action plaintiffs. The Matteawan scheme of perpetu-ally retaining its inmates without first obtaining a jury finding of danger-ousness had come to an end. It was cause for jubilation for Metesky and his attorneys, but freedom was still a distant and fleeting hope. A jury pronouncement that an inmate was not dangerous, as defined by the statute, would simply allow a transfer to a civil institution under the auspices of the Department of Mental Hygiene. Though the prospects for treatment and recovery were greatly enhanced at such a facility, it was far from the finding of competence that would then be required as a prerequisite to freedom. Metesky's legal battles, it seemed, were only just beginning.

• • •

Matteawan was hesitant to relinquish the control that it had wielded for so many years. As the legal focus shifted from the federal courts back to the state courts of New York, the institutional directors together with the Kings County prosecutors opposed every effort in Metesky's bid for due process. As the hearing on Matteawan's bid for continued retention approached, and aware of the new safeguards imposed by the federal court, a new local attorney was assigned to act on Metesky's behalf. Capable and learned in the law, Irving Engel of Brooklyn was well known and respected in the criminal court system of New York. Though court appointed and meagerly compensated, Engel valiantly came to the aid of his new client and prepared a cogent and persuasive argument against Matteawan's claim that Metesky was a dangerous incapacitated person.

On June 19, 1972, Engel appeared before Justice Beatrice Judge in a closed Brooklyn courtroom accompanied by a newly invigorated and vibrant-looking George Metesky. In an eloquent appeal designed to free his client from the dismal confines of Matteawan, Engel produced evidence of a competent and intelligent man, plainly capable of conferring with his lawyer and assisting in his defense. Though considerate of the attorney's presentation, the counter-testimony of Matteawan's psychiatrists as to their daily observations of Metesky's behavior was, in the end, overwhelmingly persuasive. Like so many other jurists in her position, Justice Judge once again concluded that Metesky was, indeed, a dangerous incapacitated person, and she recommitted him to the custody of the

Department of Correction. Visibly disappointed by the ruling, Metesky cast his eyes downward as he was led out of the courtroom to the awaiting van bound again for Matteawan.

Two weeks later, Engel filed a motion with the court seeking the jury trial that had been promised by the groundbreaking federal court decision in his client's favor. In the legal brief filed with the motion, Engel eloquently wrote, "The defendant, George P. Metesky, who is presumed innocent under our laws although under indictment, has languished in a correctional institution for the mentally insane for the past 15½ years and his constitutional rights should be treated with extreme caution." The Kings County judge agreed. A jury trial on the issue of whether George Metesky was dangerous as defined by the law was finally ordered, and on January 25, 1973, Metesky was once again transported to Kings County Hospital for further proceedings.

He would never return to Matteawan State Hospital.

. . .

On May 29, 1973, the United States Supreme Court unanimously and summarily affirmed the decision of the Federal District Court for the Southern District of New York in favor of George Metesky and his fellow plaintiffs. Adopting the lower court's opinion in its entirety, the Supreme Court had confirmed that without an adjudication of "dangerousness" by a jury of his peers, an individual indicted on a felony charge but untried because of incompetence to stand trial may not be held in a mental hospital for the criminally insane. Though noticed by few at the time, the decision would have far-reaching and broad application throughout the country, and would affect nearly five hundred patients in the New York penal system and countless others in various states. In hailing the court's decision, the state commissioner of mental hygiene, Alan D. Miller, said, "The emphasis should be on programs that treat people in treatment-oriented hospitals, and not in treatment-correctional facilities."

Across New York and beyond, individuals accused of crimes who had been adjudged too mentally ill to stand trial and thus committed to mental facilities managed by state correctional agencies found themselves transferred to kinder and gentler civil institutions and were suddenly offered hearings on their level of dangerousness—the first step on the journey to freedom.

The long road traveled by George Metesky had led him to the highest court in the land, and the injustices that he had so long and bitterly railed against had been addressed. For all the wrongs he had committed and the chaos he had wrought, the Mad Bomber had finally made a difference.

• • •

It was clear by now that seventy-year-old George Metesky would never be declared dangerous by a New York jury. Recognizing this reality, the Kings County district attorney stipulated with Irving Engel that the defendant may be moved to Creedmore State Hospital in Queens Village, New York, a civil institution operated by the Department of Mental Hygiene. Though, as stated by the federal courts, the next step in the process would have been a hearing on the thorny question of competence and capacity, such a hearing would, ironically, not be provided to Metesky. In the end, the law that he had fought so hard to change would never be applied to him. He wouldn't need it.

In 1972, as part of a sweeping set of reforms, the New York State Legislature enacted a provision of the penal statutes mandating that no untried criminally insane person could be held in an institution for a period exceeding two-thirds of the maximum term for the highest class felony charged in the original indictment. In the case of George Metesky the highest class of felony charged was attempted murder in the first degree—an offense that carried a maximum of twenty-five years. The two-thirds calculation imposed by the new law reduced Metesky's potential sentence to sixteen years and eight months—a term that would expire on September 21, 1973. In finding that the new statute had specific applicability to Metesky's case, Judge Hyman Barshay of the New York Supreme Court in Kings County wrote, "No longer is the key 'thrown away' when a mentally ill person is confined by an order of commitment which in the past has resulted in . . . [a] life [term] . . ."

. . .

On December 10, 1973, George Metesky stood before a New York judge for the final time, in a highly publicized, media-covered bid to gain his freedom. Notwithstanding the expiration of his sentence as determined by the new law, it had taken several months for the multiple charges in both counties to reach dismissal, but now, after nearly seventeen years, his long legal road appeared to be at an end.

"Sixteen years ago, you caused a great deal of turmoil in this city," began Judge Joseph Martinis.

The silver-haired Metesky silently bowed his head tensely, clutching a gray fedora close to his breast. His hopes had been dashed by many judges, and though his lawyer had told him that his long fight was finally over, a part of him could not help but worry.

"I remember it well," the judge continued. "Many of us had sleepless nights because of the terror you were causing. I expect there'll be no repetition."

Metesky looked up and gave his word.

Several days later he boarded a Greyhound bus bound for Waterbury, Connecticut. Sitting alone, he peered through the rain-streaked window, struggling to recall landmarks that he had passed so many times in earlier days. As the bus rumbled toward the city of his birth, the familiar sights of home began to fill his senses and he sighed with whimsical thoughts of what might have been. Perhaps, he wondered, things would have been better had he just let matters pass.

By the time he knocked on the door of his boyhood home, darkness had fallen on the sullen streets of Waterbury. The porch light switched on, and there in the yellow luminescence stood Mae, now frail and ailing. Anna had passed away many years earlier, and he was eager to care for his only sister. She smiled weakly and said simply, "Hello George."

He hoisted his travel bag over the threshold and surveyed the familiar surroundings with eager and longing eyes. As the porch light flickered off George Metesky warily removed his overcoat. Beneath was a double breasted suit—neatly buttoned.

· · ·

That night, as long-suffering New Yorkers locked their doors before turning in, they nervously secured the latch and checked on the children one last time for good measure.

# EPILOGUE

As George Metesky languished on the wards of Matteawan State Hospital in the late 1960s, outside a counterculture generation had begun to emerge that searched for identity as well as inscrutability. Recognizing neither bureaucratic management nor formal affiliation, elusive and radically minded bands such as Abbie Hoffman's Youth International Party—or the Yippies, as they were called—and the Diggers of Haight-Ashbury preached a message steeped in defiant attitudes and revolutionary methods.

Amid this rebellious turmoil and cultural divide, the *idea* of George Metesky had begun to take on an air of cult-hero intrigue. Attracted by his populist message of one man against the entrenched and evil corporate Goliath, many in the movement adopted Metesky as their symbolic champion and figurehead leader, and before long they were discarding their given names and assuming his in a collective cloak of anonymity. "He epitomizes the futility of joining or fighting the system," observed one member of the Diggers. "We're all Meteskys. We're a generation of schizophrenic mutants."

Perhaps attracted more to Metesky's perceived expertise in media manipulation than as revolutionary commander, Abbie Hoffman began adopting the name "George Metesky" as a public front to his various theatrics. In August 1967, Hoffman organized a planned demonstration at the New York Stock Exchange, where he and a group of others threw fistfuls of dollar bills to the trading room floor in an effort to disrupt the flow of business and to make comment on the futility of capitalism. When apprehended and cited for the act, Hoffman and each of his accomplices identified themselves as George Metesky, to the puzzlement of police and exchange security. Hoffman would author several "how to live free in New York" handbooks and one, *Fuck the System*, was even published under the Metesky pseudonym. It wasn't until 1971, when Hoffman's *Steal This Book* came out with very similar style and content, that conjecture over the authorship of the first booklet was settled.

Abbie Hoffman attempted to make contact with Metesky at Matteawan at various times in the late 1960s in an effort to identify with and take up the cause of mental health abuses. Conservative in his political views and sharing nothing in common with Hoffman's leftist antics, Metesky wanted no part of the man and rebuffed his attempts at communication. "He was known as the Eisenhower of psychotics," said attorney Franklyn Engel, who worked on the Metesky case with his father, Irving Engel. Metesky's traditional beliefs could not have been more diametrically opposed to those of Hoffman's, and the possibility of either successfully working with the other was remote.

By the end of the turbulent 1960s, a more violent form of unrest began to sweep through American cities. Fueled by a simmering and desperate anger directed at the entrenched power structures of the nation, a series of militant, neo-anarchist organizations began to surface, and violence soon erupted. Advocating armed rebellion, urban guerrilla organizations such as the Black Panthers, the Weathermen, and other radical groups bent on violence terrorized the nation with a rash of bombings that heavily damaged buildings and other property and caused multiple deaths and scores of injuries. Though it was posited by a New York psychiatrist, David Abrahamsen, who had at one time examined George Metesky, that while the fundamental grievance of those engaged in the violent bombings of the 1960s and 1970s may not have been psychotically driven, the perpetrators nonetheless bore a generalized grudge directed at society as a whole. Radical violence, according to Abrahamsen, was an expression of "the most violent and primitive emotion—revenge; here, revenge against society."

Out of this rage and social turmoil spun the so called Unabomber, who, from 1978 through 1995, terrorized universities and businesses with a series of bombings that left a trail of death and injury from Connecticut to California. Theodore Kaczynski, a highly educated mathematician with an unrelenting anger directed toward technology and the industrial complex of America, carried out a reign of terror that spanned seventeen years and killed three people. Like Metesky, the Unabomber manipulated the press and provided insights into his personality and motives through extensive writings, which would ultimately lead to his capture. And in a hauntingly familiar identifying clue, Kaczynski labeled each of his bombs and his writings with the signature mark "F.C." George Metesky had evidently inspired others beyond a ragtag band of hippies.

But Metesky was disinterested in social causes or political rebellion; he just wanted to find peace in whatever time he had left. Like most men of his age, he read his books, worked about the yard, made small repairs to his car, and painted and maintained the home. Caring for Mae, however, had become the centerpiece of his life. As she had done for him in earlier days, he now assisted her and made sure that her needs were met. He thought he owed her that.

From the moment he returned home, Metesky had said that he intended to write a book about his life and, more importantly, about his experiences at Matteawan. He had told the press that he had procured a deal with a collaborative writer and had even entered into discussions with a producer to make a motion picture centered on his life story. Neither would come. Metesky was simply too difficult to work with.

He would find that life had changed much in the seventeen years that he was away from home. "I was in hope of finding a better world," he said. "But there's no better world, It's worse, if anything, than when I went in." Despite his evident bitterness, Metesky would find solace in the changes he had prompted to the penal system for those with mental illness—changes that in 1976 reached fruition with the New York State Legislature restructuring the delivery of mental health services to the criminally insane and, with the inducement of another federal class action suit, closing Matteawan State Hospital forever.

As the years passed and new and greater concerns stole the attention of a fickle public, the story of Metesky's strange life would fade from memory and the Mad Bomber would be all but forgotten. Despite the obvious hazards of his chosen vocation and the hardships of his later institutionalized life, George Metesky would ironically outlive the doctors who diagnosed him, the lawyers who defended him, the judges who condemned him, and the institutions that confined him. He died on May 23, 1994, at the age of ninety.

"I expected to go before I was 57," he told a reporter in 1974. "I feel good. I'm lucky in a way. I don't catch too many colds and outside of colds I don't have too many ailments . . . I'm pretty well satisfied. I've been where I want to go, done what I want to do. All I want now is peace and quiet."

In his own way, George Metesky had laid the past to rest and moved forward with whatever future he could find. The perils of his life were over and he wished only calm and solitude. On occasion, however, when strolling about the yard, he would look to the small corrugated garage to the rear of the house and feel that old rush of anger welling through his veins. He could smell the bitter foulness of smokeless powder in his nostrils, and he could feel the smooth rumble of the old Daimler making its way down Fourth Street, heading south for New York.

# ACKNOWLEDGMENTS

The writing of a book is, by necessity, a collaborative effort. The gathering of source materials for a work of nonfiction is often a daunting task and, in the case of *The Mad Bomber*, well beyond this author's practical capabilities alone. I would foremost like to thank Jay Feldman, creator of the stage production *A Loud Noise in a Public Place,* which dramatizes the Mad Bomber case for theater. His willingness to share the volumes of research materials that he accumulated through the years proved invaluable to my effort. I also thank James Ledbetter for sharing his documentation on the case. As always, Kenneth Cobb at the New York City Municipal Archives graciously opened his files for viewing and provided many of the court records of the Bomber case from New York County. Robert Freeman of the State of New York Department of State Committee on Open Government provided guidance and assistance for the retrieval of police records, and his work is very much appreciated. For assistance with photographs, I thank Jeffrey Bridgers at the Library of Congress, as well as the staff at the Harry Ransom Center at the University of Texas. And of course, a special thank you to Eric Paisner for the painstaking legwork of retrieving and cataloging many of the images used in this book.

I wish to acknowledge the gracious and kind people who either were involved in the Mad Bomber case directly or knew people who were. The stepchildren of Dr. Brussel, Professor John Israel and Judith Gutmann, spent a great deal of time speaking to me on the telephone and provided a wonderful insight into Dr. Brussel's personality. Likewise, Bill Berkson, the son of Seymour Berkson, provided useful information as to his father's life and work. The lawyers who skillfully represented Metesky in the days leading up to his release, Franklyn Engel, Gene Ann Condon, and Kristin Booth Glen, were each very helpful in providing me with the legal background of the case as well as information regarding the personality of their client. I also thank Terence F. O'Rourke for documents and assistance regarding his great-grandfather, attorney Bart J. O'Rourke. In the realm of criminal profiling I wish to extend my sincere thanks to Howard Teten, who graciously read the manuscript and patiently helped me understand the concepts involved and the distinctions between his approach to the discipline and that of Dr. Brussel. His input was invaluable. Finally, I would like thank former New York City Bomb Squad detective William F. Schmitt, who actively participated in the search for the Mad Bomber and personally questioned Metesky shortly after his arrest. Detective Schmitt spent hours with me on the telephone imparting wonderful firsthand details of the case and his experiences with the Mad Bomber. I wish to thank Cliff Bieder and the staff of the Detectives Endowment Association for providing me with the leads necessary to make contact with Detective Schmitt. I also thank Officer Robert Sibilio Jr. of the Framingham, Massachusetts, Police Department who, along with Detective Schmitt, provided me with a comprehension of the technical aspects of Metesky's "units," and thus a clearer understanding of his madness.

My agent, Greg Daniel, as always, provided encouragement and enthusiasm in the formulation of this book. I appreciate his assistance, as well as that of Iris Blasi at Union Square Press, whose foresight and zeal for the topic brought *The Mad Bomber* to life.

Finally, I wish to acknowledge the longsuffering patience and indulgence of my family, Donna, Corey, and Jeffrey, who love and support me every step of the way.

# AUTHOR'S NOTE ON SOURCES

The sheer volume of endnotes in this book reveals my philosophy that any work of nonfiction be extensively documented, and though the sources relied upon were anything but voluminous, I have done my best to mine the details from the books, magazines, and newspapers that are available on the subject. A tedious list of citations, however, can only be useful when viewed in the context of the overall message delivered to the reader or researcher. It is my intention that the following source list will, thus, provide the reader with a schematic to the mind and mystery of the Mad Bomber.

Virtually every quotation in this book was an actual statement taken from primary materials and attributed directly to its source. Newspapers of the day—most notably the *New York Journal-American* and the *New York Times*—provided many of the fluid details and quotes used throughout the book. Official records of the New York City Police Department, county court files, and district attorney notes also permitted a rare glimpse into the law enforcement response to the case. Unquestionably, the most valuable resource relied upon was the actual recollections of people who were directly involved with or affected by the Mad Bomber. Recorded interviews given by Seymour Berkson to Mike Wallace on the 1957 television program *Night Beat*, currently housed at the Paley Center for Media, provided a unique insight into the thoughts and ethical dilemmas of a 1950s newspaperman covering the biggest story of his day and formed the basis for my understanding and descriptions of the open letters to the Mad Bomber. Beyond recorded transcriptions and media images, however, it was the assistance of the actual surviving witnesses to the Mad Bomber and his doings that I relied upon most in the writing of this book. Though many who lived through the terror of George Metesky are no longer with us, some are, and their assistance in formulating and substantiating the story, as I came to understand it, proved invaluable.

# NOTES

## PROLOGUE

**ix**     **"Suddenly I heard a report"**: "Blast Hurts 7 in B'klyn," *New York Journal-American,* December 3, 1956, 1.

**ix**     **"The shock and terror of what happened"**: "Explosion Victims Glad He's Caught," *New York Journal-American,* January 22, 1957, 3.

**x**     **This, the Bomber would later state"**: "Transcript of Interrogation of George Metesky, 17 4th Street, Waterbury, Connecticut, at Police Headquarters, January 22, 1957," NYC Department of Records/Municipal Archives.

**x**     **"the one place on earth"**: James A. Brussel, *Casebook of a Crime Psychiatrist* (Bernard Geis Associates, 1968), 22.

**x**     **The workspace was meticulously ordered**: Ibid.

**xi**     **"as clean and orderly as"**: "'Mad Bomber' Made Devices in Neat, Garage Workshop," *Bridgeport Post,* January 22, 1957, 12.

**xi**     **Interrupting this nefarious circuitry**: Brussel, *Casebook*, 25. Also, telephone interview with William F. Schmitt, December 10, 2009.

**xi**     **To the contrary**: Brussel, *Casebook*, 23.

**xi**     **By now the process had become**: "Report of Psychiatric Examination in the Case of George Metesky alias George Milauskas," March 1, 1957, NYC Department of Records/Municipal Archives.

**xii**     **Feeling uncomfortable as one of the only men**: Brussel, *Casebook*, 23–24.

**xii**     **With feigned nonchalance**: "Series of 'Pipe Bombs,'" Notations of the New York City Police Department, NYC Department of Records/Municipal Archives.

**xiii**     **"There are sequences and moments"**: Bosley Crowther, "Screen: '*War and Peace*'" (movie review), *New York Times*, August 22, 1956, 26.

**xiii**     **"Technicolored panorama"**: Ibid.

**xiii**     **The Paramount Theatre arose in an era**: Francis Morrone, *An Architectural Guidebook to Brooklyn* (Gibbs Smith, 2001), 3. Thus, "Warner Brothers Theatre," "Fox Theatre," and "Paramount Theatre."

xiv     **They would become:** Christopher Gray, "Streetscapes/The Brooklyn Paramount; Once a Rococo Palace, Now a Citadel of Learning," *New York Times*, July 31, 1994, R7.

xiv     **With an ornately decorated:** Morrone, *An Architectural Guidebook*, 4.

xiv     **"the plans of an outdoor moonlit Italian garden":** "New Brooklyn Theatres," *New York Times,* January 1, 1928, N19.

xiv     **"scenic effects . . . not confined":** Morrone, *An Architectural Guidebook*, 4.

xiv     **The massive glowing letters:** Ibid., 5.

xiv     **"most famous movie place":** Ibid., 3.

xiv     **Behind the opulent décor:** Christopher Gray, "Streetscapes/The Brooklyn Paramount," R7.

xv     **Rushing into the auditorium:** "6 Hurt in Bombing at Theatre Here," *New York Times*, December 3, 1956, 1. Also, author's interview with Horatio Tedesco, June 23, 2009. Tedesco knew, of course, that the explosion was caused by a force much greater than a firecracker but made the announcement in an effort to prevent further panic. As police took over the scene, Tedesco contacted the managing director of the Brooklyn Paramount, Eugene Pleshette (father of actress Suzanne Pleshette), who upon arrival at the theatre chided Tedesco for interrupting an evening out on the town. The next day, as news reports began to surface praising Tedesco's actions in avoiding a general panic, Pleshette arrogantly noted a job well done telling Tedesco, "Nice job my boy." Ibid.

xv     **Soon after, Kings County district attorney:** Ibid., 24.

xvi     **As Doris Russo fought for her life:** "Kennedy Orders Wide Manhunt for Movie Bombing Perpetrator," *New York Times*, December 4, 1956, 1.

xvi     **"easily pass as a person":** "Transcript of Court Appearance, *The People of the State of New York vs. George Metesky,* City Magistrates' Court of the City of New York Felony Court, Borough of Manhattan, Docket No. 1226. January 22, 1957," NYC Department of Records/ Municipal Archives.

xvi     **"through some quirk of fate":** "Blast Hurts 7 in B'klyn," 6.

**xvi**     **He had planted his bombs**: Transcript of Interrogation of George Metesky, January 22, 1957.

**xvi**     **"the greatest manhunt"**: "Kennedy Orders Wide Manhunt," 1.

## CHAPTER I: "A REAL BOOM TOWN"

**1**     **The call came into the 20th squad**: "Series of 'Pipe Bombs.'"

**1**     **"CON EDISON CROOKS"**: Brussel, *Casebook*, 14.

**2**     **"THERE IS NO SHORTAGE"**: Jamie James, "The Mad Bomber vs. Con Ed," *Rolling Stone Magazine,* November 15, 1979, 47.

**2**     **While being examined**: Richard Esposito and Ted Gerstein, *Bomb Squad: A Year Inside the Nation's Most Exclusive Police Unit* (Hyperion, 2007), 277.

**2**     **Though the explosion was felt**: "Crowd Unaware of Bomb Tragedy," *New York Times*, July 5, 1940, 2.

**2**     **Following the World's Fair tragedy**: Esposito and Gerstein, *Bomb Squad*, 277.

**2**     **"agitators and other suspects"**: "All Police in City on 24-Hour Duty," *New York Times,* July 5, 1940, 2.

**2**     **Adopting a more rigorous training program**: "The Twin Towers; Unit Is Oldest and Largest," *New York Times*, March 4, 1993, B4.

**2**     **"the world's most dangerous job"**: E. D. Fales Jr., "The Job That Scares Everybody," *Popular Science* 181, no. 1 (July 1962): 67.

**3**     **"'maliciously designed to explode'"**: Joseph Carter, "Wanted: The Man without a Face," *Colliers*, February 3, 1956, 23.

**3**     **"[E]very problem is a new one"**: Ibid., 56.

**3**     **Though it was not the best outcome**: Telephone interview with New York City Bomb Squad Detective William F. Schmitt (retired), December 10, 2009.

**4**     **"It's that one in a hundred"**: Joseph Carter, "Wanted: The Man without a Face," 23.

**4**     **Once it was determined that the object**: "Mad Bomber Hits Library," *New York Daily News*, December 25, 1956, 8.

4     **carried out of the building**: Joseph Carter, "Wanted: The Man without a Face," 56.

4     **The vehicle, officially named the Pyke-LaGuardia Carrier**: Fales, "The Job That Scares Everybody," 72.

4     **"designed to take a bomb"**: Esposito and Gerstein, *Bomb Squad*, 277–278.

5     **Removed to the relative safety**: Joseph Carter, "Wanted: The Man without a Face," 56.

5     **In a typical situation**: Ibid.

5     **To make matters worse**: Brussel, *Casebook*, 48–49. Also see John Douglas and Mark Olshaker, *Unabomber: On the Trail of America's Most-Wanted Serial Killer* (Pocket Books, 1996), 6.

6     **Within the company headquarters**: See, e.g., Brussel, *Casebook*, 14–15.

6     **"The episode was filed and forgotten"**: Ibid., 15.

6     **The ex-convicts and outlaws**: Esposito and Gerstein, *Bomb Squad*, 273.

6     **"Recognizing the inability of the present small force"**: "A Secret Service Squad to Hunt the Black Hand," *New York Times,* December 20, 1906, 16.

6     **"master bomb-maker for the Black Handers"**: Esposito and Gerstein, Bomb Squad, 274.

6     **"The book is not mine"**: "Get Leaders of Black Hand," *New York Times*, July 7, 1908, 1.

7     **With America's entry into the war**: Esposito and Gerstein, *Bomb Squad*, 275.

7     **Anxiety over the German espionage campaign**: See Chad Millman, *The Detonators: The Secret Plot to Destroy America and an Epic Hunt for Justice* (Little, Brown, 2006).

7     **In April 1919 militant followers**: Regin Schmidt, *Red Scare: FBI and the Origins of Anticommunism in the United States* (Museum Tusculanum Press, 2000), 148.

8    **a few months later a similar coordinated attack**: "Midnight Bombs for Officials in 8 Cities; Bombers Die at Attorney General's House; Two Victims at Judge Nott's House Here; Bombs in Boston, Cleveland, Pittsburgh," *New York Times*, June 3, 1919, 1.

8    **Anarchist literature and leaflets**: Ibid.

8    **"REMEMBER WE WILL NOT TOLERATE"**: Beverly Gage, *The Day Wall Street Exploded: A Story of America in Its First Age of Terror* (Oxford University Press, 2009), 171.

8    **"gigantic proportions"**: "The Militants Who Play with Dynamite," *New York Times*, October 25, 1970, SM20.

8    **"[a] real boom town."**: Ibid.

9    **Though some sources have concluded**: See, e.g., Brussel, *Casebook*, 14.

9    **"It wasn't loaded"**: James, "The Mad Bomber vs. Con Ed," 47.

9    **"It was a[n] empty bomb"**: Transcript of Interrogation of George Metesky, January 22, 1957.

9    **Knowing that the writing**: See e.g., Brussel, *Casebook*, 14.

9    **"That first unit was just a sample**: James, "The Mad Bomber vs. Con Ed," 47.

10    **The ultimate target**: Ibid.

10    **"I was very careful"**: "Riddle of the Mad Bomber's Personality," *Bridgeport Sunday Post*, January 27, 1957, section B.

10    **With an air of narcissistic and intellectual superiority**: See e.g., Brussel, *Casebook*, 16.

10    **As police detectives duly noted**: Ibid.

11    **"with the compliments of the 'mobsters'"**: James, "The Mad Bomber vs. Con Ed," 47.

11    **"was just the kind of unexpected thing"**: Nathan Miller, *FDR: An Intimate History* (Doubleday, 1983), 477.

12    **"I WILL MAKE NO MORE BOMB UNITS"**: Brussel, *Casebook*, 15–16.

## CHAPTER II: HELL GATE

13    **By the time of the Great Depression:** "2 Huge Generators Put in Service Here," *New York Times*, May 30, 1929, 24.

13    **The plant's interior:** Ibid.

13    **"What we are doing here":** Ibid.

13    **"Cement dust was everywhere":** "Tells of Injuries at Power Plant," *New York Journal-American*, January 24, 1957, 5.

14    **According to the plant owners:** *Generating Stations, Hell Gate—Sherman Creek.* Private publication of the United Electric Light and Power Company, 1926.

15    **His position did not utilize:** On his job application, Metesky listed "mechanical work, electrical work, machine shop practice" as the vocations in which he had experience. See "Application for Employment with the United Electric Light and Power Co.," George Peter Metesky, applicant. December 12, 1929," NYC Department of Records/Municipal Archives.

15    **As menial as many of his assigned tasks were:** "Report of Psychiatric Examination," March 1, 1957.

16    **"[He] looks like the usher":** "Sisters Shocked, Loyal to Brother," *New York Times*, January 23, 1957, 20.

16    **a "lone wolf":** "Riddle of the Mad Bomber's Personality."

16    **"spinsterish air about him":** "Metesky Taken to N.Y. under a Heavy Guard," *Bridgeport Telegram*, January 23, 1957, 1.

16    **"schoolteacher":** "Riddle of the Mad Bomber's Personality."

16    **"[e]fficient and well liked":** "Metesky's First Bombing Attempt Turned Out a Dud," *New York Journal-American*, March 23, 1957, 4.

17    **"[A]nd George would go right after":** Ibid.

17    **As a child, the younger George:** "Mad Bomber Reveals How Resentment Grew to Hate," *New York Journal-American*, March 21, 1957, 4.

17    **"George would literally not step":** Ibid.

17    **She converted "Milauskas" to "Metesky,":** Brussel, *Casebook*, 66–67.

17     **At any given time the family**: "Father Left Metesky Big Cash Bequest," *New York Journal-American*, January 28, 1957, 1. See also "Mad Bomber Reveals Kindling of His Hatred," *New York Journal-American*, March 21, 1957, 1.

17     **"I just had no interest"**: "Report of Psychiatric Examination," March 1, 1957.

17     **Upon leaving school**: Ibid. See also "Application for Employment."

17     **"Well, he was a strange one"**: "Mad Bomber Reveals How Resentment Grew to Hate," 4.

18     **In further pursuit of a technical vocation**: "Application for Employment."

18     **Several months later**: "Report of Psychiatric Examination," March 1, 1957.

18     **In an initial two-year tour**: "Mad Bomber Reveals How Resentment Grew to Hate," 4.

18     **In April 1922 he was honorably discharged**: Ibid.

18     **His record indicated**: Ibid.

18     **During this period, PFC George Metesky**: Transcript of Interrogation of George Metesky, January 22, 1957.

18     **"a dreary, shabby area"**: Brussel, *Casebook*, 66.

18     **the appellation Brass City**: Debbie Harmsen, ed., *Fodor's New England* (Random House, 2008), 317.

19     **"The house was not loved"**: Brussel, *Casebook*, 66.

19     **It wasn't long, however**: Ibid. See also "Held on 4 Counts, His Sanity Tested," *New York Herald Tribune*, January 23, 1957, 1.

19     **Content with this reclusive lifestyle**: In "Report of Psychiatric Examination," March 1, 1957, on the subject of women Metesky was quoted as saying, "Well, I didn't go out much with them because I was always in a foreign country," referring to his days in the service. The report stated that Metesky could only recall two sexual experiences in his life, both in San Domingo.

## CHAPTER III: THE SEEDS OF MADNESS

21 **"Apparently," recalled Metesky**: "Mad Bomber Reveals How Resentment Grew to Hate," 4.

22 **"There were over 12,000"**: Letter of George Metesky to the *New York Journal-American* dated January 18, 1957. See "Letters Lead to Bomber's Capture," *New York Journal-American*, January 22, 1957, 2.

23 **"active pulmonary tuberculosis"**: "Report of Psychiatric Examination," March 1, 1957.

23 **"like a tourist cabin"**: Transcript of Interrogation of George Metesky, January 22, 1957.

23 **Not two months into his stay**: "Tells of Injuries at Power Plant," 10.

23 **What remains undisputed, however**: "'Gush of Fumes' Transformed Gentle Man Into 'Mad Bomber,'" *Sunday News and Tribune* (Jefferson City, Missouri), January 27, 1957, 2.

24 **Indeed, in his yearly physical examination**: "Report of Medical Examiner, The United Electric and Power Company," NYC Department of Records/Municipal Archives.

24 **Though there remained no medical proof**: Brussel, *Casebook*, 71.

24 **For six months the company paid him**: The Association of Employees of the United Electric Light and Power Company, Sick Benefit Payroll, Courtesy of NYC Department of Records/Municipal Archives.

25 **By his own estimate**: Transcript of Interrogation of George Metesky, January 22, 1957.

25 **"I asked them to take care of me"**: Ibid.

25 **"the run around"**: "Report of Psychiatric Examination," March 1, 1957.

25 **New York's workmen's compensation system**: "A World of Hurt for Injured Workers, a Costly Legal Swamp," *New York Times*, March 31, 2009.

25 **The Lower Manhattan sweatshop**: John M. Hoenig, "The Triangle Fire of 1911," *History Magazine* (April/May 2005): 20.

25      Panic-stricken employees encountered: Ibid.

26      "the worst work-place fire": Ibid.

26      The political strength of labor unions: Ibid.

26      In exchange for this prescribed benefit: See Linda Hammond-
        Darling and Thomas J. Kniesner, *The Law and Economics of Worker's
        Compensation* (Institute for Civil Justice [U.S.] Rand Corporation,
        1980), 8.

26      This policy compromise ensured: Jack B. Hood, Benjamin A. Hardy,
        and Harold S. Lewis, *Workers Compensation and Employee Protection
        Laws in a Nutshell* (Thomson/West, 2005), 29.

28      Con Ed again asserted section 28: See "Edison Clerk Finds Case in
        File," 18; Transcript of Interrogation of George Metesky, January 22,
        1957.

28      "It took a lot of letter writing": Transcript of Interrogation of George
        Metesky, January 22, 1957.

28      "fair and honest.": "Mad Bomber Reveals How Resentment Grew to
        Hate," 4.

28      "He was a very nice man": Transcript of Interrogation of George
        Metesky, January 22, 1957.

29      "The referee was going to make an award": Ibid.

30      "I had written thousands of letters": "Report of Psychiatric Exami-
        nation," March 1, 1957.

30      He estimated that he had written: "Bomber Heard on Con Ed TV
        Show," *New York Herald Tribune*, January 23, 1957, 5.

30      "I never received so much as": James, "The Mad Bomber vs. Con
        Ed," 47.

30      YOU KNOW, I JUST REFUSE TO BE ROBBED: Ibid.

31      "It worked great too": "Coddled Bomber, Sisters Admit," *New York
        Journal-American*, March 22, 1957, 14.

31      Later, Metesky rigged a hand-pushed lawnmower: James, "The Mad
        Bomber vs. Con Ed," 47.

31      he applied for and was ultimately granted: See United States Patent

2,257,059, "Solenoid Pump," George P. Metesky, Waterbury, Conn., application July 19, 1938, serial no. 220,082, patented September 23, 1941.

31     **"I had a mission to perform"**: Testimony of Dr. Albert A. LaVerne, on March 27, 1957, during a Section 662a Hearing before Judge Samuel S. Leibowitz, Kings County Court, *The People of New York vs. George Metesky,* indictment no. 269/1957.

32     **He was sure of it**: "Report of Psychiatric Examination," March 1, 1957.

32     **In his mind's eye**: These images are based upon the Testimony of Dr. Albert A. LaVerne, March 27, 1957.

## CHAPTER IV: "SELECTED BY DESTINY"

34     **"We would deprive ourselves"**: "Coddled Bomber, Sisters Admit," 14.

34     **"classic study in over-protection"**: Ibid.

34     **He would prepare an evening meal**: "Metesky's First Bombing Attempt Turned Out a Dud," 4. Also see "Report of Psychiatric Examination," March 1, 1957.

34     **His reclusive lifestyle would later be described**: "Metesky's First Bombing Attempt Turned Out a Dud," 4.

35     **Several months later he attempted to enlist**: "Tells of Injuries at Power Plant," 10. Also see "Report of Psychiatric Examination," March 1, 1957.

35     **At the same time, he wrote**: "Metesky's First Bombing Attempt Turned Out a Dud," 4. Also see Memorandum of Interview with Detective Michael Lynch, Badge #866, with Assistant District Attorney Howard Blank dated April 15, 1957, NYC Department of Records/Municipal Archives.

35     **"He was a person who always was ready"**: "Metesky's First Bombing Attempt Turned Out a Dud," 4.

36     **"after much discussion and medical examinations"**: "Tells of Injuries at Power Plant," 10.

36     **Despite this discord, Metesky eagerly worked**: Ibid.

36 **Finally, in December 1943**: "Report of Psychiatric Examination," March 1, 1957.

36 **a state-run facility**: See Special Acts of the State of Connecticut, House Bill No. 390, approved July 28, 1909.

36 **"miserable and lonely"**: "Tells of Injuries at Power Plant," 10.

36 **A few months later he was re-examined**: "Report of Psychiatric Examination," March 1, 1957.

37 **By his own words**: Transcript of Interrogation of George Metesky, January 22, 1957.

37 **"unknown man battling for justice"**: "Metesky's First Bombing Attempt Turned Out a Dud," 4.

37 **He would later admit to planting**: See "George Did It," *Time*, February 4, 1957. Also see "Report of Psychiatric Examination," March 1, 1957. There, Metesky is quoted as claiming that he planted fifty-seven bombs. Also see Transcript of Interrogation of George Metesky, January 22, 1957; and "Metesky's First Bombing Attempt Turned Out a Dud," 4.

38 **"the world had done him wrong"**: Brussel, *Casebook*, 30.

38 **Alone against a vast conspiratorial network**: See psychiatric notes contained in files of New York County Supreme Court, "The People of the State of New York against George P. Metesky, a/k/a George Milauskas, Indictment No. 321/1957," NYC Department of Records/Municipal Archives.

38 **"[H]is fury of hatred so enveloped"**: Testimony of Dr. Albert A. LaVerne, March 27, 1957.

38 **he had become convinced**: Ibid.

## CHAPTER V: "A MAN WITH A HAMMER"

39 **The terminal had been used**: John Belle and Maxine R. Leighton, *Grand Central: Gateway to a Million Lives* (W. W. Norton and Company, 2000), 84.

39 **At the arched entrance**: Fremont Rider, *Rider's New York City: A Guide-Book for Travelers* (Henry Holt and Company, 1916), 114.

39      Covering seventy-nine acres: Ibid.

39      the station, at various times: See www.grandcentralterminal.com/
info/terminalopens.cfm accessed September 2, 2009.

39      "greatest railway terminal in the world": Rider, *Rider's New York
City*, 114.

39      such famous long-distance trains: See www.grandcentralterminal.
com/info/terminalopens.cfm accessed September 2, 2009.

39      With the advent of postwar suburban life: See www.grandcentralter
minal.com/info/grandcentraldecline.cfm accessed September 2, 2009.

39      Among the many legends: Rider, *Rider's New York City*, 115.

40      Created by the low ceramic structures: Belle and Leighton, *Grand
Central*, 84.

41      "boys or pranksters": "Bomb Blast in Terminal," *New York Times*,
March 30, 1951, 24.

41      It did not contain a pipe casing: "Series of 'Pipe Bombs.'"

41      Metesky knew that the "throat disc": Transcript of Interrogation of
George Metesky, January 22, 1957.

41      A spoonful of water: "Metesky Tells How Lozenges Set Off Bombs,"
*New York Journal-American*, January 27, 1957, 3.

41      Once the disc sufficiently dissolved: Ibid. See also Transcript of
Interrogation of George Metesky, January 22, 1957. Also, telephone
interview with William F. Schmitt, December 10, 2009.

42      "the rough stuff": James, "The Mad Bomber vs. Con Ed," 47.

42      "I've read," Metesky would later say: Ibid.

42      Every so called unit: Testimony of James B. Leggett, Chief of Detectives, Police Department of the City of New York, on March 27, 1957,
during a section 662a hearing before Judge Samuel S. Leibowitz,
Kings County Court, *The People of New York vs. George Metesky*,
Indictment No. 269/1957.

42      At 6:10 in the evening: "Series of 'Pipe Bombs.'"

42      Bomb squad detectives immediately saw: "Bomb Goes Off in
Library," *New York Times*, April 25, 1951, 31.

**43**   The New York City police downplayed: "Bomb Laid to Prankster," *New York Times*, September 13, 1951, 33.

**43**   "This is a well constructed mechanism": "Police Files Tell Weird Details of Bomber's History," *New York Journal-American*, December 30, 1956, 6.

**44**   "It would 'just build up'": "Bomb Laid to Prankster," 33.

**44**   "They got some stupid advice": James, "The Mad Bomber vs. Con Ed," 48.

**44**   The package, postmarked "White Plains, NY": Transcript of Interrogation of George Metesky, January 22, 1957.

**44**   "The weirdie patently pulled": "Bomber's Erratic Timing Baffling," *New York Journal-American*, March 24, 1957, 2.

**45**   On October 22, 1951, a longshoremen's strike: "Rail Goods Embargoed; Dock Strike Closes Port," *New York Herald Tribune*, October 23, 1951, 1; "Rail Embargo Set as Dock Strikers Tie Up Port Here," *New York Times*, October 23, 1951, 1.

**45**   at the White House an announcement: "Reds Set Off Third Atom Blast, Indicating They Have Stockpile," *New York Herald Tribune*, October 23, 1951, 1; "White House Announces Russian Detonation and Foresees New Ones," *New York Times*, October 23, 1951, 1.

**45**   "BOMBS WILL CONTINUE": "Police Find Bomb in Paramount Lounge; Note Spurs Search for One at Penn Station," *New York Times*, October 23, 1951, 30.

**46**   As 3,600 unwitting patrons: Ibid.

**46**   Following the lead of a former New York City fire marshal: "16 Year Search for Madman," *New York Times*, December 25, 1956, 31.

**47**   "one in whom flashes of lunacy": Ibid.

**47**   "This defendant is a particular source": "Sugar Bomb Suspect Is Sent to Bellevue," *New York Times*, November 8, 1951, 19.

**47**   The suspect, who silently looked on: Ibid.

**47**   "He has been sending simulated bombs": Ibid.

**47**   He was considered by police: "Laborer Says Bomb Solution

Vindicates Him," *New York Journal-American*, January 24, 1957, 2.

48    "This arrest is an outrage": "Sugar Bomb Suspect Is Sent to Bellevue," 19.

48    "They were the most harrowing days": "Laborer Says Bomb Solution Vindicates Him," 2.

48    "With horns silenced": "Raid Test Silences City in 2 Minutes; Officials Pleased," *New York Times*, November 29, 1951, 1.

49    "pattern for survival": "Air-Raid Test Better Than City Expected," *New York Herald Tribune*, November 29, 1951, 1.

49    "sounded like a stick of dynamite": "Bomb Is Exploded in Union Sq. I.R.T.," *New York Herald Tribune*, November 29, 1951, 1.

49    "TO HERALD TRIBUNE EDITOR": Brussel, *Casebook*, 17.

50    On May 15, 1952: "'Bomb' Case Dismissed," *New York Times*, May 16, 1952, 7.

50    Bomb squad detectives: Esposito and Gerstein, *Bomb Squad*, 279. Citing *Cue Magazine*, Esposito and Gerstein state that the move was required because the vibrations from the subway running beneath police headquarters on Centre Street—the original police lab location—upset the delicate instruments used by the technicians.

50    "He buys an admission ticket": Joseph Carter, "Wanted: The Man without a Face," 56.

51    A woman, innocently watching": "Bomber's Erratic Timing Baffling," 2.

51    The "sweeping arches" and "choral staircases": See www.radiocity.com/about/history.html, accessed September 16, 2009.

51    "Everything about Radio City Music Hall": Richard Alleman, *New York: The Movie Lover's Guide: The Ultimate Insider Tour of Movie New York* (Harper and Row Publishers, 2005), 54.

51    "American People's Palace": See www.radiocity.com/about/history.html, accessed September 16, 2009.

51    The hall initially opened in 1932: Richard Alleman, *New York: The Movie Lover's Guide*, 54.

52 **hundreds of film classics**: Ibid.

52 **"virtually [guaranteeing] a successful run"**: See www.radiocity.com/about/history.html, accessed September 16, 2009.

53 **a "funny" sound**: Transcript of Interrogation of George Metesky, January 22, 1957.

53 **"[It] sounded like a rocket"**: James, "The Mad Bomber vs. Con Ed," 47.

53 **"We're sorry about this"**: Brussel, *Casebook*, 19.

53 **He smiled and whispered**: James, "The Mad Bomber vs. Con Ed," 48.

53 **The morning newspapers played down**: "Psychopath's Bomb Pops in Music Hall, Burns Coat," *New York Herald Tribune*, March 11, 1953, 19.

53 **The *Herald Tribune* attributed the bomb**: Ibid.

53 **a "publicity-seeking jerk" and a "mental case."**: "A Homemade Bomb Rips Station Locker," *New York Times*, May 7, 1953, 28.

54 **"EDITOR + STAFF OF N.Y. HERALD TRIBUNE"**: See *New York Herald Tribune*, December 28, 1956, 4.

55 **"careful and wary as a cat"**: "The Mad Bomber's Story Reveals Odd Personality," *New York Journal-American*, March 20, 1957, 7.

56 **Nervously, Metesky had settled the bomb**: Brussel, *Casebook*, 24.

57 **"I thought my number was up"**: "The Mad Bomber's Story Reveals Odd Personality," 7.

57 **A blast in the lower-level men's washroom**: "Bomb Injures 3 in Grand Central," *New York Times*, March 17, 1954, 33.

57 **"fervor of excitement"**: "Bomb Lets Go at Terminal," *Charleston Gazette* (West Virginia), March 17, 1954, 1.

57 **"My ears are still deaf"**: "Bomb Explodes in Grand Central Station, Hurts 2," *Lebanon Daily News* (Pennsylvania), March 17, 1954, 1.

57 **"crude, home-made time bomb"**: "Bomb in Music Hall Injures 4 in Crowd," *New York Times*, November 8, 1954, 1.

57 **"as if a big electric bulb"**: "Bomb in the Music Hall Hurts Four in Audience," *New York Herald Tribune*, November 8, 1954, 1.

58 **"All seats were taken"**: Ibid.

58 **Within moments of the blast**: Ibid.

58 **A Port Authority attendant**: "Bomb Explodes in 8th Ave. Bus Terminal, Scares Many Commuters, Hurts No One," *New York Times*, November 29, 1954, 11.

59 **They began calling him the "Mad Bomber"**: The name "Mad Bomber" appears to have been originated by Justin Gilbert in an article found in the May 4, 1955, issue of the *New York Daily Mirror*. He wrote, "A mad bomber, so diabolically clever that he has consistently thwarted the best detectives, has planted hundreds of bombs all over mid-Manhattan for 15 years—and still is on the loose . . ." "City Hunts Mad Bomb Planter," *New York Daily Mirror*, May 4, 1955, 1.

## CHAPTER VI: CHASING SHADOWS

60 **Clearly torn between their responsibility**: "Penn Station Blast Is Ignored by Commuters," *New York Times*, January 12, 1955, 11.

60 **The effusive *New York Daily News***: "Bomb Goes Off, Panics LI Rush-Hour Throng," *New York Daily News*, January 12, 1955, 3.

60 **And, in a clear attempt to compromise**: "Penn Station Bomb Startles Commuters," *New York Herald Tribune*, January 12, 1955, 1.

61 **"to get even with the Consolidated Edison Co."**: "Radio City Bomb Found to Be Deadly," *New York Journal-American*, May 3, 1955, 4.

62 **An option that earlier had been considered**: Telephone interview with William F. Schmitt, December 10, 2009.

62 **With the device open**: "Here's How Terrorist Makes His Explosives," *New York Journal-American*, December 28, 1956, 2.

62 **"lethal weapon"**: "City Hunts Mad Bomb Planter," 30.

63 **The *New York Journal-American* chillingly proclaimed**: "Radio City Bomb Found to Be Deadly," 4.

63 **the front page banner headline**: "City Hunts Mad Bomb Planter," 1.

63 **And across America**: "Mad Bomber Being Hunted In New York," *Alton Evening Telegraph*, May 4, 1955, 15 (AP).

63    **From a detailed study of the bombings**: "City Hunts Mad Bomb Planter," 3.

64    **Following the second Radio City incident**: Ibid., 30.

64    **"You are dealing with a man"**: Joseph Carter, "Wanted: The Man without a Face," 56.

65    **"I personally have taken"**: Ibid.

65    **"once spent a solid day"**: Ibid.

65    **"The whole inside of the booth"**: "Porter Is Injured," *New York Journal-American*, February 22, 1956, 5.

65    **dismayed to find threads**: Transcript of Interrogation of George Metesky, January 22, 1957.

65    **The next day, newspapers reported**: "Penn Station Blast: FBI, Cops Hunt 'Mad Bomber,'" *New York Journal-American*, February 22, 1956, 3.

66    **he felt "sick"**: Transcript of Interrogation of George Metesky, January 22, 1957.

66    **"I took an oath to keep on placing them"**: Ibid.

66    **including one in the Empire State Building**: Ibid.

66    **As the two men talked**: "Pipe Bomb from R.C.A. Building Blasts Guard's Home in Jersey," *New York Times*, August 5, 1956, 64.

66    **"You never know when a piece of pipe"**: "Rockefeller Center Escapes a Bombing," *New York Herald Tribune*, August 5, 1956, 1.

67    **"like two cars coming together"**: Ibid., 6.

67    **"a mess . . ."**: "PipeBomb from R.C.A. Building Blasts Guard's Home in Jersey," 64.

67    **"I haven't been as religious"**: "Rockefeller Center Escapes a Bombing," 1.

67    **"His face remains a blank"**: Joseph Carter, "Wanted: The Man without a Face," 56.

68    **". . . WHILE VICTIMS GET BLASTED"**: "Psychiatrist Depicts the Bomber," *New York Herald Tribune*, December 27, 1956, 1. Also see Brussel, *Casebook*, 21–22.

## CHAPTER VII: THE "TWELFTH STREET PROPHET"

69    **Parakeets flying freely**: Telephone interview with John Israel, James A. Brussel's stepson, May 29, 2009.

69    **"It is a comfortable enough face"**: Brussel, *Casebook*, 3.

69    **"Bow-tied, Mustachioed and Natty"**: "My New York," *Titusville Herald*, August 8, 1959, 6.

69    **From his office**: Telephone interview with John Israel, May 29, 2009.

69    **His submissions were so frequent**: Ibid.

69    **A prolific and incessant writer**: Telephone interview with Judith Gutmann, James A. Brussel's stepdaughter, June 5, 2009.

69    **"[A] man has to be paranoid"**: "My New York," 6.

70    **On one of many working vacations**: Telephone interview with John Israel, May 29, 2009.

70    **"There is a kind of poetic justice"**: Brussel, *Casebook*, ix.

70    **A native-born New Yorker**: Biographical information is derived from Brussel, *Casebook*, 4; *The New York Red Book, Volume 71* (Williams Press, 1963), 645; and a telephone interview with John Israel, May 29, 2009.

71    **Though he focused some of his**: See James A. Brussel, "Military Psychiatry," *Military Surgeon* 88 (1941).

71    **he developed an intriguing interest**: See James A. Brussel, "Charles Dickens: Child Psychologist and Sociologist," *Psychiatric Quarterly* 12, no. 1 (1938); James A. Brussel, "Van Gogh: Masochist Genius of the Canvas, A Psychiatric Study," *Psychiatric Quarterly* 14, Supplement 1 (1940): 7–16; and Judith A. Peraino, *Listening to the Sirens: Musical Technologies of Queer Identity from Homer to Hedwig* (University of California Press, 2006), 83.

71    **Established in 1926, the stated function**: "Preliminary Guide to Mental Health Documentary Sources in New York State," www.archives.nysed.gov/a/research/res_topics_health_mh_recguide_dmh.shtml, accessed October 9, 2009.

71    **"The history of mental disease"**: New York State Department of

Mental Hygiene, *Annual Report*, 1948, 46.

72    "the great mystery of human behavior": Brussel, *Casebook*, 4.

72    "with an attitude of cool scientific inquiry": Ibid., 5.

72    "common psychiatric principles in reverse": Ibid., 3.

73    "That the human mind works at all": Brussel, *Casebook*, xii.

73    "Sherlock Holmes of the Couch": Ibid., 3.

## CHAPTER VIII: "THE GREATEST MANHUNT IN THE HISTORY OF THE POLICE DEPARTMENT"

74    In Sir Arthur Conan Doyle's classic: A. Conan Doyle, *The Sign of Four* (Spencer Blackett, 1890), 93.

74    "greatest manhunt in the history": "Kennedy Orders Wide Manhunt," 1.

74    "New York's 'finest career officer'": "Portrait of Our No. 1 Cop," *New York Times*, November 15, 1959, SM16.

74    "number one headache": Marjorie Dent Candee, ed., *Current Biography Yearbook 1956* (H.W. Wilson, 1956), 334.

75    "Deceptively gentle in appearance": "Portrait of Our No. 1 Cop," SM16.

75    He grew up in the tough Greenpoint section: "Strong Arm of the Law," *Time*, July 7, 1958.

75    Soon after, he attended: Candee, ed., *Current Biography Yearbook 1956*, 334.

75    In 1951 he was promoted: "Strong Arm of the Law."

75    though he had a reputation: "'All Cop' Commissioner, Stephen P. Kennedy," *New York Times*, February 14, 1956, 21.

75    "Mr. Kennedy is a man": Ibid.

75    Though this authoritative deportment: Gerald Astor, *The New York Cops: An Informal History* (Charles Scribner's Sons, 1971), 209.

76    By 1958, the department would boast: "Strong Arm of the Law."

76    "to make every effort": "'Get Bomb Maniac,' All Police Told," *New York Daily News*, December 4, 1956, 2.

76    "**The man is not**": "Kennedy Orders Wide Manhunt," 47.

76    "**an outrage that cannot**": Ibid., 1.

76    **He concluded the conference**: Ibid.

77    "**I appeal to members**": "'Get Bomb Maniac,'" 2.

77    "**DO YOU RECOGNIZE**": "Do You Recognize This Writing?" *New York Daily News*, December 11, 1956, 10.

77    "**A 'faceless man'**": "'Mad Bomber' Believed to Be Man About 45," *New York Journal-American*, December 4, 1956, 11.

77    "**He is searching desperately**": "His Secret Notes Paint the Portrait of Mad Bomber," *New York Daily News*, December 11, 1956, 10.

77    **The *New York Journal-American***: "Bomber Mystery," *New York Journal-American*, December 26, 1956, 19.

77    **the *World-Telegram and Sun***: "The Mad Bomber," *Time*, Janaury 7, 1957, 17.

78    **BIU detectives canvassed**: "16-Year Search for Madman," *New York Times*, December 25, 1956, 1.

79    "**reached the end**": "Publicity Heat Turned Toward Mad Bomber," *New York Journal-American*, December 5, 1956, 6.

## CHAPTER IX: A CITY IN TURMOIL

80    "**I didn't see any reason**": Deborah Kops, *Racial Profiling Open for Debate* (Marshall Cavendish, 2006), 27.

80    "**A whole generation**": James, "The Mad Bomber vs. Con Ed," 46.

80    "**He had the whole city**": "Injured Victims Express Relief," *Waterbury Republican-American*, January 23, 1957, 1.

81    "**It is one thing**": "Terror in the Age of Eisenhower," New York Times, September 10, 2004, B1.

82    "**He has been described**": "New Man Heads Troubled Police Force," *Bee* (Danville, Virginia), June 28, 1962, 2-B. (AP).

82    "**Book of Rules**": Jeane Toomey, *Assignment Homicide: Behind the Headlines* (Sunstone Press, 2006), 94.

82    **His 1956 contribution**: Morris Ploscowe, *Manual for Prosecuting*

*Attorneys* (Practising Law Institute, 1956), 432.

83 **Through 1956**: James A. Brussel, M.D., "History of the New York State Department of Mental Hygiene," *N.Y. State Journal of Medicine* 57, no. 3 (1957): 559.

83 **Though the arcane methodology**: Ibid.

83 **"I had real people"**: Brussel, *Casebook*, 28.

84 **"I don't know what"**: Ibid., 12.

## CHAPTER X: PROFILE OF A BOMBER

85 **Homer's eighth century BC**: Richard N. Kocsis and George B. Palermo, *Criminal Profiling: Principles and Practice* (Humana Press, 2006), 4.

86 **Published in 1486**: Brent E. Turvey, *Criminal Profiling: An Introduction to Behavioral Evidence Analysis*, (Elsevier, 2008), 6–10.

86 **"born criminals"**: Ibid., 17.

86 **"I seemed to see"**: Colin Wilson and Damon Wilson, *Written in Blood: A History of Forensic Detection* (Carroll and Graff, 2003), 591.

86 **Pursuant to his anthropological theory**: Turvey, *Criminal Profiling*, 17–18.

86 **"mark of Cain"**: Ibid., 18.

86 **Though most of these**: Kocsis and Palermo, *Criminal Profiling*, 4.

87 **"Conan Doyle continually referenced"**: Turvey, *Criminal Profiling*, 21.

87 **By a careful examination**: Tim Newburn, *Handbook of Criminal Investigation* (Willan Publishing, 2007), 493–494.

87 **". . . A man subject to periodical attacks"**: Kocsis and Palermo, *Criminal Profiling*, 5.

88 **The Whitechapel murders**: Ibid.

88 **Of strategic significance**: Newburn, *Handbook of Criminal Investigation*, 494.

88 **Though Langer's assessment**: Kocsis and Palermo, *Criminal Profiling*, 6.

89 **"I knew I wasn't going to fool him"**: Brussel, *Casebook*, 13.

89    "I'd seen that look before": Ibid.

90    "I felt that my profession": Ibid., 13–14.

90    "I stood up from my desk": Ibid., 11–12.

90    "He seemed like a ghost": Ibid., 28.

91    "At large somewhere": Ibid., 14.

91    "A psychiatrist's dominant characteristic": Ibid., 5.

91    Each such item: Email from Howard Teten to author dated July 9, 2009, in which a detailed analysis of Dr. Brussel's approach to criminal profiling was provided. Dr. Teten was an instructor at the FBI's Behavioral Science Unit at Quantico, Virginia, and developed the Bureau's original approach to profiling which was adapted, in 1970, as a lecture course titled "Applied Criminology."

91    It would, in effect: See Charles Patrick Ewing and Joseph T. McCann, *Minds on Trial: Great Cases in Law and Psychology* (Oxford University Press, 2006), 14.

92    "These mechanical affairs": Brussel, *Casebook*, 28–29.

92    "alien to the feminine personality": "Bomber a Woman? Idea Called 'Silly,'" *New York Herald Tribune*, December 28, 1956, 11.

92    Consequently, Brussel indicated: Brussel, *Casebook*, 29.

93    The threats had continued: "Psychiatrist Depicts the Bomber," 1.

93    "a chronic disorder": Brussel, *Casebook*, 30.

93    "These are the people": "Psychiatrist Depicts the Bomber," 1.

93    "The paranoiac is the world's": Brussel, *Casebook*, 30–32.

94    "He's symmetrically built": Ibid., 32.

94    Brussel spoke in assured tones: Douglas and Olshaker, *Unabomber*, 10.

94    In a study: Ernest Kretschmer, *Physique and Character* (University of Michigan, 1925; reprinted by Read Books, 2008), 16–36.

94    Brussel told the officers: Brussel, *Casebook*, 32–33.

95    "He's middle-aged": Ibid., 33.

95    It was a logical assumption: Ibid. See also "Bomber a Woman? Idea Called 'Silly,'" 11.

95      Since the Bomber's overriding contempt: Ibid.

95      "He wants to be flawless": Brussel, *Casebook*, 41.

96      Repeated use of odd phrasings: "Mad Bomber Believed 'Ordinary Man' in 40s," *New York Journal-American*, December 26, 1956, 3. See also "Search for the Bomber," *New York Times*, January 6, 1957, E2.

96      Another theory: Joseph Carter, "Wanted: The Man without a Face," 56.

96      "It was like a slouching soldier": Brussel, *Casebook*, 36.

96      "something inside him": Ibid.

96      "Something about sex": Ibid.

97      "Once again, I realized": Ibid., 37.

97      "Could the seat symbolize": Ibid.

98      Brussel was convinced: Ibid., 37–38.

98      "And now," thought Brussel: Ibid., 39.

98      "inferential mosaic": Ibid., 38–39.

98      "A loner": Ibid., 39–40.

98      He has no friends: "Bomber a Woman? Idea Called 'Silly,'" 11.

98      "He [is] unmarried": Brussel, *Casebook*, 40–41.

99      Since men typically don't reside alone: Ibid., 40.

99      "at least two years of high school": Ibid., 41.

99      He flipped through the pages: Ibid., 34.

99      The letters almost read: Douglas and Olshaker, *Unabomber*, 11.

100     "Historically," responded Brussel: Brussel, *Casebook*, 42 (emphasis added).

100     "To play the odds again": Ibid.

100     Recognizing that thousands: Ibid., 42–43.

101     "Heart disease is my guess": Ibid., 43.

101     a failure "to make every possible allowance": Ibid., 42.

101     "The Bomber was God": Ibid., 43.

101     "Tell me something,": Ibid., 43–44

102     "By putting these theories": Ibid., 45.

102     "I guess it has to be done": Ibid., 46.

103   "When you catch him": Ibid.

## CHAPTER XI: CHRISTMAS IN MANHATTAN

104   With typical holiday fanfare: "Christmas Tree Rises in Midtown," *New York Times*, November 27, 1956, 27.

104   The twenty-fourth annual: "A Tree Is Lighted in Rockefeller Center, and Suddenly It's Christmas Time Again," *New York Times*, December 7, 1956, 29.

107   "MAD BOMBER STRIKES AGAIN": "Mad Bomber Strikes Again in Main Library," *New York Daily News*, December 25, 1956, 1.

107   "BOMB IN 5TH AVE. LIBRARY": "Bomb in 5th Ave. Library Spurs Hunt for Psychotic," *New York Times*, December 25, 1956, 1.

107   "Yuletide gift": "Mad Bomber Strikes Again in Main Library," 1.

107   "a kind of portrait": "Bomb in 5th Ave. Library Spurs Hunt for Psychotic," 31.

107   "conceived this image": Ibid.

108   "Single man, between 40 and 50": Ibid.

108   "[The *Times* story] didn't contain": Brussel, *Casebook*, 47.

## CHAPTER XII: "AN INNOCENT AND ALMOST ABSURDLY SIMPLE THING"

109   "window on the world": William Randolph Hearst Jr., *The Hearsts: Father and Son* (Roberts Rinehart Publishers, 1991), 301.

109   Later, back in New York: *Seymour Is Dead at 53; Publisher of Journal-American*, New York Times, January 5, 1959, Page 29.

110   "Get it first, but first get it right": William Safire, No Uncertain Terms: More Writing From the Popular "On Language" Column in The New York Times Magazine (Simon and Schuster, 2003), 725. See also, William Safire, Words of Wisdom: More Good Advice (Simon and Schuster, 1990), 205.

110   "To ask Seymour Berkson to relax": Bob Considine, *It's All News to Me: A Reporter's Deposition* (Meredith Press, 1967), 106.

110    **"Empress of Seventh Avenue"**: "Eleanor Lambert, Empress of Fashion, Dies at 100," *New York Times*, October 8, 2003, C17.

110    **In the early part of December**: See *Night Beat*, WABD-TV interview of Seymour Berkson by host Mike Wallace, Thursday, February 14, 1957, 11:00 p.m. Courtesy of the Paley Center for Media.

111    **"rather innocent"**: Ibid.

111    **"stab in the dark"**: "Bizarre Case Is Unique in Police Annals," *Bridgeport Telegram*, January 23, 1957, 6 (AP).

## CHAPTER XIII: "PLENTY OF WHACKS"

113    **"At first we requested"**: "13 Bomb Threats Harry City in Day," *New York Times*, December 5, 1956, Page 80.

113    **"Every hopeful lead has vanished"**: "His Secret Notes Paint the Portrait of Mad Bomber," 10C.

113    **"Any one who has any helpful information"**: "The Search for the Bomber," *New York Herald Tribune*, December 27, 1956, editorial page.

113    **"This then clearly is a case"**: "The Mad Bomber," *New York Journal-American*, December 27, 1956, editorial page.

114    **"For more than 15 years"**: "Police Distribute Circular Warning of 'Mad Bomber's' Deadly Danger," *New York Journal-American*, December 11, 1956, 5.

114    **"The hysteria"**: "Bomb Hoax Wave Compels Police to Limit Checks," *New York Times*, December 29, 1956, 1.

114    **As Christmas approached**: "Hoaxers Tormented Bomb Squad with 160 Calls in December, Then Shifted to Schools," *New York Times*, January 23, 1957, 18.

114    **One New York police officer**: Ibid.

115    **"Every time we find a real bomb"**: "The Mad Bomber," *New York Times*, December 30, 1956, E2.

115    **"I paid $258 for that durned TV set"**: "Not A 'Bomb' Just TV Tube!" *New York Journal-American*, December 31, 1956, 1.

115 "He's my husband": "Tips on Bomber Funny and Tragic," *New York Journal-American*, January 23, 1957, 13.

116 **Bomb scares and homemade devices:** "Hoaxers Tormented Bomb Squad with 160 Calls in December, Then Shifted to Schools," 18.

116 **"Not since the 'Jack the Ripper' murders":** "Siege by Bomber Recalls Terror of 'Jack the Ripper,'" *New York Journal-American*, December 27, 1956, 5.

116 **"The Mad Bomber . . . is a man":** "Bomber Mystery Baffles Hitchcock," *New York Journal-American*, December 30, 1956, 7.

116 **would soon begin production:** "Fox Plans Movie on 'Mad Bomber,'" *New York Times*, January 3, 1957, 27.

116 **"a suitably dramatic ending":** "Talk of the Town, Notes and Comments," *New Yorker*, January 12, 1957.

117 **"calculated risk":** "Police Get New Leads on Bomber, Kennedy Backs Publicity Policy," *New York Herald Tribune*, January 7, 1957, 1.

117 **"The public can cope":** "Hoaxers Tormented Bomb Squad with 160 Calls in December, Then Shifted to Schools," 18.

117 **He publicly warned:** "Hoax Calls Slow Hunt for Mad Bomber," *New York Journal-American*, January 2, 1957, 15.

117 **"Our policy is to arrest these people":** "Firm Penalty Due for Bomb Cranks," *New York Times*, January 1, 1957, 23.

117 **and in Brooklyn two girls:** "2 B'klyn Girls in Court Today on Bomb Hoax," *New York Journal-American*, January 5, 1957, 4.

117 **a thirty-seven-year-old fruit store clerk:** "'Bomb' Disrupts Subway Travel," *New York Times*, December 31, 1956, 26.

118 **Arraigned on a charge of disorderly conduct:** Ibid.

118 **"If I, or any of my colleagues":** Ibid.

118 **In the early morning hours:** "New Bomb Found in Seat at B'Way Theatre," *New York Journal-American*, December 28, 1956, 6.

118 **"Fire in the Hole":** "Bomb Hoax Wave Compels Police to Limit Checks," 30. Also see "Explode Mad Bomber's Bombs; They're Real!" *New York Daily News*, December 29, 1956, 6.

119     "Resolved . . . that the City of New York": "26G for Bomber," *New Daily Mirror*, December 29, 1956, 2.

119     "of the killer type": "Bomb Hoax Wave Compels Police to Limit Checks," 30.

120     "atmosphere of a siege prevailed": James, "The Mad Bomber vs. Con Ed," 47.

120     During two hours of interrogation: "Tell of Talk in Library with Suspect," *New York Journal-American*, December 26, 1956, 1.

121     Of particular interest to police: "Pair Believe They Saw Bomber with Woman," *New York Daily News*, December 30, 1956, 3.

121     The idea that the Bomber: See "Push Bomber; Could Be a Woman," *New York Daily News*, December 27, 1956, 2.

121     "poorly dressed, thin, pale-faced . . . [man]": "Find Pipe, Watch Mechanism at Grand Central," *New York Journal-American*, December 27, 1956, 2.

121     "I am NOT the Mad Bomber": About New York, Itinerant Watch Repairer Is Leading a Freer Life with Arrest of the 'Mad Bomber,' *New York Times*, January 28, 1957, 18.

122     As 1956 came to a close: "Crime Sets New Record," *New York Journal-American*, December 30, 1956, 6.

## CHAPTER XIV: "THE FOUR FISHERMEN"

123     "uncharted course": "The Journal's Role—Step by Step—in Capture of Elusive Bomber," *New York Journal-American*, January 23, 1957, 2.

123     "We've heard of people": Ibid.

123     "a fair deal under American justice": See *Night Beat*, February 14, 1957.

123     "pique his interest and tempt him": "The Journal's Role—Step by Step," 2.

123     While Berkson maintained a good faith belief: See *Night Beat*, February 14, 1957.

124     "four fishermen": Bob Considine, "How They Caught the Mad Bomber," *American Weekly*, April 7, 1957, 25.

124     "More than one rival paper": Ibid., 23.

125     Stearn had, in fact, received several letters: "How the Journal Helped Police in Solving of Case," *New York Journal-American*, January 22, 1957, B.

125     "To the sick person": "Walter Winchell of New York," *New York Daily Mirror*, January 14, 1957.

125     "Reporters, advertising salesmen, secretaries": Hearst, *The Hearsts: Father and Son*, 283.

126     "finest hour": Ibid., 293.

126     The building itself: Ibid., 284.

126     "Arthur, you've done it to me again!": Ibid.

127     "I MAY PAY YOU A VISIT": "How the Journal Helped Police," B.

127     "TO JOURNAL-AMERICAN": Ibid.

128     "BEFORE I AM FINISHED": Ibid.

128     "Unquestionably genuine": Considine, "How They Caught the Mad Bomber," 23.

129     130 from Christmas Eve: "'Bomb' on 57th St. Is a Firecracker," *New York Times*, January 2, 1957, 48.

129     The task of distinguishing: Considine, "How They Caught the Mad Bomber," 24.

130     Each of the three politicians: "City Tests Clear Dead Bronx Man," *New York Journal-American*, January 12, 1957, 10.

130     "blind alley": Ibid., 1.

131     Investigators had always found: "Bomber Hunted in White Plains," *New York Times*, January 4, 1957, 42.

131     Samples of the Bomber's distinctive block printing: See "Search for the Bomber," E2; "Cops Check Jury List In Search for Bomber," *New York Journal-American*, January 9, 1957, 1; "150,000 Jury Forms Sifted for Bomber," *New York Times*, January 18, 1957, 14; and "Comb Alien Files for Bomber Clue," *New York Journal-American*, January 16, 1957, 1.

131     To aid in this monumental task: "Police Rush New Search for Bomber," *New York Journal-American*, January 9, 1957, 1.

131    **Meanwhile, the department:** "'Bomber' Presses Threat on Utility," *New York Times*, January 11, 1957, 16.

132    **The resulting list of forty-two matches:** "Suspects Tailed by Top Sleuths," *World-Telegram and Sun*, January 11, 1957, 1.

132    **On the recommendation of Dr. Brussel:** "Bomber Hunt Centers on Doctors, Hospitals," *New York Daily Mirror*, January 11, 1957, 3.

133    **Initial descriptions of Kleewen's handwriting:** "Mystery Man Dies—Sparks Bomber Hunt," *New York Daily Mirror*, January 12, 1957, 3. See also "Dead Bronx Machinist's Home Searched for Clues to Bomber," *New York Times*, January 12, 1957, 10.

133    **when a stack of bills:** "Dead Bronx Machinist's Home Searched for Clues to Bomber," 10.

133    **The following day:** "Mad Bomber's Letter Hints Brief Truce," *New York World-Telegram and Sun*, January 7, 1957, 1.

134    **"psychopathic 'enemy of society'":** "Hunt Workshop of Mad Bomber in White Plains," *New York Journal-American*, January 4, 1957, 1.

134    **"TO NEW YORK JOURNAL AMERICAN":** Considine, "How They Caught the Mad Bomber," 23.

136    **"F. P. We are publishing for you":** "An Open Letter to the Mad Bomber," *New York Journal-American*, January 10, 1957, 1.

136    **The January 10, 1957, issue:** Considine, "How They Caught the Mad Bomber," 23.

137    **"I WILL EXTEND THIS ONE SIDED 'TRUSE'":** "Bomber's New Letter Tells Motive, Extends His 'Truce,'" *New York Journal-American*, January 15, 1957, 1; "The Bomber's Grievances Came to Light in a Series of Letters," *New York Times*, January 23, 1957, 19.

137    **Lehman, Pelotti, and Andrews:** Ibid.

138    **"I DID NOT GET A SINGLE PENNY":** Ibid.

138    **"WHEN A MOTORIST INJURES A DOG":** Ibid.

138    **The embossed postal cancellation:** "Bomber Tells Motives in New Note to Journal," *New York Journal-American*, January 15, 1957, 6.

138    "Can you name the perjurers?": "Another Open Letter to F.P.," *New York Journal-American*, January 15, 1957, 1.

139    "Your story is convincing": Ibid.

140    "On January 16, the paper published": "We Want to Help," *New York Journal-American*, January 16, 1957, 1.

140    "If an injustice has been done": "State Promises Review of Case," *New York Journal-American*, January 16, 1957, 1.

140    As with the letter from Con Ed: Ibid., 11.

140    "the most scientific medical care": "Wait Reply to Promise of Fairness," *New York Journal-American*, January 17, 1957, 1.

140    opinions from lawyers: "Check Old Files to Help Bomber Get Fair Hearing," *New York Journal-American*, January 18, 1957, Page 1.

141    Perhaps overstepping its journalistic bounds: "Wait Reply to Promise of Fairness," 11.

141    "top legal counsel": *State Spurs Effort To Help 'Bomber,' New York Journal-American*, January 21, 1957, Page 3.

141    "THANKS VERY MUCH FOR YOUR EFFORT": "Letters Lead to Bomber's Capture," 5.

141    "I was injured on September 5th, 1931": Ibid.

## CHAPTER XV: ALICE KELLY

143    Finally, it was agreed: Considine, "How They Caught the Mad Bomber," 25.

143    "You can decide where": Ibid.

144    According to Con Ed: "Con Ed Girl Aide to Skip Reward," *New York Journal-American*, January 24, 1957, 7; "Con-Ed and Cops Wrangle Over Who Gets the Credit for What," *New York Daily News*, January 23, 1957, 4; "Investigate Con Edison Bomb Role," *New York Journal-American*, January 25, 1957, 5.

144    Con Ed reported that: "Edison Clerk Finds Case in File; Bomber's Words Alerted Her," *New York Times*, January 23, 1957, 18.

145    At approximately 4:20 p.m.: Ibid.

145 **The file contained the same**: Brussel, *Casebook*, 63.

145 **There were several typewritten letters**: "Edison Clerk Finds Case in File," 18.

146 **"The word 'injustices' sort of remained**: "Girl's Memory Uncovered Clue," *New York Journal-American*, January 22, 1957, 2.

146 **"I think we have it!"**: "Con-Ed and Cops Wrangle Over Who Gets the Credit for What," 4.

146 **"kind attitude of the Police Commissioner"**: "Letters Lead to Bomber's Capture," 5.

147 **"WHAT ABOUT MY PEOPLE"**: Ibid.

147 **"Were I alone"**: Ibid.

147 **On the following morning**: "Didn't Call at His Home For 70 Hrs.," *New York Herald Tribune*, January 24, 1957, 1.

148 **Pakul, a veteran officer**: Brussel, *Casebook*, 65–66.

148 **Under the pretext**: Ibid., 66.

148 **At 4:37 that afternoon**: Ibid., 67. "Didn't Call at His Home For 70 Hrs.," 2, and "Metesky Given 1-Day Stay in City Court Here," *Waterbury Republican-American*, January 22, 1957, 12.

149 **Commissioner Kennedy would later protest**: "Police Give Clerk Bomb-Clue Credit," *New York Times*, January 24, 1957, 23.

149 **At 9:00 a.m. on Monday, January 21**: Brussel, *Casebook*, 67.

## CHAPTER XVI: "THE PRICE OF PEACE"

150 **"very vague religion"**: Patrick Allitt, *Religion in America Since 1945: A History* (Columbia University Press, 2005), 31, quoting William Lee Miller.

150 **the twentieth amendment to the U.S. Constitution**: The amendment had been ratified under FDR, and this marked the first time the event had fallen on a Sunday.

150 **"[n]ew forces . . . stir across the earth"**: *U.S. Presidential Inaugural Addresses* (Kessinger Publishing 2004) 242–245.

150 **a chilling fog had begun to gather**: James, "The Mad Bomber vs. Con Ed," 45.

151     **He called a relative**: Memorandum of interview with Detective Michael Lynch, April 15, 1957.

152     **Kelly, recollecting his prior rancorous dealings**: Ibid.

152     **"a good bet."**: Ibid.

152     **Several of the detectives**: James, "The Mad Bomber vs. Con Ed," 46.

153     **"It was almost like the guy"**: Ibid.

153     **"George Metesky?" asked Captain Pakul**: The circumstances of and exchanges during Metesky's arrest are derived from Memorandum of interview with Detective Michael Lynch, April 15, 1957; Brussel, *Casebook*, 69; James, "The Mad Bomber vs. Con Ed," 46; "To Face Check by Psychiatrists in N.Y. Hospital," *Waterbury Republican-American*, January 23, 1957, 3.

154     **He was wearing"**: "Sisters Shocked," 20. See also Brussel, *Casebook*, 69.

155     **"George couldn't hurt anybody"**: Ibid.

156     **"an innocent, happy, strange smile"**: *Year End Review 1957,* WRCA-TV, Host Bill Ryan, December 29, 1957. Courtesy of the Paley Center.

156     **He spoke in soft and courteous tones**: "Metesky Given 1-Day Stay in City Court Here," 12.

156     **"got a bum deal"**: "Suspect Is Held as 'Mad Bomber'; He Admits Role," *New York Times*, January 22, 1957, 1.

157     **"Waterbury went coast-to-coast"**: "Waterbury Arrest Brings Coast-to-Coast Hookup," *Waterbury Republican-American*, January 22, 1957, 1.

157     **"There is absolutely no question"**: "'Mad Bomber' Captured at Home," *New York Herald Tribune*, January 22, 1957, 1.

157     **Pakul commended Metesky's "remarkable memory"**: Ibid.

158     **Their dialogue was captured**: Transcript of interrogation of George Metesky, January 22, 1957.

159     **Following the formal interrogation**: Telephone interview with William F. Schmitt, December 10, 2009. See also Esposito and Gerstein, *Bomb Squad*, 279–280.

159 **"Find what, George?"**: Telephone interview with William F. Schmitt, December 10, 2009.

160 **"the items [taken from the Metesky home]"**: Memorandum of Opinion from Detective William Schmitt, Shield #909, Bomb Squad concerning, *List of Items Found At 17 Fourth Street, Waterbury, Connecticut,* dated January 24, 1957, NYC Department of Records/ Municipal Archives.

161 **"Metesky was smiling"**: Brussel, *Casebook*, 70.

## CHAPTER XVII: "YOUR NEXT DOOR NEIGHBOR"

162 **The police had privately feared**: "Police Use Extreme Caution in Dismantling 'Bomber's' Shop," *Bridgeport Telegram*, January 23, 1957, 6.

163 **"This is the man"**: "N.Y. 'Mad Bomber' Seized in State," *Bridgeport Post*, January 22, 1957, 1.

163 **The usually tranquil and dignified courthouse**: "Letters to Journal Trap the Mad Bomber," *New York Journal-American*, January 23, 1957, 4.

163 **"It is a bit unusual"**: "Judge Permits Cameramen in Court," *Waterbury Republican-American*, January 23, 1957, 2.

164 **"Do you understand these proceedings?"**: See "Didn't Call at His Home for 70 Hrs.," 1, for details of arraignment and dialogue between Metesky and Judge McGill.

164 **As they approached the steel bars**: See "Kin Refuse to Believe He's Guilty," *New York Journal-American*, January 22, 1957, 1, for statements of Metesky's sisters and brother.

165 **Prior to Metesky's departure**: See "Bomber Heard on Con Ed TV Show," 5, for facts, circumstances, and all quotes regarding the John Tillman interview.

165 **"The story of the century"**: "The 'Bomber Story,'" *Waterbury Republican-American*, January 23, 1957, editorial page.

166 **"The man police arrested today"**: "'Bomber' Seems to Like Being in Public Eye," *Bridgeport Telegram*, January 23, 1957, 6.

166 **"could well have passed"**: "N.Y. 'Mad Bomber' Seized in State," 1.

166    **"[t]he prisoner resembled"**: "Bomber Is Booked; Sent to Bellevue for Mental Tests," *New York Times*, January 23, 1957, 18.

166    **As word spread**: See "Bomber Is Booked; Sent to Bellevue for Mental Tests," 18, for entire scene.

166    **"impress both the officer and the prisoner"**: *Fodor's New York City 2010* (Random House, 2009), 69.

167    **"You glad it's over"**: Ibid. See also "'Mad Bomber' Booked, Sent to Bellevue," *New York Herald Tribune*, January 23, 1957, 1, for entire dialogue.

167    **The initial charges alone**: "Bomber Is Booked; Sent to Bellevue for Mental Tests," 1.

168    **"the poor man's legal representative"**: "Benjamin Schmier Dies at 65; A Retired Brooklyn Prosecutor," *New York Times*, November 16, 1975, 75.

168    **"I must however state"**: For all dialogue of Metesky's New York City arraignment" see "Transcript of Court Appearance . . . January 22, 1957."

## CHAPTER XVIII: REWARDS, ACCOLADES, AND ACCUSATIONS

171    **"rare photographic memory"**: "Girl's Memory Uncovered Clue," 4.

171    **invited to the reviewing stand**: "Wants Alice Kelly to Review St. Patrick's Day Parade," *World-Telegram and Sun*, January 26, 1957, letters page.

171    **considered to fill an open seat**: "Con Edison Votes Stock Increase," *New York Times*, May 21, 1957, 49.

171    **". . . [W]e say it's not so"**: "Con-Ed and Cops Wrangle Over Who Gets the Credit for What," 4.

171    **Though Arm acknowledged**: "Who Traced Bomber: Police or File Girl?" *New York Herald Tribune*, January 23, 1957, 1.

172    **Kennedy made special public mention**: "Con-Ed and Cops Wrangle Over Who Gets the Credit for What," 4. See also, *23 On Bomb Case To Be Promoted*, *New York Times*, January 23, 1957, 19.

172    **"The main thing is**: "Didn't Call at His Home For 70 Hrs.," 2.

173    "This was not good police work": Ibid.

173    "A man has been arrested": "Police Give Clerk Bomb-Clue Credit," 23.

173    "Police were working for five or six years": "Didn't Call at His Home For 70 Hrs.," 2.

173    On January 14, 1957: "Investigate Con Edison Bomb Role," 5. See also "Bomb-Hunt Delay Laid to Con Edison By Police Sources," *New York Times*, January 25, 1957, 1.

174    "Our employees have worked": See "Hunt for All Data on Bomber Case," *New York Journal-American*, January 25, 1957, 7, for Brady and Forbes quotes.

174    "The complete investigation showed": Ibid.

175    "[Alice] was like an executive secretary": James, "The Mad Bomber vs. Con Ed," 48. Detective Will Schmitt concurs with virtually every aspect of Lehane's recollection but states that the Metesky file was held by Con-Ed lawyers in a locked safe which Alice Kelly had access to. See telephone interview with William F. Schmitt, December 10, 2009.

175    "[a]nybody who files a just claim": "Police Yield Credit on Con Ed Bomber File," *New York Daily Mirror*, January 24, 1957, 1.

176    "Why, with all the available clues": "New York, Bomber at Bay," *New York Times*, January 27, 1957, E2.

176    "I have no more right": "'Bomber' Reward Might Go Begging," *New York Times*, February 16, 1957, 18.

177    "long and serious consideration": "Spurns Bomb Case Reward," *New York Journal-American*, February 8, 1957, 1.

177    "I realize of course": "Clerk Raps Proxies' Bomber Reward Bid," *New York Post*, February 8, 1957, 3.

177    "I haven't had any ill feeling": "Confession Pleases a Penn Station Porter Incapacitated for 11 Months by Explosion," *New York Times*, January 23, 1957, 20.

177    "Most people can work their way": "Aged Victim of Mad Bomber Sorry for Him," *New York Daily Mirror*, January 23, 1957, 3.

178    "Why not contribute the reward money": "Letters to the Times, Use for 'Mad Bomber' Reward," *New York Times*, February 19, 1957, 30.

178    Harland Forbes called the matter: "'Bomber' Reward Might Go Begging," 18.

179    "You tell me": See telephone interview with William F. Schmitt, December 10, 2009.

179    There, among the stench of stale beer: Hearst, *The Hearsts: Father and Son*, 295.

179    "I congratulate the *Journal-American*": "Tributes Heaped on Journal over Bomber Capture," *New York Journal-American*, January 23, 1957, 5.

179    "The *New York Journal-American*": Ibid.

180    "exceptional vision and dedication": Ibid.

180-181 "The capture of the Mad Bomber": "The Mad Bomber," *New York Journal-American*, January 23, 1957, editorial page.

181    "one of the great journalistic coups": "Editor's Report: Paper Helped Trap 'Bomber,'" *San Antonio Light*, January 27, 1957, 1.

181    "Under no circumstances": "The Reward," *New York Journal-American*, January 25, 1957, editorial page.

182    Upon the arrest: See *Night Beat*, February 14, 1957.

182    "esteemed compeers": "Telegram Lauds J-A," *New York Journal-American*, January 25, 1957, 7.

182    The January 21 issue of *Time* magazine: "Bombs Away," *Time*, January 21, 1957.

## CHAPTER XIX: A QUESTION OF COMPETENCY

184    Though Bellevue Hospital Center: Arthur Zitrin, *The Psychiatric Division—Bellevue Hospital Center, Frontiers in General Hospital Psychiatry,* ed. Louis Linn, M.D. (International Universities Press, Inc., 1961), 414.

184    None other than Kris Kringle: Mark Harris, "Checkout Time at the Asylum," *New York Magazine*, November 16, 2008.

185      **"most happy fellow"**: "Test Bomber's Sanity," *New York Journal-American*, January 23, 1957, 1.

185      **"He mingles freely**: "Metesky Takes Plight Nonchalantly," *New York Journal-American*, January 23, 1957, 9.

185      **"He's always smiling"**: "'Popular' Bomber a Checker Champ," *New York Journal-American*, March 14, 1957, 3.

185      **The notorious and oft quoted phrase**: Zitrin, *The Psychiatric Division*, 422.

186      **"in such a state of idiocy"**: N.Y. Laws 1939, c. 861. See also "New York Procedure for Determination of Sanity of Defendant. Desmond Act," *Columbia Law Review* 39, no. 7 (November 1939): 1262.

186      **In earlier years**: "New York Procedure for Determination of Sanity of Defendant. Desmond Act," 1260.

187      **"[T]here is no question"**: "Expert at Work to Help Metesky," *New York Journal-American*, January 23, 1957, 15.

188      **"I understand"**: "Tells of Injuries at Power Plant," 10 (emphasis added).

188      **"I believe a new claim"**: "Hunt for All Data on Bomber Case," 7.

188      **"champion of lost causes"**: William F. Longgood, "Lawyer for the Defense," *Saturday Evening Post*, November 2, 1957, 87.

188      **"He's very much the fox"**: Ibid., 88.

189      **"I guess I was born with"**: Ibid., 26.

189      **"To me, the man on trial"**: Ibid., 87.

190      **"He is as jovial and gay today"**: See "Insanity Plea for Mad Bomber," *New York Journal-American*, January 26, 1957, 4.

190      **Prosecutors had earlier stated**: "Doctors Study Bomber," *New York Herald Tribune*, January 24, 1957, 2.

191      **"alert, cooperative, and eager"**: "Report of Psychiatric Examination," March 1, 1957.

191      **"exhibited abnormal thinking and acting"**: Ibid.

193      **"imminently dangerous to others"**: The People of the State of New York against George Metesky, alias George Milauskas, Court of General Sessions County of New York, Indictment No. 321–57.

193     **The charges:** "Jury Indicts Metesky on 47 Bomber Counts," *New York Journal-American*, January 30, 1957, 1.

194     **"Gee whizz!":** "'Bomber' Indicted For B'klyn Blast," *New York Journal-American*, February 19, 1957, 1.

194     **The average stay:** Zitrin, *The Psychiatric Division*, 422.

194     **"This fellow is smarter":** "Metesky Hearing Postponed; Wait Full MD Report," *New York Journal-American*, February 20, 1957, 1.

195     **During the 1955 murder trial:** "Justice John A. Mullen Dies; Served on State Supreme Court," *New York Times*, September 30, 1972, obituaries.

196     **"Did he indicate to you":** See "Bomber Planned to Darken N.Y.," *New York Journal-American*, March 5, 1957, 17.

197     **"All delays in cases of this sort":** See "Trial Is Ordered for 'Mad Bomber,'" *New York Times*, March 1, 1957, 31.

198     **"I have thought about it":** Testimony of Albert A. LaVerne, on March 27, 1957, during a Section 662a Hearing before Judge Samuel S. Leibowitz, Kings County Court, *The People of New York vs. George Metesky,* Indictment No. 269/1957.

## CHAPTER XX: "AS PLAIN AS THE NOSE ON YOUR FACE"

199     **"While generally compliant":** "Report of Psychiatric Examination," March 1, 1957.

199     **"I don't believe in letting people":** "Sanity Report on Bomber Goes to Officials Today," *New York Journal-American*, March 4, 1957, 3.

200     **"We cannot keep a man":** "Fear Tombs Suicide Try by Metesky," *New York Journal-American*, March 1, 1957, 1.

200     **"I am going to do":** "Jail for 'Bomber' Leads to Dispute," *New York Times*, March 2, 1957, 23.

200     **"I don't know what [those powers] are":** "Sanity Report on Bomber Goes to Officials Today," 3.

201     **"The law is right there":** See "Judge, Lawyer Clash at 'Bomber' Hearing," *New York Times*, March 23, 1957, 1, 20, for all quotes and circumstances of the March 22, 1957, hearing.

201 **"a rather bizarre conflict"**: Transcript of a Section 662a Hearing held on March 27, 1957 before Judge Samuel S. Leibowitz, Kings County Court, *The People of New York vs. George Metesky,* Indictment No. 269/1957.

202 **"one county is looking for"**: Ibid.

202 **"out of courtesy and respect"**: Ibid.

203 **"we will proceed"**: Ibid.

203 **On March 29 Metesky**: See "Bomber Ordered to Stand Trial," *New York Times*, March 30, 1957, 21; and "Mad Bomber's Lawyer Fights 'Sanity' Ruling," *New York Journal-American*, March 30, 1957, 3; for quotes and circumstances of the March 29, 1957, hearing.

204 **"I am claiming"**: "Expert Asks Compensation for Bomber," *New York Journal-American*, April 7, 1957, 6.

## CHAPTER XXI: "HIS DAYS ON EARTH ARE NUMBERED"

205 **"Well it's no use living"**: Testimony of Dr. Albert A. LaVerne, March 27, 1957.

205 **"This man could at any time"**: "Reveal Bomber Stricken by TB," *New York Journal-American*, April 3, 1957, 1.

207 **"How many reports would you say"**: All quotations are taken from the transcript of a Section 662a Hearing held on April 10, 1957 before Judge Samuel S. Leibowitz, Kings County Court, *The People of New York vs. George Metesky,* Indictment No. 269/1957.

208 **"It is my feeling"**: All quotations are taken from the transcript of a Section 662a Hearing held on April 15, 1957 before Judge Samuel S. Leibowitz, Kings County Court, *The People of New York vs. George Metesky,* Indictment No. 269/1957.

210 **"The decision of this Court"**: All quotations are taken from the transcript of a Section 662a decision delivered on April 18, 1957 by Judge Samuel S. Leibowitz, Kings County Court, *The People of New York vs. George Metesky,* Indictment No. 269/1957.

## CHAPTER XXII: THE BIRTH OF CRIMINAL PROFILING

212 **"amazingly accurate"**: "Proven Profile," *Newsweek*, February 4, 1957, 82.

212 **"had not done badly"**: "Bomber Is Booked; Sent to Bellevue for Mental Tests," 18.

212 **"textbook case of paranoia"**: "'Textbook Case of Paranoia,'" *New York Herald Tribune*, January 23, 1957, 2.

213 **"word picture"**: Telephone interview with William F. Schmitt, December 10, 2009.

213 **Brussel himself had been accused**: Malcolm Gladwell, "Dangerous Minds," *New Yorker*, November 12, 2007, 36, 44; Don Foster, *Author Unknown* (Henry Holt and Company, 2000), 116.

213 **some of the publicized character portraits**: "'Mad Bomber' Believed to Be Man about 45"; "Mad Bomber Believed 'Ordinary Man' in 40s."

213 **though Brussel would later be criticized**: See Gladwell, "Dangerous Minds," 36, 44; Don Foster, *Author Unknown*, 116.

213 **In point of fact**: See "Proven Profile," 82; "16 Year Search for Madman," 31; "Bomber Is Booked; Sent to Bellevue for Mental Tests," 18; "Psychiatrist Depicts the Bomber," 1; and "Bomber a Woman? Idea Called 'Silly,'" 11.

214 **"A profile isn't a test"**: Gladwell, "Dangerous Minds," 36, 43.

214 **In some circles**: See e.g. Diana Concannon, Bruce Fain, and Diane Fain, *Kidnapping: An Investigator's Guide to Profiling* (Academic Press, 2008), 2, and Stephen G. Michaud, *Beyond Cruel* (Macmillan, 2007), 211.

214 **"private blend of science"**: Brussel, *Casebook*, 4.

215 **"the first crude manual"**: John E. Otto and Stephen Band, *Into the Minds of Madmen: How the FBI's Behavioral Science Unit Revolutionized Crime Investigation* (Prometheus Books, 2004), 66.

215 **"I am not the best writer"**: "Sirhan Expert Wanted 'Vivid' Report," *New York Times*, March 19, 1969, 26.

216 **"the Gentle Titan"**: Otto and Band, *Into the Minds of Madmen*, 153.

216    **Teten had developed**: Turvey, *Criminal Profiling*, 35.

217    **"He was a wonderful old gentleman"**: Otto and Band, *Into the Minds of Madmen*, , 118.

217    **Teten recognized that Dr. Brussel's method**: Email from Howard Teten to author dated July 8, 2009.

217    **"In what might be termed"**: Email from Howard Teten to author dated July 9, 2009.

217    **"Dr. Brussel had an exhaustive"**: Email from Howard Teten to author dated July 8, 2009.

218    **"comprehensive and probing"**: Email from Howard Teten to author dated July 9, 2009.

218    **Finally, Teten believed**: Ibid.

218    **Though the two men generally agreed**: Email from Howard Teten to author dated July 8, 2009.

218    **Conversely, Teten's approach**: Ibid.

218    **"I would much rather"**: Ibid.

218    **In the years that followed**: Otto and Band, *Into the Minds of Madmen*, , 116–117.

219    **"He was an innovator"**: Email from Howard Teten to author dated July 8, 2009.

## CHAPTER XXIII: RIGHT FROM WRONG

220    **"To the layman and the lawyer alike"**: Transcript of a Section 662a decision delivered on April 18, 1957 by Judge Samuel S. Leibowitz, Kings County Court, *The People of New York vs. George Metesky*, Indictment No. 269/1957.

221    **the McNaughten rule**: New York Penal Law, Section 1120.

221    **Irresistible Impulse rule**: *Parsons v. State*, 81 Ala. 577, 2 So. 854 (1887).

221    **"an accused is not criminally responsible"**: *Durham v. United States*, 214 F.2d 862 (1954).

221    **"I trust that the State of New York"**: Transcript of a Section 662a decision delivered on April 18, 1957 by Judge Samuel S. Leibowitz,

Kings County Court, *The People of New York vs. George Metesky,* Indictment No. 269/1957.

221 **"a fine example":** Ibid.

221 **"Metesky may have had a delusional mission":** Ibid.

223 **"Application of [the McNaughton Rule]":** Robert Allan Carter, *History of the Insanity Defense in New York State* (New York State Library Legislative Research Service 1982), 10, quoting Public Papers of Governor Averell Harriman, 1957, 1070–1071.

223 **Finally, in 1965:** Robert Allan Carter, History of the Insanity Defense in New York State, 12.

223 **a defense based upon the inability:** Ibid., 13; See also American Law Institute, Model Penal Code: Tentative Draft No. 4, April 1955, 27.

223 **"if at the time of such conduct":** Former New York Penal Law, Section 30.05; L. 1965, Chapter 1030 (emphasis added).

223 **The intent and effect:** Robert Allan Carter, *History of the Insanity Defense in New York State,* 12, citing *People v. Buthy,* 38 A.D. 2d. 10, 326 N.Y.S. 2d. 512 (1971).

## CHAPTER XXIV: MATTEAWAN

225 **"storage bin":** Ron Casanova, Each One Teach One: Up and Out of Poverty, Memoirs of a Street Activist (Curbstone Press, 1996), 47.

225 **"Abandon hope":** Dante, *Inferno,* Canto iii. 1.9. (Cary, trans.)

225 **Prior to the age of reform:** Grant H. Morris, "The Confusion of Confinement Syndrome: An Analysis of the Confinement of Mentally Ill Criminals and Ex-Criminals by the Department of Correction of the State of New York," 17 *Buff. L. Rev.,* 651 (1968).

226 **In 1855 the New York Legislature:** Henry M. Hurd, William F. Drewry, Richard Dewey, Charles W. Pilgrim, G. Adler Blumer, and T. J. W. Burgess, *The Institutional Care of the Insane in the United States and Canada,* volume 3 (Johns Hopkins Press, 1916), 241–242.

226 **Those "twice cursed":** Morris, "The Confusion of Confinement Syndrome," 651, 652.

226     The nine-hundred-acre estate: Federal Writers Project, *New York: A Guide to the Empire State* (US History Publishers, 1989), 576.

226     in 1892 the newly constructed: Morris, "The Confusion of Confinement Syndrome," 651, 653.

226     "isolation of dangerous and vicious patients": Chapter 45, Section 1, N.Y. Sess. Laws (1888).

226     "gives primacy to the problems": Application for the Commitment of ANONYMOUS, an Alleged Dangerously Mentally Ill Patient to Matteawan State Hospital, 69 Misc.2d 181, 183 329 N.Y.S.2d 542, 545 (1972).

226     Sadistic beatings and involuntary medication: See e.g., Casanova, *Each One Teach One*, 47. *Schuster v. Herold,* 410 F.2d 1071 (1969), *Neely v. Hogan,* 62 Misc.2d 1056, 310 N.Y.S.2d 63 (1970). Special Committee on the Study of Commitment Procedures and the Law Relating to Incompetents of the Ass'n of the Bar of the City of New York, Mental Illness, Due Process, and the Criminal Defendant, 23–26 (1968).

226     Unlike the more benign conditions: Morris, "The Confusion of Confinement Syndrome," 651, 658.

226     The dangers, restraints, and poor conditions: *Schuster v. Herold,* 410 F.2d 1071, 1078 (1969).

227     "a place more likely": *Wolfersdorf v. W. C. Johnston, M.D.*, 317 F.Supp. 66, 67 (1970).

227     Denied any effective therapeutic measures: Morris, "The Confusion of Confinement Syndrome," 651, 656.

227     In 1965, prior to the introduction of reform measures: Ibid., 651, 657.

227     "marooned and forsaken": *Schuster v. Herold,* 410 F.2d 1071, 1079 (1969).

229     "They used to take him out": James, "The Mad Bomber vs. Con Ed," 48.

229     "I became fully convinced": Letter of George Metesky dated November 24, 1963 to District Attorney Frank Hogan.

230     "So many injustices have been done": Transcript of hearing dated

December 15, 1966, *George Metesky v. Dr. W. C. Johnston, Superintendent Matteawan State Hospital*, Supreme Court of the State of New York Dutchess County.

230 **"I made this application"**: Ibid.

231 **"Inappropriate emotional reaction"**: Ibid.

231 **"He doesn't pay much attention"**: Ibid.

231 **"[Metesky] has failed to establish"**: Opinion of Judge Joseph F. Hawkins, *George Metesky v. Director of Matteawan State Hospital*, Supreme Court of the State of New York Dutchess County, Index No. 217/1964.

232 **"for further care and treatment"**: Ibid.

232 **With specific regard to Matteawan**: See *Baxtrom v. Herald,* 383 U.S. 107, 86 S.Ct. 760 (1966), and *Schuster v. Herold,* 410 F.2d 1071, 1073, (1969).

232 **"We have, thankfully, come a long way"**: *Schuster v. Herold,* 410 F.2d 1071, 1073, (1969).

233 **In a long and often incoherent handwritten plea**: Petition for Dismissal of Indictment dated November 16, 1970, *George Metesky v District Attorney Frank Hogan*, Supreme Court Borough of Manhattan, Indictment No. 321/57.

233 **"The laws are explicit"**: #1 Supplement To Petition for Dismissal of Indictment dated December 5, 1970, *George Metesky v District Attorney Frank Hogan*, Supreme Court Borough of Manhattan, Indictment No. 321/57.

235 **"AS THE COURT WELL KNOWS,"**: Response to Application for Order of Detention, dated January 12, 1972, *George Metesky v District Attorney Frank Hogan*, Supreme Court Kings County, Indictment No. 269/57.

237 **"The defendant, George P. Metesky"**: Memorandum on Behalf of George P. Metesky, Defendant, *The People of the State of New York v. George P. Metesky,* Supreme Court of the State of New York, County of Kings, Indictment No. 269/1957.

237    "The emphasis should be on programs": "High Court Backs Commitment Cure," *New York Times*, May 30, 1973, 14.

239    "No longer is the key 'thrown away'": Memorandum of Decision dated September 20, 1973, *The People of the State of New York v. George P. Metesky,* Supreme Court of the State of New York, County of Kings, Indictment No. 269/1957.

239    "Sixteen years ago": "Bomber Wins His Freedom," *Times* (San Mateo, California), December 13, 1973, 9 (UPI).

## EPILOGUE

241    Attracted by his populist message: Jonah Raskin, *For the Hell of It: The Life and Times of Abbie Hoffman* (University of California Press, 1998), 100–101.

241    "He epitomizes the futility": Richard Goldstein, "In Search of George Metesky," *Village Voice*, March 16, 1967, 5, 6.

242    "He was known as the Eisenhower": Telephone interview with Franklyn Engel of February 9, 2010.

242    Though it was posited: "Expert Fears Violence in U.S. Is Going to Get Worse," *New York Times*, March 13, 1970, 1.

243    "I was in hope of finding a better world": "Metesky recalls years as bomber," *Anniston Star*, December 18, 1974, 2F (AP).

244    "I expected to go before I was 57": Ibid.

# BIBLIOGRAPHY

## BOOKS

Alleman, Richard. *New York: The Movie Lover's Guide: The Ultimate Insider Tour of Movie New York.* Harper & Row, 2005.

Allitt, Patrick. *Religion in America Since 1945: A History.* Columbia University Press, 2005.

Astor, Gerald. *The New York Cops: An Informal History.* Charles Scribner's Sons, 1971.

Belle, John, and Maxine R. Leighton. *Grand Central: Gateway to a Million Lives.* W. W. & Norton, 2000.

Brussel, James A., M.D. *Casebook of a Crime Psychiatrist.* Bernard Geis Associates, 1968.

Casanova, Ron. *Each One Teach One: Up and Out of Poverty, Memoirs of a Street Activist.* Curbstone Press, 1996.

Concannon, Diana, Bruce Fain, and Diane Fain. *Kidnapping, An Investigator's Guide to Profiling.* Academic Press, 2008.

Considine, Bob. *It's All News to Me: A Reporter's Deposition.* Meredith Press, 1967.

Dante. *Inferno.* Canto iii. l.9. Cary, trans.

Dent Candee, Marjorie, ed. *Current Biography Yearbook 1956.* H. W. Wilson, 1956.

Douglas, John, and Mark Olshaker. *Unabomber: On the Trail of America's Most-Wanted Serial Killer.* Pocket Books, 1996.

Doyle, A. Conan. *The Sign of Four.* Spencer Blackett, 1890.

Esposito, Richard, and Ted Gerstein. *Bomb Squad: A Year Inside the Nation's Most Exclusive Police Unit.* Hyperion, 2007.

Ewing, Charles Patrick, and Joseph T. McCann. *Minds on Trial: Great Cases in Law and Psychology.* Oxford University Press, 2006.

Federal Writers Project. *New York: A Guide to the Empire State.* US History Publishers, 1989.

*Fodor's New York City 2010.* Random House 2009.

Foster, Don. *Author Unknown.* Henry Holt and Company, 2000.

Gage, Beverly. *The Day Wall Street Exploded: A Story of America in its First Age of Terror.* Oxford University Press, 2009.

Hammond-Darling, Linda, and Thomas J. Kniesner. *The Law and Economics of Worker's Compensation.* Institute for Civil Justice (U.S.) Rand Corporation, 1980.

Harmsen, Debbie, ed. *Fodor's New England.* Random House, 2008.

Hearst, William Randolph, Jr. *The Hearsts: Father and Son.* Roberts Rinehart Publishers, 1991.

Hood, Jack B., Benjamin A. Hardy, and Harold S. Lewis. *Workers Compensation and Employee Protection Laws in a Nutshell.* Thomson/West, 2005.

Hurd, Henry M., William F. Drewry, Richard Dewey, Charles W. Pilgrim, G. Adler Blumer, and T. J. W. Burgess. *The Institutional Care of the Insane in the United States and Canada*, vol. 3. Johns Hopkins Press, 1916.

Kocsis, Richard N., PhD, and George B. Palermo. *Criminal Profiling Principles and Practice.* Humana Press, 2006.

Kops, Deborah. *Racial Profiling: Open for Debate.* Marshall Cavendish, 2006.

Kretschmer, Ernest. *Physique and Character.* University of Michigan, 1925; reprinted by Read Books, 2008.

Morrone, Francis. *An Architectural Guidebook to Brooklyn.* Gibbs Smith, 2001.

Michaud, Stephen G. *Beyond Cruel.* Macmillan, 2007.

Miller, Nathan. *FDR: An Intimate History.* Doubleday, 1983.

Millman, Chad. *The Detonators: The Secret Plot to Destroy America and an Epic Hunt for Justice.* Little, Brown, 2006.

Newburn, Tim. *Handbook of Criminal Investigation.* Willan Publishing, 2007.

Otto, John E., and Stephen Band. *Into the Minds of Madmen: How the FBI's Behavioral Science Unit Revolutionized Crime Investigation.* Prometheus Books, 2004.

Peraino, Judith A. *Listening to the Sirens: Musical Technologies of Queer Identity from Homer to Hedwig.* University of California Press, 2006.

Ploscowe, Morris. *Manual for Prosecuting Attorneys.* Practising Law Institute, 1956.

Raskin, Jonah. *For the Hell of it: The Life and Times of Abbie Hoffman.* University of California Press, 1998.

Rider, Fremont. *Rider's New York City: A Guide-Book for Travelers.* Henry Holt & Company, 1916.

Safire, William. *No Uncertain Terms: More Writing from the Popular "On Language" Column in the New York Times Magazine.* Simon and Schuster, 2003.

———. *Words of Wisdom: More Good Advice.* Simon and Schuster, 1990.

Schmidt, Regin. *Red Scare: FBI and the Origins of Anticommunism in the United States.* Museum Tusculanum Press, 2000.

Toomey, Jeane. *Assignment Homicide: Behind the Headlines*. Sunstone Press, 2006.

Turvey, Brent E. *Criminal Profiling: An Introduction to Behavioral Evidence Analysis*. Elsevier, 2008.

*U.S. Presidential Inaugural Addresses*. Kessinger Publishing, 2004.

Wilson, Colin, and Damon Wilson. *Written in Blood: A History of Forensic Detection*. Carroll and Graff Publishers, 2003.

Zitrin, Arthur. *The Psychiatric Division—Bellevue Hospital Center, Frontiers in General Hospital Psychiatry*. Edited by Louis Linn, M.D. International Universities Press, 1961.

## MAGAZINES, ARTICLES, JOURNALS, PAMPHLETS

American Law Institute. Model Penal Code: Tentative Draft No. 4. April 1955. Page 27.

"Bombs Away." *Time*, January 21, 1957.

Brussel, James A. "Charles Dickens: Child Psychologist and Sociologist." *Psychiatric Quarterly Supplement*, 1938.

———. "History of the New York State Department of Mental Hygiene." N.Y. State Journal of Medicine 1957, no. 3 (February 1, 1957): 555–559.

———. "Military Psychiatry." *Military Surgeon* 88 (May 1941).

———. "Van Gogh: Masochist Genius of the Canvas, A Psychiatric Study." *Psychiatric Quarterly* 14, supplement 1 (March 1940): 7–16.

Carter, Joseph. "Wanted: The Man without a Face." *Colliers*, February 3, 1956, 23.

Carter, Robert Allan. *History of the Insanity Defense in New York State*. New York State Library Legislative Research Service, 1982.

Considine, Bob. "How They Caught the Mad Bomber." *American Weekly*, April 7, 1957, 5.

Editorial Staff. "New York Procedure for Determination of Sanity of Defendant. Desmond Act." *Columbia Law Review* 39, no. 7 (November 1939): 1260.

Fales, E. D., Jr. "The Job That Scares Everybody." *Popular Science* 181, no. 1 (July 1962): 67.

"George Did It." *Time*, February 4, 1957.

*Generating Stations, Hell Gate—Sherman Creek*. Private publication of the United Light and Power Company, 1926.

Gladwell, Malcolm. "Dangerous Minds." *New Yorker*, November 12, 2007, 36.

Goldstein, Richard. "In Search of George Metesky." *Village Voice*, March 16, 1967, 5.

Harris, Mark. "Checkout Time at the Asylum." *New York Magazine*, November 16, 2008.

Hoenig, John M. "The Triangle Fire of 1911." *History Magazine*, April/May 2005, 20.

James, Jamie. "The Mad Bomber vs. Con Ed." *Rolling Stone*, November 15, 1979, 47.

Longgood, William F. "Lawyer for the Defense." *Saturday Evening Post*, November 2, 1957, 26.

"The Mad Bomber." *Time*, January 7, 1957, 17.

Morris, Grant H. "The Confusion of Confinement Syndrome: An Analysis of the Confinement of Mentally Ill Criminals and Ex-Criminals by the Department of Correction of the State of New York," 17 *Buff. L. Rev.* 651 (1968).

New York State Department of Mental Hygiene. Annual Report 1948, 46.

"Proven Profile." *Newsweek*, February 4, 1957, 82.

Special Committee on the Study of Commitment Procedures and the Law Relating to Incompetents of the Ass'n of the Bar of the City of New York, Mental Illness, Due Process, and the Criminal Defendant, 1968.

"Strong Arm of the Law." *Time*, July 7, 1958.

"Talk of the Town, Notes and Comments." *New Yorker*, January 12, 1957.

United States Patent 2,257,059, "Solenoid Pump," George P. Metesky, Waterbury, Conn., application July 19, 1938, serial no. 220,082, patented September 23, 1941.


## TELEVISION INTERVIEWS

*Night Beat,* WABD-TV interview of Seymour Berkson by host Mike Wallace, Thursday, February 14, 1957, 11:00 p.m. Courtesy of the Paley Center for Media.

*Year End Review 1957,* WRCA-TV, host Bill Ryan, December 29, 1957. Courtesy of the Paley Center for Media.


## TRANSCRIPTS, COURT RECORDS, POLICE FILES, DISTRICT ATTORNEY'S NOTES

Transcript of Interrogation of George Metesky, 17 4th Street, Waterbury, Connecticut, at Police Headquarters, January 22, 1957. Contained in files of New York County Supreme Court, *The People of the State of New York against George P. Metesky, a/k/a George Milauskas*, indictment no. 321/1957. Courtesy of NYC Department of Records/Municipal Archives.

Transcript of Court Appearance, *The People of the State of New York vs. George Metesky,* City Magistrates' Court of the City of New York Felony Court, Borough of Manhattan, Docket No. 1226. January 22, 1957. Courtesy of NYC Department of Records/Municipal Archives.

Memorandum of Interview with Detective Michael Lynch, Badge #866, with Assistant District Attorney Howard Blank dated April 15, 1957. Contained in files of New York County Supreme Court, *The People of the State of New York against George P. Metesky, a/k/a George Milauskas,* Indictment No. 321/1957. Courtesy of NYC Department of Records/Municipal Archives.

Memorandum of Opinion from Detective William Schmitt, Shield #909, Bomb Squad concerning List of Items Found at 17 Fourth Street, Waterbury, Connecticut. January 24, 1957. Contained in files of New York County Supreme Court, *The People of the State of New York against George P. Metesky, a/k/a George Milauskas,* Indictment No. 321/1957. Courtesy of NYC Department of Records/Municipal Archives.

Psychiatric notes contained in files of New York County Supreme Court, *The People of the State of New York against George P. Metesky, a/k/a George Milauskas,* Indictment No. 321/1957. Courtesy of NYC Department of Records/Municipal Archives.

Testimony of James B. Leggett, Chief of Detectives, Police Department of the City of New York, on March 27, 1957, during a Section 662a Hearing before Judge Samuel S. Leibowitz, Kings County Court, *The People of New York vs. George Metesky,* Indictment No. 269/1957.

Testimony of Dr. Albert A. LaVerne, on March 27, 1957, during a Section 662a Hearing before Judge Samuel S. Leibowitz, Kings County Court, *The People of New York vs. George Metesky,* Indictment No. 269/1957.

Testimony of Dr. Albert A. LaVerne, on April 10, 1957, during a Section 662a Hearing before Judge Samuel S. Leibowitz, Kings County

Court, *The People of New York vs. George Metesky,* Indictment No. 269/1957.

Transcript of entire Section 662a Hearing held on April 10, 1957 before Judge Samuel S. Leibowitz, Kings County Court, *The People of New York vs. George Metesky,* Indictment No. 269/1957.

Transcript of entire Section 662a Hearing held on April 15, 1957 before Judge Samuel S. Leibowitz, Kings County Court, *The People of New York vs. George Metesky,* Indictment No. 269/1957.

Transcript of a Section 662a decision delivered on April 18, 1957 by Judge Samuel S. Leibowitz, Kings County Court, *The People of New York vs. George Metesky,* Indictment No. 269/1957.

Indictment. *The People of the State of New York against George Metesky, alias George Milauskas,* Court of General Sessions County of New York, Indictment No. 321-57.

Letter of George Metesky dated November 24, 1963, to District Attorney Frank Hogan, contained in files of New York County Supreme Court, *The People of the State of New York against George P. Metesky, a/k/a George Milauskas,* Indictment No. 321/1957.

Opinion of Judge Joseph F. Hawkins, *George Metesky v. Director of Matteawan State Hospital,* Supreme Court of the State of New York Dutchess County, Index No. 217/1964.

Transcript of hearing dated December 15, 1966, *George Metesky v. Dr. W. C. Johnston, Superintendent Matteawan State Hospital,* Supreme Court of the State of New York Dutchess County.

Petition for Dismissal of Indictment dated November 16, 1970, *George Metesky v District Attorney Frank Hogan,* Supreme Court Borough of Manhattan, Indictment No. 321/57.

#1 Supplement to Petition for Dismissal of Indictment dated

December 5, 1970, *George Metesky v District Attorney Frank Hogan*, Supreme Court Borough of Manhattan, Indictment No. 321/57.

Response to Application for Order of Detention, dated January 12, 1972, *George Metesky v District Attorney Frank Hogan*, Supreme Court Kings County, Indictment No. 269/57.

Memorandum on Behalf of George P. Metesky, Defendant, *The People of the State of New York v. George P. Metesky*, Supreme Court of the State of New York, County of Kings, Indictment No. 269/1957.

Memorandum of Decision dated September 20, 1973, *The People of the State of New York v. George P. Metesky*, Supreme Court of the State of New York, County of Kings, Indictment No. 269/1957.

Report of Psychiatric Examination in the case of George Metesky alias George Milauskas. March 1, 1957. Contained in files of New York County Supreme Court, *The People of the State of New York against George P. Metesky, a/k/a George Milauskas*, Indictment No. 321/1957. Courtesy of NYC Department of Records/Municipal Archives.

"Series of 'Pipe Bombs'" Notations of the New York City Police Department contained in files of New York County Supreme Court, *The People of the State of New York against George P. Metesky, a/k/a George Milauskas*, Indictment No. 321/1957. Courtesy of NYC Department of Records/Municipal Archives.

Application for Employment with the United Electric Light and Power Co., George Peter Metesky applicant. December 12, 1929. Contained in files of New York County Supreme Court, *The People of the State of New York against George P. Metesky, a/k/a George Milauskas*, Indictment No. 321/1957. Courtesy of NYC Department of Records/Municipal Archives.

Report of Medical Examiner, the United Electric and Power

Company. Contained in files of New York County Supreme Court, *The People of the State of New York against George P. Metesky, a/k/a George Milauskas*, Indictment No. 321/1957. Courtesy of NYC Department of Records/Municipal Archives.

The Association of Employees of the United Electric Light and Power Company, Sick Benefit Payroll. Contained in files of New York County Supreme Court, *The People of the State of New York against George P. Metesky, a/k/a George Milauskas*, Indictment No. 321/1957. Courtesy of NYC Department of Records/Municipal Archives.

## AUTHOR INTERVIEWS AND CORRESPONDENCE

Telephone interview of New York City Bomb Squad detective William F. Schmitt (Retired), December 10, 2009.

Telephone interview of Horatio Tedesco, assistant manager of Brooklyn Paramount Theatre. June 23, 2009.

Telephone interview of John Israel, James A. Brussel's stepson. May 29, 2009.

Telephone interview of Judith Gutmann, James A. Brussel's stepdaughter. June 5, 2009.

Telephone interview of Franklyn Engel, Metesky's lawyer. February 9, 2010.

Telephone interview of Gene Ann Condon, Metesky's lawyer. February 9, 2010.

Telephone interview of Kristin Booth Glen, Metesky's lawyer. February 9, 2010.

Telephone interview of Terence F. O'Rourke, great-grandson of Bart J. O'Rourke. June 19, 2009.

Telephone interview of Dr. Arthur Zitrin, former director of psychiatric services at Bellevue Hospital. June 24, 2009.

Telephone interview with Bill Berkson, son of Seymour Berkson. December 15, 2009.

Email from Howard Teten to author dated July 8, 2009.

Email from Howard Teten to author dated July 9, 2009.

## WEBSITES

www.grandcentralterminal.com/info/grandcentraldecline.cfm, accessed September 2, 2009.

www.grandcentralterminal.com/info/terminalopens.cfm, accessed September 2, 2009.

Preliminary Guide to Mental Health Documentary Sources in New York State, www.archives.nysed.gov/a/research/res_topics_health_mh_recguide_dmh.shtml, accessed October 9, 2009.

www.radiocity.com/about/history.html, accessed September 16, 2009.

# INDEX

Note: Photographs in middle section are shown as P1–P16.

# ABOUT THE AUTHOR

Michael Greenburg is a practicing attorney and former member and editor of the Pepperdine Law Review. He is the author of the nonfiction book, *Peaches and Daddy, A Story of the Roaring 20s, the Birth of Tabloid Media, and the Courtship that Captured the Heart and Imagination of the American Public.* He lives in suburban Boston with his wife, Donna, and two boys, Corey and Jeffrey.